Chaucer
and the
Politics of Discourse

CHAUCER
and the
Politics of Discourse

Michaela Paasche Grudin

UNIVERSITY OF SOUTH CAROLINA PRESS

Chapter 8 originally appeared as "Chaucer's *Manciple Tale* and the Poetics of Guile" in *Chaucer Review* 25 (1991): 329–42; Chapter 9 appeared as "Discourse and the Problem of Closure" in *PMLA* 107, no. 5 (1992): 1157–67.

Library of Congress Cataloging-in-Publication Data

Grudin, Michaela Paasche, 1941–
   Chaucer and the politics of discourse/Michaela Paasche Grudin.
    p. cm.
   Includes bibliographical references and index.
   ISBN 1-57003-102-9
   1. Chaucer, Geoffrey, d. 1400—Technique. 2. Speech in literature. 3. Discourse analysis, Literary. 4. Chaucer, Geoffrey, d. 1400. Canterbury tales. 5. Politics and literature—Great Britain. 6. Rhetoric, Medieval. 7. Christian pilgrims and pilgrimages in literature. 8. Tales, Medieval—History and criticism. 9. Storytelling in literature. I. Title.
PR1933.S73G78   1996
821'.1—dc20
                                  95-50230

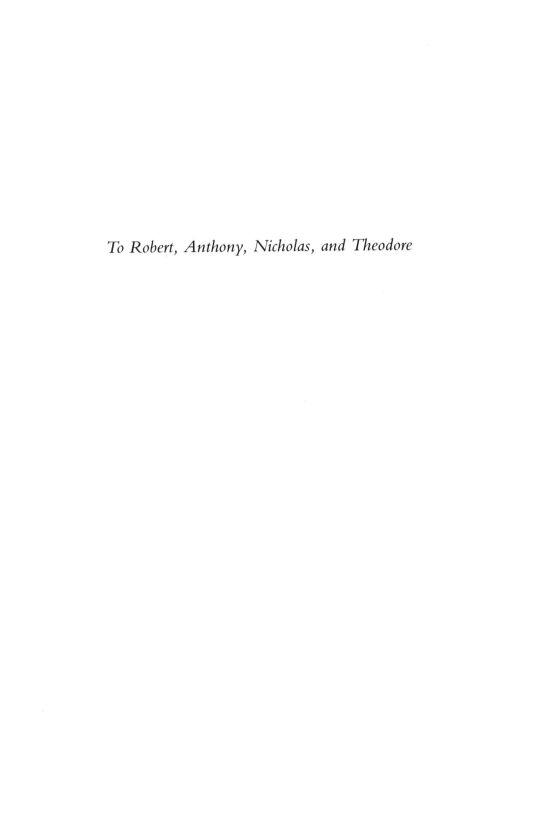

To Robert, Anthony, Nicholas, and Theodore

CONTENTS

ACKNOWLEDGMENTS

A National Endowment for the Humanities Summer Institute, led by C. David Benson, Charles A. Owen, Jr., and Linda Giorgianna, gave my work critical impetus. For scholarly counsel and encouragement I am grateful to Robert O. Frank, Derek Brewer, George Economou, Walter Kaiser, Gloria Johnson, Derek Pearsall, James W. Earl, Maurice Holland, the late Stanley B. Greenfield, and most of all to Charles Muscatine, with whom I first undertook the study of Chaucer. The National Endowment for the Humanities, the University of Oregon, the American Council of Learned Societies, and Lewis and Clark College provided essential research support. Marty Davis, Peggy Hill, Warren Slesinger, and Linda Fogle of the University of South Carolina Press have handled the manuscript with unfailing care and good humor. I also owe much, for refuge and support, to Paula Burkhart, Alice Carnes, Susan Plass, Susanna Dakin, John Murray, Manga Samerakkody, Buzzy and Gigi Crompton, Charmian Byers-Jones, the Hon. Edward S. Northrop, Lucinda Olney, Henry and Vergilia Dakin, Marianne Buchwalter, Mary Fink, Lucy Lamkin, and David Lunney. I am grateful, too, to my parents for inspiration and to my husband, Robert, for conversations without which this book would never have been written.

1

Speech and the Commonwealth

This book is a study of Chaucer's concern with discourse. Even the most casual of his readers will recognize his perennial interest in talk, talkers, and dialogue. The central feature of his early *Book of the Duchess* is a conversation, and the most memorable parts of the other dream visions are mainly talk: the squabble of the birds in the *Parliament of Fowls,* the delicious loquaciousness of the eagle—and also the extended remarks on rumor—in the *House of Fame. Troilus and Criseyde* would be unimaginable without the lyrical speech of Troilus, the virtuoso elocution of Pandarus, and the exquisite dramatics of the latter's dialogue with Criseyde. The *Canterbury Tales,* of course, with the Wife of Bath and the Pardoner brings us in passing some of the most famous talkers in all of literature; but Chaucer also imagines the action of the work as a whole to take its very origin in dialogue—

> So hadde I spoken with hem everichon
> That I was of hir felaweshipe anon—[1]

and most of the ensuing characterizations of the pilgrims in the *General Prologue* are involved with significant traits of their speech.

---

[1] *General Prologue* to the *Canterbury Tales* I (A) 31–32. This and all subsequent Chaucer citations are from *The Riverside Chaucer,* ed. Larry D. Benson et al., 3rd ed. (Boston: Houghton Mifflin Co., 1987).

In the still-oral culture of England,[2] talk for Chaucer could be expected to have almost instant practical significance, psychological, social, and political.[3] But this inquiry will be concerned also with Chaucer's underlying views about discourse. If human voices are so various as we hear them in the *Parliament of Fowls* and the *Canterbury Tales,* how can talk promote social order? What, indeed, constitutes a cultural discourse? What is the place of the poet's own discourse within the human community? Why, finally, is it so important to Chaucer to bring *speche* to our attention?

Chaucer's interest in speech, in the *General Prologue* and elsewhere, his almost intuitive yoking of language, character, and experience, points to numerous and profound similarities between him and the Italian humanists. For Chaucer, as for the early humanists, the study of speech promises to uncover the hidden premises of society.[4] Speech is the sovereign cultural artifact and the most intelligible human institution—an institution, like chivalry, monarchy, or the estates, worthy of poetic scrutiny. In the writings of Petrarch, Boccaccio, and others, we recognize not only Plato's estimation in the *Timaeus,* that "the river of speech, which flows out of a man and ministers to the intelligence, is the fairest

---

[2] For a recent study (including extensive bibliography) of this complex situation, especially as it affects our understanding of the poetry of the period, see *Oral Poetics in Middle English Poetry,* ed. Mark C. Amodio (New York: Garland, 1994). Amodio's introduction, "Oral Poetics in Post-Conquest England," reminds us that in this period, "orality and literacy exist along a continuum and are integral and interrelated parts of a subtle and complex cultural change rather than (largely) unrelated moments of cultural evolution . . ." (5). In this same volume, Ward Parks, "Oral Tradition and The *Canterbury Tales,*" 150, urges that the *Canterbury Tales* "could be fruitfully characterized and studied as a literate author's representation of the proceedings of an oral tradition."

[3] On this subject, Walter J. Ong, *Orality and Literacy: The Technologizing of the Word* (New York: Methuen, 1982), comments on the power of words in an oral (or transitional) culture: "For anyone who has a sense of what words are in a primary oral culture, or a culture not far removed from primary orality, it is not surprising that the Hebrew term *dabar* means 'word' and 'event.' Malinowski (1923, pp. 451, 470–81) has made the point that among 'primitive' (oral) peoples generally language is a mode of action and not simply a countersign of thought. . . . Neither is it surprising that oral peoples commonly, and probably universally, consider words to have great power" (32).

[4] On the centrality of speech (and the arts of communication) and civic life to the program of the Italian humanists, see particularly Eugenio Garin, *L'umanesimo italiano: filosofia e vita civile nel Rinascimento* (Italian Humanism: Philosophy and Civic Life in the Renaissance) (Bari: Laterza, 1952); Hans Baron, *The Crisis of the Early Renaissance* (Princeton: Princeton UP, 1955); and Charles Trinkaus, "A Humanist's Image of Humanism: The Inaugural Orations of Bartolommeo della Fonte" in *The Scope of Renaissance Humanism* (Ann Arbor: U of Michigan P, 1983) 52–87.

and noblest of all streams,"[5] but also the ancient sense that a consonance between words and deeds is necessary to the moral life and to human civilization. In the Homeric epics (as in *Beowulf*), speech is the measure of a human being and, as Odysseus reminds Agamemnon in the Underworld when he can give him no news of his son, "empty words are evil."[6] Odysseus, the man "skilled in all ways of contending," not least in the area of artful speech, voices a distinction between his more specific and limited deceptions and his overall integrity, as evidenced by his desire to return home and reestablish his household.[7]

In their concern with the consistency between speech and action and particularly in their estimation of speech, the humanists challenge the traditional Christian conviction that speech brings with it (indeed, precipitates) all that is evil and sensuous. While speech retained through the Middle Ages its ritual function as a conduit to God,[8] it was bridled by church authority on the popular front. Early Christian writings had repeatedly urged the containment of speech, describing it as something that, if not evil in itself, would surely lead to evil. These strictures remained influential for centuries. Thus Abelard in his *Letters of Direction* assembles for Heloise an arsenal of *sententia* against speech:

> An idle or superfluous word and too much talk are the same thing. Hence St Augustine says in the first book of his *Retrac-*

---

[5] *Timaeus* 75e, in *The Collected Dialogues of Plato,* ed. Edith Hamilton and Huntington Cairns, Bollingen Series, no. 71 (Princeton: Princeton UP, 1961) 1198.

[6] Homer, *The Odyssey*, vol. 1, Loeb Classical Library (1919, repr. 1960) XI.463-64, " '. . . οὐδέ τι οἶδα, ζώει ὅ γ᾽ ἢ τέθνηκε· κακὸν δ᾽ ἀνεμώλια βάζειν.' " The English translation is taken from Homer, *The Odyssey*, trans. Robert Fitzgerald (New York: Doubleday, 1963) 200.

[7] This distinction is also evident in Alkinoos's comment to Odysseus that the latter speaks with art, but that his intent in speaking is honest (*The Odyssey*, trans. Fitzgerald, 197).

[8] On the subject of the spoken word as a conduit to God—and especially women's role in this—see Sharon Farmer, "Persuasive Voices: Clerical Images of Medieval Wives," *Speculum* 61 (1986): 517–43. Farmer reminds us that "even here there were hesitations about the positive potential of spoken language alone. Medieval authors often asserted that by itself speech could not bring about conversion, the desired effect of evangelism. Those saintly men who spread the faith with their preaching were heirs to the apostles, who had received the gift of tongues from the Holy Spirit on the day of Pentecost: their preaching was aided by divine grace." Farmer describes a tradition extending from the 1030s (and the charters concerning Ermengard, the wife of Count Odo II) to Thomas of Chobham's *Manual for Confessors* (ca. 1215) that allowed that "pious women, like evangelists, were agents of the civilizing process . . ." (541).

3

tions: "Far be it from me to hold that there is too much talk when necessary words are spoken, however long-winded and prolix they may be." And in the person of Solomon it is also said that "Where men talk too much sin is not far away; the man who holds his tongue is wise." . . . Just how difficult it is to bridle the tongue, but how beneficial, the apostle James carefully considers when he says that "All of us often go wrong: the man who never says a wrong thing is perfect. . . . The tongue is a small member of the body, but how great a fire! How vast a forest it can set alight! . . . It is a world of wickedness, an intractable evil, charged with deadly venom. . . ."

Any excess of words or signs must be firmly corrected, words especially, in which lies the greater danger—a frequent and serious danger which St Gregory was most anxious to forestall when he instructs us in the seventh book of his *Morals*: "When we are careless about guarding against idle words, we come to harmful ones. By these provocation is sown, quarrels arise, the torches of hatred are set alight and the whole peace of the heart is destroyed."[9]

Augustine describes speech as a bridge to spiritual understanding and as something that is finally transcended; thus words are sounds of the mouth and have "a beginning and an ending," while God's, are "fruits of the spirit" and eternal.[10] In the thirteenth century, St. Thomas Aquinas reasons that "as Plato says, speech was given to us so we could know signs of others' wills," but "the word of the heart—that which is actually considered by the intellect—is predicated properly of God, because it is entirely free of matter, corporeity, and all defects."[11] In the fourteenth

---

[9] Abelard, in *The Letters of Abelard and Heloise,* trans. Betty Radice (New York: Penguin, 1974) 187–89, citing St. Augustine, *Retractiones* 1, preface; Proverbs 10.19 (Vulgate); James 3.2, 5; St. Gregory, *Moralia* 7.37.

[10] *The Confessions of St. Augustine* 9.10, trans. Rex Warner (New York: New American Library, 1963) 201.

[11] St. Thomas Aquinas, *Truth,* vol. 1, questions 1–9, trans. Robert W. Mulligan, S.J. (Chicago: Regnery, 1952) 423 and 172–73, resp. In the thirteenth century, too, the vices of the tongue were given "a separate category subordinated to or added to the seven capital sins." See Elaine Fantham, trans. and ed., introduction to Erasmus's "The Tongue / Lingua," in *The Collected Works of Erasmus: Literary and Educational Writings* vol. 29, *Literary and Educational Writings* (Toronto: U of Toronto P, 1989) 252. Fantham cites Morton Bloomfield's *The Seven Deadly Sins: An Introduction to the History of a Reli-*

century, prayer itself, by more radical authorities, is abridged and abbreviated, sometimes to a single word.[12] And even as late as the sixteenth century, Erasmus would devote at least three quarters of his *Lingua* (1525) to describing the evils of the tongue.[13]

In early Italian humanist thought, the Christian advice to bridle or at least to minimize speech is replaced by a celebration of its potentialities. Thus, if speech in St. Gregory's estimation can destroy the heart's peace, it is for Dante "an instrument as necessary to our thought as a horse is to a knight."[14] In his defense of the vernacular in the early fourteenth century, Dante will ask, "for what greater power is there than that which can change human hearts, making men do what they would not, and refrain from what they would, as this language has done and still does?"[15] For Petrarch speech is an "index of the soul."[16] But perhaps

---

gious Concept (East Lansing: U of Michigan P, 1952) for discussion of specific medieval works treating the sins of the tongue. Robert Mannyng of Brunne's *Handlyng Synne* (1303) reflects this attention to classification in its treatment of the sins of the tongue. In *Handlyng Synne*, sins of speech are found both among the Ten Commandments and the Seven Deadly Sins. For an example in the *Canterbury Tales* of this penchant for classification, see the fiend's rather erudite distinction between intentional and unintentional cursing in the *Friar's Tale*, esp. III (D) 1556–68 ("It is nat his entente . . . / The carl spak oo thing, but he thoghte another") and III (D) 1624–27.

[12] *The Cloud of Unknowing and Other Works,* ed. and trans. Clifton Wolters (New York: Penguin Books, 1961) 104. "If they are in few words, as they seldom are, then they are very few words; the fewer the better. If it is a little word of one syllable, I think it is better than if it is of two, and more in accordance with the work of the spirit."

[13] See "The Tongue / Lingua," trans. and ed. Elaine Fantham, in *The Collected Works of Erasmus,* vol. 29, bk. 7 (Toronto: U of Toronto P, 1989) 249–412. As Fantham points out in her introduction, "The final positive and hortatory section on 'Christian use of the tongue' is shortest of all, occupying only 10 pages"; this, she explains is partly because "Erasmus had already formed the ambition of writing a larger and more comprehensive study of the art of preaching, a counterpart of the fourth book of Augustine's *De doctrina christiana* on harnessing rhetoric in the service of God" (255–56).

A succinct statement of the Christian view of language can be found in Phillip Pulsiano, "Redeemed Language and the Ending of *Troilus and Criseyde,*" in *Sign, Sentence, Discourse: Language in Medieval Thought and Literature,* ed. Julian N. Wasserman and Lois Roney (Syracuse: Syracuse UP, 1989) 153–74.

[14] *De vulgari eloquentia* II.1, in Dante Alighieri, *De vulgari eloquentia,* ed. Aristide Marigo (Firenze: Felice Le Monnier, 1957) 168. "Et cum loquela non aliter sit necessarium instrumentum nostre conceptionis quam equus militis. . . ." The English translation is taken from Dante Alighieri, *Literature in the Vernacular (De vulgari eloquentia),* trans. Sally Purcell (Manchester, Eng.: Carcanet New P, 1981) 38.

[15] *Literature in the Vernacular* 35.

[16] Petrarch, *Rerum familiarium libri* 1.9, ed. Rossi-Bosco (Firenze, 1933) 45ff.; cited in Eugenio Garin, *Italian Humanism: Philosophy and Civic Life in the Renaissance,* trans. Peter Munz (Oxford: Blackwell, 1965) 19.

the most expansive humanist statement concerning speech is Boccaccio's:

> But the origin of man was truly from Heaven; he was created for the purpose of reflecting upon things celestial and was given speech not only as a necessity but as an enhancement. By this means we communicate our most profound reflections on higher things, on changes in the elements, on the advancement of various matters, and on our perception of iniquities. We join with other men in intelligent understanding. We praise virtues; we deprecate vices; we receive and transmit the results of teaching. In short, we reveal whatever the mind experiences through reason, and we comprehend the significance of what we learn.[17]

The very power in speech that drives the Christian fathers to seek to minimize it, whether in the individual soul or in the commonwealth, inspires the humanists,[18] following Cicero, to encourage its study. Cicero's *De inventione*,[19] the work to which especially Petrarch and Boccaccio

[17] *De casibus virorum illustrium* 6.13.5, in *Tutte le Opere di Giovanni Boccaccio* (Milano: Arnoldo Mondadori, 1983) 546. All subsequent citations in Latin are taken from this edition. "Homini vero, cui celestis erat origo et ad celestia consideranda producto, non solum decora fuit sed oportuna locutio. Hac etenim profundissimas superiorum corporum meditationes, elementorum alterationes, rerum variarum productiones atque corruptiones perceptas communicamus solo homini intellectas; amicitias iungimus virtutes laudamus, vitia deprimimus, doctrinas accipimus et exhibemus et breviter quicquid rationalis anima sentiat propalamus et sentita percipimus." The English translation is from Boccaccio, *The Fates of Illustrious Men*, trans. Louis Brewer Hall (New York: Ungar, 1965) 165–66. All subsequent citations in translation are taken from the Hall edition.

[18] Trinkaus regards Petrarch (1304–74) as "the chief founder of Renaissance humanism" and judges that Boccaccio (1313–75) is the "most important link between Petrarch's pioneering phase of humanism and its later development as a widely diffused, increasingly favored cultural movement in the Quattrocento" (*The Scope of Renaissance Humanism* 11, 15–16).

[19] On the different conceptions of Cicero in the Middle Ages and the Renaissance, particularly as these concern his emphasis on civic life, see Hans Baron, *In Search of Florentine Civic Humanism: Essays on the Transition from Medieval to Modern Thought*, vol. 1 (Princeton: Princeton UP, 1988), esp. chap. 5, "The Memory of Cicero's Roman Civic Spirit in the Medieval Centuries and in the Florentine Renaissance" (94–133). Baron remarks that "one could find no better framework for the history of Humanism in the early Renaissance, especially in Florence, than the story of how the aspect of Cicero the Roman citizen and thinker was but timidly recognized throughout the medieval centuries, only to be seized upon in the Quattrocento by humanists as an essential aid in their efforts to break away from many of the assumptions held during the Middle Ages" (96–97).

most frequently return, had established the art of rhetoric as part of politics and had immediately addressed the problem of the deceiver. Cicero drew attention to the "depraved imitation of virtue" (*prava virtutis imitatrix*) that masquerades as eloquence and corrupts the state. Though true eloquence is always accompanied by wisdom,[20] this depraved imitation of eloquence, accompanied by cunning and helped by talent, often passes as eloquence so successfully that it is a powerful corrupter of men and states: "But when a certain agreeableness of manner—a depraved imitation of virtue—acquired the power of eloquence unaccompanied by any consideration of moral duty, then low cunning supported by talent grew accustomed to corrupt cities and undermine the lives of men."[21]

If only to combat this abuse of eloquence, Cicero urges good men to learn the skills of speaking well. Whether it be an art, a study, a skill, or a gift of nature, eloquence must be an attribute of good citizens. In

---

[20] The tradition of the good man speaking well is as ancient as the Homeric epics; it is significant in Plato and Isocrates, and is powerfully developed by Cicero. In the *De inventione,* Cicero argues that eloquence first brought about the transformation of mankind from savage to civilized and that its study by good men is necessary for the protection of society. Cicero's emphasis on the role and power of eloquence is suffused with his fundamental concern that it be inseparable from wisdom.

"Ac me quidem diu cogitantem ratio ipsa in hanc postissimum sententiam ducit, ut existimem sapientiam sine eloquentia parum prodesse civitatibus, eloquentiam vero sine sapientia nimium obesse plerumque, prodesse numquam. Quare si quis omissis rectissimis atque honestissimis studiis rationis et offici consumit omnem operam in exercitatione dicendi, is inutilis sibi, perniciosus patriae civis alitur; qui vero ita sese armat eloquentia, ut non oppugnare commoda patriae, sed pro his propugnare possit, is mihi vir et suis et publicis rationibus utilissimus atque amicissimus civis fore videtur."

[For my own part, after long thought, I have been led by reason itself to hold this opinion first and foremost, that wisdom without eloquence does too little for the good of states, but that eloquence without wisdom is generally highly disadvantageous and is never helpful. Therefore if anyone neglects the study of philosophy and moral conduct, which is the highest and most honourable of pursuits, and devotes his whole energy to the practice of oratory, his civic life is nurtured into something useless to himself and harmful to his country; but the man who equips himself with the weapons of eloquence, not to be able to attack the welfare of his country but to defend it, he, I think, will be a citizen most helpful and most devoted both to his own interests and to those of his community]. *De inventione* 1.1, in *De inventione, De optimo genere, Oratorum topica,* trans. H. M. Hubbell, Loeb Classical Library (Cambridge: Harvard UP, 1949) 4–5. All further citations from *De inventione* are taken from the Loeb edition.

[21] *De inventione* 1.3. "postquam vero commoditas quaedam, prava virtutis imitatrix, sine ratione offici, decendi copiam consecuta est, tum ingenio freta malitia pervertere urbes et vitas hominum labefactare assuevit." This issue is addressed immediately after Cicero has defended the good accomplished by eloquence.

addition to employing eloquence for the welfare of the state, these citizens will recognize the false imitation of it in others and be armed against that abuse, for eloquence is a "weapon" that can be used for good as well as for evil. It is precisely because of the danger of speech, particularly in the mouths of evil people who use it to disguise their aims, that its study by others is so critical.[22]

In the fourteenth century, Petrarch complains that the Scholastics do not find eloquence worthy of a man of letters,[23] and he more than once describes eloquence—and speech—in terms that recall Cicero's emphasis in the *De inventione* on its political nature.[24] In the *Remedies for Prosperity,* Petrarch explicitly distinguishes between "the ready flow of words (the *dicendi peritia,* or rhetorical skill) which often abounds in wanton and depraved people," and true eloquence, which must be accompanied by goodness.[25] The consonance between words and deeds, which is the ideal of speech—and indeed, Cicero's and Petrarch's definition of true eloquence—is not the political reality. "Articulate language," Petrarch continues, "a big vocabulary, and a certain rhetorical know-how can be possessed, equally, by good and by evil people," and speech is potentially all-powerful, for good or for harm. For Petrarch, as for Cic-

---

[22] *De inventione* 1.5. James J. Murphy reminds us that Cicero's *De inventione* was so esteemed in the Middle Ages as to be referred to as *rhetorica prima* or *rhetorica vetus.* See Murphy, *Rhetoric in the Middle Ages: A History of Rhetorical Theory from Saint Augustine to the Renaissance* (Berkeley: U of California P, 1974) 10. See also Richard McKeon, "Rhetoric in the Middle Ages," *Speculum* 17 (1942): 1–32.

[23] See Michael Mooney, *Vico in the Tradition of Rhetoric* (Princeton: Princeton UP, 1985) 42, who quotes Petrarch (quoting Cicero) as follows: "Thus only 'infantile inability to speak' and perplexed stammering, 'wisdom' trying hard to keep one eye open and 'yawning drowsily,' as Cicero (*De or.* 3.51.198; 233.144–45) calls it, is held in good repute nowadays. . . . From Aristotle's ways they swerve, taking eloquence to be an obstacle and a disgrace to philosophy, while he considered it a mighty adornment and tried to combine it with philosophy, 'prevailed upon,' it is asserted (*De or.* 3.35.141) 'by the fame of the orator Isocrates.' " See Petrarch, *De sui ipsius et multorum ignorantia, Opera omnia,* trans. Hans Nachod, 3 vols. (1554; rpt. Ridgewood, NJ: Gregg P, 1965) 2: 1143. See also *The Renaissance Philosophy of Man,* ed. Ernst Cassirer, P. O. Kristeller, and J. H. Randall Jr. (Chicago, U Chicago P, 1948) 53ff.

[24] In *Rhetoric and the Middle Ages,* Murphy describes the works of Cicero, Quintilian, and the author of *Rhetorica ad Herennium* as partaking of a common tradition which could properly be called "Ciceronian," and he reminds us that they "all follow the fundamental teaching of Isocrates to the effect that rhetoric is a part of political science" (8). See also his "Epilogue: Rediscovery and Implications" (357–63) on the rediscovery of Quintilian's *Institutio* and Cicero's *De oratore,* two works that were not available in their entirety in the 1300s.

[25] *Petrarch's Remedies for Fortune Fair and Foul: Book I: Remedies for Prosperity,* ed. and trans. Conrad H. Rawski (Bloomington: Indiana UP, 1991) 26–27.

ero, it is a "double-edged weapon, and it matters very much how you use it": "Some compare not ineptly the eloquence of a fool or a scoundrel to a sword in the hands of a madman—since it is important to the community that neither of the two be armed." Clearly, the political consequences of speech are extreme:

> Death and life are in the power of the tongue, the tongue, not of one man alone, but the tongues of many. And their tongues have overthrown whole commonwealths, and shall continue to overthrow them. The tongue is the worst and the most harmful member of evil persons. There is nothing softer than the tongue and nothing harder.[26]

Like Petrarch, Boccaccio asserts that neglecting speech is detrimental to the community. In *De casibus virorum illustrium,* a work which ostensibly seeks to arouse princes from their corrupt ways, Boccaccio gives specificity to his conviction that the mastery of speech is essential for individual and political well being. He returns repeatedly to a nexus of issues surrounding what Cicero had called in *De inventione* (1.3.) the depraved imitation of virtue. Flattery, hypocrisy, deceit, and the gullibility on which they depend, Boccaccio argues, must be combatted with a knowledge of the arts of speech. In the first book of *De casibus,* following the story of Theseus's "fall"—a fall that involves decisions made on the basis of others' words—Boccaccio pauses to consider the problem of credulousness. To combat credulousness involves, at the very least, the ability to listen astutely:

> Do you think all opinions make equal sense? Certainly nothing is more foolish than a credulous mind. The prudent man refuses no one's ideas, weighs each according to its worth, then deliberates carefully so that he does not make a mistake by a too precipitous conclusion concerning something he does not know anything about. He is like a mental watchtower observing with discrimination who is speaking, and judging what the speaker has to gain; he wants to know what actually took place, where and when. He takes anger or calm

---

[26] Petrarch, *Remedies for Prosperity* 26–28.

into account, and whether the speaker is friend or enemy, honorable or infamous.[27]

Here, in his emphasis on the art of listening, Boccaccio reasserts the objectives of Cicero's rhetoric (particularly in the *De inventione*) as a means of regaining contact with political reality. In his subsequent comment that "if we are human, if we examine ourselves, if we are careful, we will follow the authority of ancient laws which abhorred ready credulousness,"[28] Boccaccio points his audience to the study of eloquence and speech, not only as a means of moving people, but as a means of understanding their inner nature. Theseus's misjudgment, brought about by credulousness, can be avoided by greater alertness to speech. The study of speech is a means of anticipating or "reading" others, including the flatterer or the deceiver; in short, it is a kind of sociology, a means of understanding human nature and society.

Boccaccio claims that the care for the safety of a prince concerns itself with everything except the most critical source of danger:

> Often I remember laughing when I saw princes walking in public surrounded by a retinue of servants. The doors of their houses had guards who examined everyone for arms. At meals they had food-tasters in case they might swallow anything poisonous. On the other hand they kept their ears wide open and their minds receptive to anyone who was speaking, as if words could not influence, deceive, or poison them. Oh, how foolish was their ingenuousness! We have never heard of a village, no matter how small, the inhabitants of which were all killed by poison, nor any group of people, regardless of its size, who could not prevent an equal misfortune with a little care. Countless tragedies known in every hamlet proclaim that it was the honeyed phrase, the deceptive tongue

---

[27] *De casibus*, I.XI.3–5. "Et cum ita sit, omnesne putabis uno eodemque animo verba proferre? Nil profecto hac existimatione stolidius. Circumspecti quidem viri atque constantis est negligere neminem, sed unumquemque pro meritis pendere, et, ne possit de incognitis precipiti sententia falli, se in se ipsum colligere, et, quasi e specula mentis librato iudicio, intueri quis verba faciens, quod ob meritum, quis in quem facta, quo in loco, quo in tempore, iratus an quietus animo, hostis an amicus, infamis aut honestus homo sit."

[28] *De casibus*, I.XI.17. ". . . si viri erimus, si oculati, si cauti venerandarum legum auctoritatem imitabimur, que in tantam festinantiam abhorrent credulitatis. . . ."

believed too easily which brought about the downfall of the credulous, the ruin of cities, and the destruction of whole regions and their inhabitants, and the subversion of kingdoms.[29]

Deceit is elsewhere described as "the worst kind of evil" because with "a pleasing face, honeyed words, a humble step she is ever watchful to snare the pure in faith." Religion, law, wisdom, and arms are all potentially successful arenas for her work.[30]

If it is servants who protect the prince from the armed assassin and from poisons, what, according to Boccaccio, can protect him from "the honeyed phrase" and "the deceptive tongue?" Not servants, surely. The urgency with which Boccaccio calls for the study of rhetorical skills exactly reflects Cicero's thought in *De inventione,* and the reasons for the urgency are also the same:

There are still many other forces, however, which, unless they are controlled by oratory, might develop from insig-

---

[29] *De casibus,* I.XI.10–12. "Risisse sepissime memini dum viderem in publico principes caterva satellitum stipatos incedere; domi, clausis ianuis vigiles hostiarios habere, neminem preter inermem et examinatum introducere; in mensa poculorum et epularum pregustatores tenere, ne forsan aliquid nocuum saluti corporee immicti queat; aures vero atque animum quibuscunque loquentibus habere propatulum, quasi non aculeos non insidias non venena ingerant verba. O potentum solertia inanis! Nullos usquam etiam parvi oppidi cives simul veneno sublatos audivimus, nullos populos, quantulacunque parva cautela previsos, pari cede deletos comperimus. Mellita verba et bilinguium suasiones iniecte credulis ruinas urbium et incendia creba, regionum populationes, et regnorum subversiones, sino exitia, stulte credentium suscitasse fere per omne trivium flebiles clamitant tragedie."

[30] The passage describing deceit from *De casibus,* II. XXIII.1–2. is as follows: "Est enim fraus species pessima mali. Nam facie placida, mellitis verbis ac humili incedens gradu, pervigil semper sincere insidiatur fidei, et ut plurimum ad aculeos veneniferos infigendos pro instrumento superficie tenus utitur Deo. Hec enim tanti roboris est, si astutus sit artifex, ut venerandam legum potestatem prosternat, mortalium sapientiam fallat, armorum vim atque potentiam frangat, artem decipiat, et omnem vigilantiam persepe confundat."

[Deceit is truly the worst kind of evil, for with a pleasing face, honeyed words, and a humble step, she is ever watchful to snare the pure in faith. And to inject her poisonous sting she invokes the name of God often for frivolous purposes. She is so strong, so clever, so artful that she overthrows the venerable power of the law. She deceives the wisdom of man and conquers the power of arms. She beguiles any skill and very often confounds any vigilance. The most shamefully evil men, and those without any principles make great use of her, for she has no constancy of virtue or strength of mind. Beneath her cloak of honor she always carries snares, lures and craftiness. She tramples

nificance into the greatest calamity to mankind. If we do not possess the skill in oratorical composition appropriate to the occasion: words now rough or sharp, but now calm and placid, now agreeably discerning, now containing beautiful figures of speech, now serious wisdom, and—in addition to these embellishments—a public delivery suitable to the immediate need, then we would not be able to restrain ordinary men lost in the passion of anger (let alone a king).[31]

In explicitly or implicitly subsuming Chaucer's sense of discourse into a patristic model, critics have generally ignored the force of the humanist tradition and Chaucer's place in it.[32] Much evidence, notably that which connects the *Monk's Tale* with Boccaccio's *De casibus virorum illustrium*,[33] suggests that Chaucer was aware of this tradition. Chaucer's

the simple and credulous under her feet and frequently brings them to ruin with her sham].

[31] *De casibus*, VI. XIII.9. "Preterea multa supersunt que, nisi moderata oratione tractentur, in mortalium perniciem maximam ex minimis quandoque consurgunt. Si nobis non sint pro tempore arte composita, nunc aspera atque mordentia verba, nunc placida atque clementia, nunc summo lepore sapida, nunc colorata pulchritudine splendida, nunc gravitate sententiarum succiplena et cum his pronuntiatio secundum necessitudinem instantem apta, qualiter, sinamus regem, sed plebeium hominem ira incensum furentemque perdite in mansuetudinem retrahemus. . . ."

[32] Eugene Vance, for example, grants that "the notion that the order of language constitutes the living order of society was already central to a tradition of classical oratory that any poet such as Chaucer, Dante, or Petrarch knew very well." See Vance, "Marvelous Signals: Poetics, Sign Theory, and Politics in Chaucer's *Troilus*," *New Literary History* 10 (1979): 294. But in this same essay, Vance claims that "in England attitudes towards rhetoric as a political instrument remained ambivalent" and that Chaucer, in contrast to Lydgate, sees the "rhetor" as "a powerful and dangerous figure who subverts the well-being of society" (299). For Lydgate on the status of rhetoric, Vance cites Lois Ebin, "Lydgate's Views on Poetry," *Annuale Mediaevale* 18 (1977): 76–106. Vance's essay, which makes no reference to Italian humanist ideas of discourse and rhetoric, argues that Chaucer's Nun's Priest is "a paradigm of Christian eloquence" and that Chaucer sees the "rhetor" in figures like the Summoner, the Pardoner, and the Wife of Bath (299).

[33] For discussion of this connection, see particularly Peter Godman, "Chaucer and Boccaccio's Latin Works," in *Chaucer and the Italian Trecento*, ed. Piero Boitani (Cambridge: Cambridge UP, 1983) 269–95; and Piero Boitani, "The *Monk's Tale*: Dante and Boccaccio," *Medium Aevum* 45 (1976): 50–69. Chaucer's receptivity to Italian humanism is also the subject of Renate Haas's "Chaucer's *Monk's Tale*: An Ingenious Criticism of Early Humanist Conceptions of Tragedy," *Humanistica Lovaniensia* 36 (1987): 44–70. The substantial Anglo-Italian economic and social links in the fourteenth century, and the day-to-day effect of these on Chaucer, are described by Wendy Childs, who reminds us that "London was the busiest Italian centre in England, the Italian merchant

treatment of speech is characterized by a remarkable appreciation of its potentialities and nuances, in the individual and in the commonwealth.[34] Issues prominent in the humanist discussions of speech—the integrity of words and deeds, and the misuses of speech in the form of deceit, flattery, and hypocrisy—surface repeatedly in Chaucer's poetry. So, too, does the problem of credulousness and the relationship between speech and the commonwealth. Sometime in the 1380s or '90s, Chaucer's "Lak of Stedfastnesse" counsels Richard II to "wed thy folk agein to stedfastnesse," defining "stedfastnesse" as the consonance between words and deeds, and thus making true eloquence the central and urgent necessity of good governance. But the relationship between speech and the commonwealth, as we shall see, is prominent throughout Chaucer's work, and particularly in the *General Prologue* and in the frame narrative that it introduces, where Chaucer embraces a group that more or less mirrors society itself[35] and looks at that society in part through the prism of its discursive habits and aims.

Chaucer's handling of speech shows both intense interest and exquisite discrimination. For Chaucer, as for Boccaccio, speech is a way of reading society. In the portraits of the *General Prologue*—just one of the poems where Chaucer's differentiation of speech habits is notable—even those pilgrims who are described as customarily talkative, who make a habit of vivacious (gregarious) speech, are different from one another. So, for example, the comment on the Wife of Bath that "In felaweshipe wel koude she laughe and carpe" distinguishes her speech from the

---

community was an integral part of his working world, the more so since the only alien group to take part in the export of English wool by this time was the Italian." See Childs, "Anglo-Italian Contacts in the Fourteenth Century," in *Chaucer and the Italian Trecento,* ed. Piero Boitani (Cambridge: Cambridge UP, 1983) 68.

[34] The situation in England regarding the study of rhetoric in the two centuries before Chaucer has been briefly, but pointedly, noted by James J. Murphy. His analysis of *The Owl and the Nightingale* (ca. 1180) implies a remarkable "environment of discourse" and "advances what can only be seen as a sad and depressing conjecture about the welfare of Middle English literature in the two centuries following the poem." See *Medieval Eloquence: Studies in the Theory and Practice of Medieval Rhetoric,* ed. James J. Murphy (Berkeley: U of California P, 1978) 198–230.

[35] Paul Strohm refers to the *Canterbury* pilgrims as a "discursive community" and the *General Prologue* as a "mixed commonwealth of style"; see *Social Chaucer* (Cambridge: Harvard UP, 1989), esp. 145–82. In spite of the fact that some social classes in medieval society (i.e., the peasantry and the aristocracy) are missing from the *General Prologue,* Nevill Coghill's comment about the *Canterbury Tales* is still generally valid: "In all our literature, there is not such another picture of a whole society"; see Coghill, *The Poet Chaucer* (London: Oxford UP, 1949) 87.

Miller, "a janglere and a goliardeys" who talks mostly of "synne and harlotries" (I [A] 560–61). In turn, the report of the Host's boldness of speech is bent towards the complimentary, being coupled with Ciceronian virtues:

> A fairer burgeys was ther noon in Chepe—
> Boold of his speche, and wys, and wel ytaught. (I [A] 754–55)

Chaucer, like Petrarch and Boccaccio, draws attention to the gulf between rhetorical skills and the public understanding of them and to the humanist issue of consonance between words and deeds. His list of pilgrims in the *General Prologue* notably begins and ends with two figures whose discursive habits are in this respect most contrasted. First is the Knight, who "never yet no vileynye ne sayde" in his whole life to anyone. His speech, characterized by what it does not include, is of a piece with his generally idealized nature:

> . . . though that he were worthy, he was wys,
> And of his port as meeke as is a mayde.
> He nevere yet no vileynye ne sayde
> In al his lyf unto no maner wight. (I [A] 68–71)

Last in the group of portraits is the Pardoner, for whom the use of language is all virtuoso performance and private gain. His speech is an amalgam of the discursive skills of many of his fellow pilgrims, and he uses these to blatantly manipulative effect:

> Wel koude he rede a lessoun or a storie,
> But alderbest he song an offertorie;
> For wel he wiste, whan that song was songe,
> He moste preche and wel affile his tonge
> To wynne silver, as he ful wel koude. (I [A] 709–13)

Like Boccaccio when he comments that deceit "is ever watchful to snare the pure in faith," Chaucer here alerts us that though the Knight and the Parson may represent ideal discursive positions, it is the Pardoner with whom society (and especially the Parson) must reckon. His rhetorical skills uncover a mine of public gullibility:

. . . And thus, with feyned flaterye and japes,
He made the person and the peple his apes. (I [A] 705–6)

However various and nuanced, the portraits of the *General Prologue* return repeatedly to the issue of the integrity of speech and action. So, for example, it is the style of the Clerk—along with the Knight and Parson—to speak with restraint. Fulfilling not a courtly but a clerical and scholarly ideal, the Clerk's speech is economical in the extreme:

Noght o word spak he moore than was neede,
And that was seyd in forme and reverence,
And short and quyk and ful of hy sentence;
Sownynge in moral vertu was his speche,
And gladly wolde he lerne and gladly teche. (I [A] 304–8)

As "moral" as the Clerk's, the Parson's use of language is more practical and has a greater range of tone. Though usually discreet and benign, his speech, in contrast to the Clerk's, is capable of sharpness:

But it were any persone obstinat,
What so he were, of heigh or lough estat,
Hym wolde he snybben sharply for the nonys. (I [A] 521–23)

The Parson's portrait is wrapped up with reference both to the matter and the manner of his discourse. Thrice-evoked, the Gospel—its content and its style—is specifically the authoritative source of the Parson's speech:

He was also a lerned man, a clerk,
That Cristes gospel trewely wolde preche. (I [A] 480–81)

This noble ensample to his sheep he yaf,
That first he wroghte, and afterward he taughte.
Out of the gospel he tho wordes caughte
And this figure he added eek therto,
That if gold ruste, what shal iren do? (I [A] 496–500)

But Cristes loore and his apostle twelve
He taughte; but first he folwed it hymselve. (I [A] 527–28)

15

For the Prioress, the Monk, and the Friar, on the other hand, speech is one of the symptoms of the tailoring of spiritual calling to worldly interests. Briefly, but pointedly and variously, it indicates the worldly circumferences of their natures. For the Prioress, speech is a social trait that one can try to imitate. The ingenuousness of her speech—her dainty oaths, her refined singing, and finishing-school French—is remarkably of a piece with her desire to imitate courtliness and to be held worthy of respect:

> Hire gretteste ooth was but by Seinte Loy;
> And she was cleped madame Eglentyne.
> Ful weel she soong the service dyvyne,
> Entuned in hir nose ful semely;
> And Frenssh she spak ful faire and fetisly,
> After the scole of Stratford atte Bowe,
> For Frenssh of Parys was to hire unknowe. (I [A] 120–26)

For the Monk, on the other hand, speech is a more direct means of expression. Paradoxically, there is integrity between his words and his deeds: his speech is an honest confrontation of his quarrel with authority. The savvy and shrewdness of common speech (whether the Monk's own or as reported by the narrator) assert themselves against the aridity of "that text" and "thilke text":

> He yaf nat of that text a pulled hen,
> That seith that hunters ben nat hooly men,
> Ne that a monk, whan he is recchelees,
> Is likned til a fissh that is waterlees—
> This is to seyn, a monk out of his cloystre.
> But thilke text heeld he nat worth an oystre;
> And I seyde his opinion was good.
> What sholde he studie and make hymselven wood
> Upon a book in cloystre alwey to poure,
> Or swynken with his handes, and laboure,
> As Austyn bit? How shal the world be served?
> Lat Austyn have his swynk to hym reserved! (I [A] 177–88)

There is a certain admiration (mixed with moral disapprobation) in Chaucer's view of the Friar's discourse, something that will turn up in

16

the Pardoner's later performance, too. The Friar has mastered a courtly discourse that effectively (and amiably) disguises his material objectives. He hears confession sweetly; his discourse is pleasant (I [A] 221–22); lisping like the courtly lover, his English is sweet upon his tongue (I [A] 265); in all the four orders, there is no one that knows so much of dalliance and fair language (I [A] 210–11). While the Monk's speech openly debunks authority, the Friar's neglect of the sick and the poor (I [A] 243–48) is sarcastically portrayed as rationalization.

In some portraits, discourse serves to give the impression of professional and monetary well-being; in contrast to the Clerk, whose speech is "sownynge in moral vertu" (I [A] 307), the Merchant speaks

> . . . ful solempnely,
> Sownynge alwey th'encrees of his wynnyng.
> He wolde the see were kept for any thyng
> Bitwixe Middelburgh and Orewelle. (I [A] 274–77)

Of the Sergeant of Law we are told:

> Discreet he was and of greet reverence—
> He semed swich, his wordes weren so wise. (I [A] 312–13)

And the Physician's speech is purely professional:

> In al this world ne was ther noon hym lik,
> To speke of phisik and of surgerye,
> For he was grounded in astronomye. (I [A] 412–14)

People are credulous, and key elements of a particular style are easily mimicked. Thus, the Summoner,

> . . . whan that he wel dronken hadde the wyn,
> Thanne wolde he speke no word but Latyn.
> A fewe termes hadde he, two or thre,
> That he had lerned out of som decree—
> No wonder is, he herde it al the day;
> And eek ye knowen wel how that a jay
> Kan clepen "Watte" as wel as kan the pope.
> But whoso koude in oother thyng hym grope,

> Thanne hadde he spent al his philosophie;
> Ay "*Questio quid iuris*" wolde he crie. (I [A] 637–46)

Given this variety of discourse in the *General Prologue,* the absence of speech can also be meaningful. In the portraits of the Yeoman, the Shipman, the Reeve, and especially the Manciple, the mastery of a given specialty—whether it be the Shipman's "craft" (I [A] 401), the Manciple's "achaat" (I [A] 571), or the Reeve's "rekenynge" (I [A] 600)—seems to take precedence over speech itself and exerts felt power over others. The Reeve is, of course, the most extreme example of this: there is something completely disquieting in the power of his silence, his secrets, and his knowledge of the secrets of others (I [A] 603–5).

Encircling, but still set apart from, the great spectrum of the pilgrims' speech is the speech of the poet-narrator himself, which Chaucer comments upon in the *General Prologue* and in the *Miller's Prologue.* Bringing to bear both Christ's authority and Plato's,[36] these comments powerfully embrace for the poet the whole range of discourse suggested in the portraits of the Knight and the Pardoner:

> But first I pray yow, of youre curteisye,
> That ye n'arette it nat my vileynye,
> Thogh that I pleynly speke in this mateere,
> To telle yow hir wordes and hir cheere,
> Ne thogh I speke hir wordes proprely.
> For this ye knowen al so wel as I:
> Whoso shal telle a tale after a man,
> He moot reherce as ny as evere he kan
> Everich a word, if it be in his charge,
> Al speke he never so rudeliche and large,
> Or ellis he moot telle his tale untrewe
> Or feyne thyng, or fynde wordes newe. (I [A] 725–36)

The emphasis on inclusiveness and truth to his "mateere" (I [A] 727; also 3172–75) recalls, by contrast, both the Knight's purity—the absence of "vileynye" in his speech (I [A] 70)—and the Pardoner's "feyned flaterye" (I [A] 705). The poet-narrator describes himself as speaking

---

[36] See P. B. Taylor, "Chaucer's *Cosyn to the Dede,*" *Speculum* 47 (1982): 315–27.

"pleynly" (I [A] 727), relaying to the audience, as nearly as he is able, what he has heard.

But it is when Chaucer turns to the storytelling game, and we realize he is going to subject different modes of discourse to each other, that a larger, distinctively Chaucerian approach to discourse becomes most apparent. The Host's proposed game—arrived at by discussion, voted on, and itself consisting of discourse (I [A] 783–84)—is further testament to the universality of the word. But it is more: for Chaucer, discourse does not attain its full meaning until it becomes dialogue—until an audience enters the equation.

The dialogic[37] mode—with its questions, disputes, pretensions, and misunderstandings—gives a special realism to issues raised more theoretically by early humanists on the Continent. Chaucer's repeated return in the *Canterbury Tales* to issues of speech suggests that he creates in the tale-telling game a fictive world in which to explore manifest conflicts in the nature and aims of discourse. By subjecting disparate discourses to one another—the authoritative, idealized discourse of the Knight and his tale to the Miller's and his tale, the Miller's to the Reeve's, and then down the fragments to the irrational energies of the pilgrim society generally—Chaucer suggests that no single frame, except a dialogic one, can hope to be inclusive or objective. The contrast between the discursive world of the *Knight's Tale* and that of the fabliaux is only one example of the tendency of extremes to suggest each other, rather than to achieve resolution.[38] In a period when discourse is typically more pre-

---

[37] Here and in the pages that follow, I use the terms "dialogic" and "dialogical" in Bakhtin's sense to describe discourse as an interaction, whether actual or implied, between speaker and listener. Bakhtin describes the "dialogic orientation of discourse" as "the natural orientation of any living discourse. On all its various routes toward the object, in all its directions, the word encounters an alien word and cannot help encountering it in a living, tension-filled interaction. Only the mythical Adam, who approached a virginal and as yet verbally unqualified world with the first word, could really have escaped from start to finish this dialogic inter-orientation with the alien word that occurs in the object." See "Discourse in the Novel" in *The Dialogic Imagination: Four Essays by M. M. Bakhtin*, ed. Michael Holquist, trans, Caryl Emerson and Michael Holquist (Austin: U of Texas P, 1981) 279. Jill Mann has recently applied this dialogic process, or "dialogism," to the interaction between Chaucer's text and the reader; see her Presidential Address, "Chaucer and Atheism," *Studies in the Age of Chaucer* 17 (1995) 5–19, esp. 8–9. Also see Jill Mann, "The Authority of the Audience in Chaucer," in *Poetics: Theory and Practice in Medieval English Literature: The J. A. W. Bennett Lectures*, ed. Piero Boitani and Anna Torti (Woodbridge: D. S. Brewer, 1991) 1–11.

[38] Kathleen M. Ashley recognizes the significance to our understanding of the *Canterbury Tales* of Bakhtin's "insight into language as a field of ideological contention." She

scriptive than descriptive—when, in Derek Pearsall's words, "we have to reckon with the immensity of the weight of 'authority' "[39]—Chaucer repeatedly explores the ways in which speech refuses to be prescribed and contained.

Chaucer's sense of the critical nature of discourse (and its political character) was not only radical but dramatically timely. It came at a time in English history when severe and arbitrary restrictions were being put on the spoken word both in the city and in the court.[40] In *The Westminster Chronicle,* for example, two out of three of the ordinances ascribed to Nicholas Brembre (mayor of London from 1377 to 1378 and from 1383 to 1386) curtail free speech, making punishable by death the utterance of "any abuse or scurrility, in public or in private, against the mayor or

---

asserts that "contrary to the assumption which seems to underlie much Chaucer criticism of the past thirty years, Chaucer is bent on destabilizing meaning precisely by revealing the process of ideological contention at work" and that "Chaucer mirrors a world which is recognizably Early Modern in its dispersal of power." "The world he represents," she concludes, "is one in which no social or political group can establish hegemony and silence its rivals." See Ashley, "Renaming the Sins: A Homiletic Topos of Linguistic Instability in the *Canterbury Tales,*" in *Sign, Sentence, Discourse: Language in Medieval Thought and Literature,* ed. Julian N. Wasserman and Lois Roney (Syracuse: Syracuse UP, 1989) 272–89. Peggy Ann Knapp, similarly armed with Bakhtin's theory of the dialogic, challenges the assumptions of exegetical interpretations of the *Canterbury Tales.* See Knapp, *Chaucer and the Social Contest* (New York: Routledge, 1990), esp. 4–5. See also John Ganim, *Chaucerian Theatricality* (Princeton: Princeton UP, 1990) 30.

[39] Derek A. Pearsall has commented on the dangers of skepticism in the Middle Ages: "Now, we may think that the unknowableness of things is something of a weary platitude, and that a poet is not going to sustain interest for long in talking about something so obvious, but we have to reckon with the immensity of the weight of 'authority' in the Middle Ages and the difficulties, even the dangers, of skepticism. Skepticism is cheap nowadays, but William of Ockham, who at some distance, with the other *moderni,* is Chaucer's philosophical ancestor here, had to pay for it with exile and imprisonment." See Pearsall, *The Life of Geoffrey Chaucer: A Critical Biography* (Cambridge, MA: Blackwell, 1992) 114.

[40] Carl Lindahl's *Earnest Games: Folkloric Patterns in the "Canterbury Tales"* (Bloomington: Indiana UP, 1987) analyzes the "folkloric patterns" and "traditional strategies" used by Chaucer's pilgrims "to express their most negative and heretical thoughts—thoughts which, if given any other form, would invite frightening consequences" (10). Lindahl's study is unusual in being founded on the recognition that "Chaucer's contemporaries faced severe restrictions on what they could say and whom they could freely address" and argues that "if the *Canterbury Tales* is realistic on the level of language, similar restrictions should govern the verbal behavior of the pilgrims" (83). See particularly Lindahl's chap. 6, "The Social Base of Angry Speech in Chaucer's London" (73–86), where he comments that "the magnitude of slander can be gauged by the fact that *medieval Londoners, for all intents and purposes, considered words and deeds to be of equal significance*" (77; his italics).

20

an alderman or any respectable and substantial member of the commons of the city."[41]

Theoretically, a medieval king was urged to listen to counsel; the success of his policies depended on his hearing disinterested, prudent, and frank opinion. But in the complex factionalism that characterized most of Richard's reign (1377–99), verbal criticism could constitute treason.[42] In *The Westminster Chronicle* for 1386, the statute that accompanied the letters patent detailing conditions forced upon Richard II by his councillors in the Parliament of 1 October 1386 consisted primarily of an explicit prohibition against counseling the king.[43] It was "enacted in full parliament" so as to give, in the chronicler's words, "greater strength" to the councillors' provisions.[44] The statute warned that "no person of whatsoever estate or condition he may be, greater or less, shall give to our said lord the king, in private or openly, counsel, exhortation, or impulse" that would in any way undermine the provisions or their enforcement. If convicted a first time, "he shall forfeit all his goods and chattels to the king and nevertheless shall be imprisoned at the king's

---

[41] See *The Westminster Chronicle,* ed. L. C. Hector and Barbara F. Harvey (Oxford: Clarendon, 1982) 137.

[42] See J. G. Bellamy, *The Law of Treason in England in the Later Middle Ages,* Cambridge Studies in English Legal History (Cambridge: Cambridge UP, 1970), particularly chap. 5, "The Scope of Treason, 1352–1485" (102–37). Bellamy points out that "in the matter of defining treason the law to be observed was primarily the statute of 1352" (102). His discussion of this statute includes the detail that in the reign of Henry IV "several men were executed for high treason committed merely by the uttering of words; this was also held as imagining the king's death" (107).

[43] The statute is found in *The Westminster Chronicle,* 174–77. In *The Hollow Crown: A Life of Richard II* (New York: John Day, 1961), Harold F. Hutchison describes England at the time of these provisions (and statute) as a country dreading "for the second time a full-scale French invasion from the Low Countries." Gloucester and his faction "pose as the defenders of the realm"; the "Commons apprehensive and surly; the city of London was equally apprehensive, and still split between victualler and draper factions; the King and his court circle were without popular support." Hutchison points out that the parliament attacked the king indirectly through his chief ministers, demanding "the dismissal and impeachment of the Treasurer, John Fordham, and the Chancellor, Michael de la Pole, Earl of Suffolk" (104–5). See also Ruth Bird's *The Turbulent London of Richard II* (London: Longman's, Green, and Co., 1949), esp. chapter 5: "The Merciless Parliament and London," 86–101.

[44] *The Westminster Chronicle* 167–75. These provisions included, among other things, the names of the members of the "great counsel," which was now forcing its absolute powers on the nineteen-year-old Richard in order (in the words of the letters patent of 19 November 1386) "to survey and examine with our said great officers both the estate and government of our household, with all our courts, places, and offices, and the estate and government of all our realm. . . ."

will."[45] If convicted a second time, "then shall the said person . . . have judgement of life and limb." In other words, "misprision was to be punished with the penalty for treason."[46]

The Proclamation of 1387 (the earliest entry in English in the Letter-Books) "made in the City, by the King's command," casts a large net, in terms of the means of communication and the circumstances that were prohibited, whether private or public. A broad range of discourse could fall within its catch. The Gloucester faction is here using considerations of security as an excuse to eliminate powerful courtiers and to limit royal discourse:

> Oure Lord the kyng, that God saue and loke, comaundeth to alle his trewe liges in the cite of Londone, and the suburbe, of what condicion that euer thei ben, up the peyne of here liues, and forfaiture of here godes, that non be so hardy to speke, ne mouen, ne publishe, en priue ne appert, onithyng that might soune in euel or dishoneste of oure lige Lord the Kyng, ne of oure Ladi the Quene or ony lordes that haue bien duellyng with the Kyng bi for this time, or of hem that duellen aboute his persone nowe, or shul duelle, in hinder-yng of here state in any manere: ne that non of his trewe liges melle hem of suche matirs, but that oure Lord the Kyng, oure souereyn juge mowe ordenye therof that hem semeth best.[47]

The proclamations and restrictions were made in the name of the king and on behalf of the king's safety (and that of Queen Anne). As we know, at least two people close to Chaucer, Nicholas Brembre and Thomas Usk, were arrested and hanged in the proceedings of the "Merciless Parliament" of 1388, for crimes that involved loyalty to, and asso-

---

[45] Under the present political circumstances, the phrase "at the king's will" (in Anglo-Norman: *al volunte le roi*) was, of course, empty language. For a sense of the degree to which the lords appellant took justice (and the king) hostage, see the description of Richard's response to the charges of treason brought against Brembre in *The Westminster Chronicle* 310–11.

[46] *The Westminster Chronicle* 175–77.

[47] *Memorials of London and London Life in the XIIIth, XIVth and XVth Centuries*, A.D. 1276–1419, ed. and trans. Henry Thomas Riley (London: Longmans, 1868) 500. Riley notes that "the issuing of this Proclamation in the City, formed one of the charges of high treason against Brembre and his accomplices."

ciation with, Richard and the court.[48] In the 1390s, Richard was himself exceedingly sensitive to criticism of his person and policies—the contemporary chronicles describe an edict sent out to all sheriffs to arrest, detain, and punish by death anyone in their shire who *speaks* critically of him publicly or privately. Walsingham's *Historia Anglicana* for 1399 describes this edict as causing "a great destruction of the realm" and striking fear "into all members of the community." "From this it happened," Walsingham writes, "that many of his [Richard's] lieges were maliciously accused of saying something, either publicly or secretly, which could turn to the slander, disgrace, or dishonour of the king's person; and they were taken and imprisoned and led before the Constable and Marshal of England in the court of chivalry."[49]

But these proclamations and edicts against freedom of speech, whether they issued from mayors of the city of London, from baronial factions vying for power with Richard, or from the court itself, only make more pronounced what was already the reality of London in the late 1370s and throughout the '80s and '90s. The contemporary records are rife with punishments accorded speech—whether it be slander, false

---

[48] For an extensive account of the charges, or appeal, brought on 3 February 1388 by the Gloucester faction against "Alexander archbishop of York, Robert de Vere duke of Ireland, Michael de la Pole earl of Suffolk, Robert Tresilian false justice, and Nicholas Brembre false knight of London," see *The Westminster Chronicle* 280–83. John Blake and Thomas Usk were arraigned 3 March 1388; see *The Westminster Chronicle* 284–85.

[49] The complete edict, reproduced from Walsingham's *Historia Anglicana* for 1399, appears in *English Historical Documents IV, 1327–1485,* ed. A. R. Myers (New York: Oxford UP, 1969) 177–78. It reads as follows:

> Moreover, he [Richard] made the sheriffs throughout the realm swear unaccustomed oaths, that they should obey all the king's commands, whether they were directed to them under the Great or the Privy Seal, and also letters directed to them under the signet. And if the sheriffs should know any of his bailiffs, of whatever condition they were, who should utter or speak any evil, publicly or privately, in dishonour or disgrace of the king's person, they should imprison them, until they should receive orders from the king. From this it happened that many of his lieges were maliciously accused of saying something, either publicly or secretly, which could turn to the slander, disgrace, or dishonour of the king's person; and they were taken and imprisoned and led before the Constable and Marshal of England in the court of chivalry. And they were not exonerated unless they had defended and acquitted themselves personally in single combat, notwithstanding the fact that their accusers and appealers were strong and healthy young men, whereas those who were accused were mostly weak, maimed, and infirm. This was not only a great destruction of the realm, but struck fear into all members of the community.

rumor, lies, deceptions, falsehoods, vulgarity, or simply the language of a "common scold."[50]

In November 1378, in the second year of Richard's reign, "Thomas Knapet, clerk of the Church of St. Peter the Little, near Pouleswharf in London, was arrested by the Mayor and John Boseham, one of the Sheriffs," for speaking "disrespectful and disorderly words of the puissant and most honourable Lordship of Lancaster. . . ." In spite of "the great scandal of the said lord" and "the annoyance of all good folks of the city," it was the "puissant" Lancaster himself, "at the suit of the wife of the said clerk," who orchestrated the clerk's release.[51]

Simple criticism, as the case of John Pountfreit attests, was also to be muzzled. On 26 March 1382, Pountfreit's servant, a "common ostler," was charged with demanding extortionate rates for oats. This action, apparently against a city ordinance, was reported to the mayor, John Northampton, and Pountfreit was duly fined for the actions of his servant. But on the same day, after dinner "at the house of Thomas Screveyn, at Graschirche, in presence of John More, one of the Aldermen," Pountfreit "censured the judgment and doings of the said Mayor as to the matter aforesaid," for which criticism he was on 27 March again brought in to be questioned by the mayor and the alderman. Again, Pountfreit only made matters worse: "he said nothing by way of excusing himself, but answered the said Mayor in unbecoming language, and in Court in some degree cast censure upon the said John More." For this he was given into the custody of the sheriffs until 29 March. When Pountfreit was then released—"seeing that the same John Pountfreit so humbly humiliated himself, and asked for favour"—he agreed "that for the future he should cast no censure upon any acts or judgments of the Mayor, Aldermen, Sheriffs, or other officers of the City; nor should speak ill of them, nor make any assembly or covin which might tend to a breach of the peace, or to harm. . . ."[52]

On 4 April 1384, letters patent (formally, or ostensibly, from Richard) were addressed to "all bailiffs and his faithful subjects" describing the circumstances of a recent beheading in London, in order (as the letter itself states) that the people involved in the arrest and punishment and any of their heirs should not "by us or our heirs be in any way molested, disquieted, or aggrieved":

---

[50] Instances of the speech of the "common scold" are discussed in chap. 5, below.
[51] *Memorials of London* 425.
[52] *Memorials of London* 460–62.

whereas, when of late a great outbreak of our people, against our peace, was threatened in our city aforesaid, one John Constantyn, cordwainer, going among, counselling, comforting, and inciting the people of the said city to close their shops, and through his iniquitous contrivances, in the way of rumour, commotion, disturbance, and insurrection, on Thursday, the 11th day of February last past, the same was in part carried out, against our peace and the sound governance of the said city; he was therefore taken, as the one among them who was the first to close his shops and windows, affording to the others an example therein; and upon this was recently arraigned, and on the testimony of witnesses sworn and examined, and upon his own acknowledgment theron, and for other reasons, sentenced to death, and beheaded.[53]

Is it possible, given such highly charged political circumstances both in the court and in the city particularly as regards free speech, that there is more urgency in Chaucer's concerns with speech than has been understood? That, indeed, at a time when free speech was severely threatened, Chaucer found a way to sponsor it through the agency of dialogue, thus working with an instrument which is potentially subversive to all authority?

Chaucer's development of frame narration in the *Canterbury Tales* suggests an immediate and vital understanding of human behavior and the role of speech in the commonwealth. But his sense of the dialogic nature of discourse does not begin with the *Canterbury Tales*. It is a recurrent interest of a whole poetic career. Taken together, phenomena such as Chaucer's treatment of discourse as a transaction (usually open) between listener and speaker, his concern with the lines of co-dependence and reciprocity that build up between listener and speaker, his captivation with miscommunication and with the multiple perspectives of a narrator, his discontent with conventional structural closure, his acute interest in the literary artist's audience and, of course, his frequent return to frame narration and the evidence of the *Canterbury Tales* itself, all point to a more than usual fascination with speech as a social and political phenomenon. Chaucer's interest in discourse thus offers almost limitless possibility for study. I have chosen examples that will illustrate salient issues.

---

[53] *Memorials of London* 482–83.

One final note on method. Contemporary literary interpretation has been strongly influenced by various forms of discourse theory. Though these forms vary broadly in detail, they generally agree upon the premise that the writers of a given period operate within the limited awareness ("syntax," "hermeneutic circle") of that culture and that these writers are unaware of these cultural limitations. I am not convinced of this premise. Rather it seems to me that much of great literature is "great" precisely because it recognizes and grapples with the limiting contingencies of its culture. When this struggle is successful, it creates a moment of cultural self-consciousness, a graced episode during which some ingrained cultural vector—faith or authority or language itself—is suddenly the object of an aroused awareness. Such moments are metatheoretical in that they achieve a theoretical perspective within a literary context which at once justifies and transcends that perspective.

It follows from this that a cultural self-consciousness as subtle as Chaucer's should be presented insofar as possible in the author's own words, rather than be intruded upon by the contemporary jargon of awareness. In appreciating Chaucer's alienation, why compound it with our own? Accordingly I have addressed Chaucer as much as possible in his own language.

2

The Dream Visions:
Discourse at Play

THE *BOOK OF THE DUCHESS*

The *Book of the Duchess* is early evidence of Chaucer's sense of discourse as an open and unfinished interaction between speaker and listener. Although Chaucer's naive and quizzical narrator[1] usually dominates discussions of the *Book of the Duchess,* he is only one part, and a shifting part at that, of a poem in which discourse—whether it be spoken, read, or reported, as in a dream—is presented as a series of complex transactions.[2] Because they are habitually left open, the poem's

---

[1] In my use of the word "narrator" in this and subsequent chapters, I subscribe to the distinction made by David Lawton between narratorial voice and narratorial *persona*. As Lawton puts it in *Chaucer's Narrators,* Chaucer Studies 13 (Cambridge, Eng.: Brewer, 1985): "I have placed the emphasis on narratorial voice rather than narratorial *persona* because it seems to me that in medieval poetry most narrators are part of, rather than subsume, the rhetoric of a work. They are elements in a larger strategy. Sometimes a narrator is no more than a product of rhetorical imperative, the decorum either of the style or the set of structural conventions adopted" (8). More specifically concerning the *Book of the Duchess,* Lawton comments that the poem's "difference can be gauged, and was in large measure shaped by, Chaucer's radical change of *persona*" (52). On this subject, see also John Finlayson, "The *Roman de la Rose* and Chaucer's Narrators," *Chaucer Review* 24 (1990): 187–210. Finlayson takes up the whole issue of Chaucer's dream narrators and whether they are, indeed, "distinctive personalities who play a dramatic role in his fictions" (187).

[2] The poem bears out D. W. Davenport's observation that "Middle English writing tends to aspire to the condition of speech and exploits the relationship between speaker

---

27

transactions are at once a means of joining together its episodes and illustrating the fundamental reciprocity of discourse. They suggest that reciprocity demands a listening talent in speaker as well as listener and that discourse is an open process that precipitates and generates new initiative, controversy, and revision. In creating what we might call "dynamic aperture" in the *Book of the Duchess,* Chaucer seems to be exploring a discourse that is deeply reciprocal, if not political, and that will find its culmination in the frame narration of the *Canterbury Tales.*

Of course, not all literary transactions—and, as Chaucer shows, not all those in the *Book of the Duchess*—have the potential to generate discourse so dynamically, if at all. Some do not because they are failed transactions. And some do not because they are completed. Of these additional possibilities, the *Book of the Duchess* portrays most vividly the failed transaction, especially in the description of Juno's messenger in the story of Ceys and Alcyone. The partially humorous treatment of this message and its journey allows us to experience every aspect of the process of communication, from the thought's inception in Ceys's grief and her prayer to Juno, to Juno's calling her messenger, to his trip to the dark valley, and the first stage of the delivery of the message to the god of sleep. Although the resolution of Ceys's distress and her knowledge of whether her "lord" is alive or dead (121) depends on successful delivery of the message, the message is, at first, spoken in vain:

> This messenger com fleynge faste
> And cried, "O how! Awake anoon!"
> Hit was for noght; there herde hym non.
> "Awake!" quod he, "whoo ys lyth there?"
> And blew his horn ryght in here eere,
> And cried "Awaketh!" wonder hyë.
> This god of slep with hys oon yë
> Cast up, and axed, "Who clepeth ther?" (178–85)

Chaucer's obvious engagement with communication, as poet and public man, is surely finding comic expression in this scene. Its vivid portrayal of an almost failed communication can also be read as a humorous meta-

---

and hearer; in some works dialogue becomes a state of being." See Davenport, "Patterns in Middle English Dialogue," *Medieval English Studies Presented to George Kane,* ed. Edward Donald Kennedy, Ronald Waldron, and Joseph S. Wittig (Wolfeboro, NH: Boydell and Brewer, 1988) 144.

phor for the necessary reciprocity of discourse. Juno's messenger cannot deliver his message to Morpheus until Morpheus is awake to hear it. Without a listener, all that is spoken, no matter what its significance to human joy and sorrow, is in vain. If Chaucer, in the words of one critic, seems to spend "disproportionate space" on the "mechanics of how messages are transferred,"[3] might it be that it is specifically these "mechanics" and the engagement between speaker and listener, discourse and audience, that fascinate him? That he cannot, in fact, think of discourse except in terms of an engagement between speaker and listener?

There are other failed transactions. One is indicated in the dream, in the Black Knight's thrice-repeated (once with minor variation) statement:

> "Thow wost ful lytel what thow menest;
> I have lost more than thou wenest." (743–44, 1137–38, 1305–6)

Both in the Ceys and Alcyone episode, and in the dream, the failure of the transaction results from inadequate reception—the listener has either not fully heard the speaker or not heard at all. The question, frequently debated by critics, of whether the dreamer initially overhears the man in black as he laments the death of "my lady bryght" (475–86) may be moot. To overhear is not to hear. The sense of discourse as a mutual process is so emphasized in the *Book of the Duchess* as to suggest that it is defined by this mutuality. Similarly, in the curious description of the Knight's song (471–72), the Knight may be using speech, but it is an inwardly directed speech, he "argued with his owne thoght, / And in his wyt disputed faste" (504–5); thus while the dreamer overhears and rehearses the "lay," there is not yet communication between him and the man in black. Finally, the unrequited love indicated in the poem's opening would also seem to be an instance of a failed transaction.

The completed transaction—a transaction in which resolution is achieved and nothing further generated by the transaction itself—is simply not typical of Chaucer. Even in this early poem, in the one place we might most expect to find such a transaction—when the dreamer has

---

[3] Barry A. Windeatt, *Chaucer's Dream Poetry: Sources and Analogues* (Totowa, NJ: Rowman and Littlefield, 1982) xiii. But Windeatt also notes more generally the poem's attention to communication and observes that this "is part of the wider concern with processes of communication and understanding . . . which seems to underlie Chaucer's poems."

fully understood the Black Knight's loss—we will find that the transaction, instead, serves to precipitate another. And not only because the poem does not end here.

Most of the transactions in which the *Book of the Duchess* abounds are notably open. The conversational style of the poem's beginning invites a listener into an engagement with the speaker and then proceeds to evade, rather than to elucidate, the conflict it raises. Closely modeled on Froissart's opening in *Le Paradys d'Amour*,[4] Chaucer's is marked, unlike the latter, by elusiveness and indirection. It raises more questions than it answers. Froissart's speaker describes sleeplessness and melancholy and, having done so, immediately enlightens the reader regarding their cause. The speaker finds himself in the paradoxical situation of at once suffering sleeplessness and not wanting to loosen the melancholy thoughts that bind him: loosening them might cause him to forget "la belle" for whom he entered into this suffering and sleeplessness.[5]

The opening of the *Book of the Duchess* may assume the same paradox, but does not state it. And rather than immediately resolve his reader's curiosity about the source of his sorrowful imagination (14), the speaker voices the inner conflict and invites emotional response. So instinctively dialogic is Chaucer's style even here that what may begin as simply the utterance of a personal condition—

> I have gret wonder, be this lyght,
> How that I lyve . . . (1–2)—

is soon transformed into a lively exchange between speaker and listener. The overt signs of this listener are frequent—"And wel ye wot" (16);

---

[4] For a comprehensive study of Chaucer's relationship to the fourteenth-century French poets, see James I. Wimsatt, *Chaucer and His French Contemporaries: Natural Music in the Fourteenth Century* (Toronto: U of Toronto P, 1991), esp. chap. 6, "Chaucer and Jean Froissart" (174–209). It is Wimsatt's sense that "the relationship of the *Duchess* (c 1368) to the *Paradys* (c 1365) provides the clearest instance of Froissart's instructing Chaucer in the use of Machaut" (181). In addition to the *Roman de la Rose*, Chaucer's sources include Machaut's *Le Jugement dou Roy de Behaingne*, *La Fonteinne amoureuse*, *Remede de Fortune*, *Le Dit dou Lyon*, and Froissart's *Le Paradys d'Amour*. John Fisher reminds us that in spite of the fact that over two-thirds of its lines "have direct parallels in the *Roman de la Rose* and the poems of Machaut and Froissart," the *Book of the Duchess* is "thoroughly idiomatic" and distinctively Chaucer. See Fisher, ed., *The Complete Poetry and Prose of Geoffrey Chaucer* (New York: Holt, 1977) 543.

[5] Jean Froissart, *Le Paradys d'Amour*, ed. Peter F. Dembowski (Geneva: Librairie Droz S.A., 1986) 40. Loosening the bonds might cause him "la belle oubliier / Pour quelle amour en ce travel / Je sui entres et tant je vel" (lines 9–12).

"But men myght axe me" (30); "who aske this" (32)—and the tone is imperative: "Passe we over untill eft" (41); "Our first mater is good to kepe" (43).

Chaucer's speaker insists more than once on "our first mater" (43, 218), his sleeplessness, but he indicates, as speaker, the real matter[6]— unrequited love and the failed communication it implies—with the same artfulness and indirection that he will show, as listener, to the Black Knight. Here, as in the lament of the Black Knight, discourse *requires* a listening talent. The speaker deftly directs and controls, locating issues rather than putting them to rest. The poem's first major transaction between speaker and listener resolves nothing. On the contrary, it looses an undercurrent of questions.

The open-endedness of the poem's first transaction also quite literally generates the next, as continued sleeplessness causes the speaker to ask someone to give him a book. One of the book's fables is transmitted to us by the speaker, turned reader, who shows us specifically how he responds to it as audience (95–100). By presenting the Ceys and Alcyone story as an affecting transaction between book and reader, Chaucer draws attention again to the importance of response:

> Such sorowe this lady to her tok
> That trewly I, that made this book
> Had such pittee and such rowthe
> To rede hir sorwe that, by my trowthe,
> I ferde the worse al the morwe
> Aftir to thenken on hir sorwe. (95–100)

Though we might expect allusions to sorrow in a poem whose central passage concerns the Black Knight's bereavement, it is curious that the same speaker whose own sorrow (his eight-year sickness) at the poem's opening has made him almost numb, "a mased thyng" (12), is here, as reader and audience, fully alert to sorrow. The so-called narrative *persona* of the *Book of the Duchess* may be less a distinctive personality than a means of incorporating speaker and listener, discourse and audience, into the very texture of the poem. Here, the speaker's re-

---

[6] In these denials, Chaucer's speaker establishes what Natalie Sarraute calls a "sous-conversation"—a sub-conversation that will now dominate our perception of what follows. See Sarraute, *L'Ère du Soupçon* (Paris: Gallimard-Idées: 1956) 95–147.

sponse—as reader—would seem to tell us that the story of Ceys and Alcyone in the book exists fully only in the context of a reader. That this sympathetic reader is at once also author and narrator only serves to underscore the reciprocity of these roles.

Like other transactions in the *Book of the Duchess,* the one between reader and the book of Ceys and Alcyone is characteristically left open. Chaucer ignores the conclusion of the story as he finds it in his sources, portraying the poem's speaker as suddenly possessed by an aspect of the story quite peripheral to the sorrow to which he—as book-reader—has just showed such responsiveness:

> Whan I had red thys tale wel
> And overloked hyt everydel,
> Me thoghte wonder yf hit were so,
> For I had never herd speke or tho
> Of noo goddes that koude make
> Men to slepe, ne for to wake,
> For I ne knew never god but oon.
> And in my game I sayde anoon
> (And yet me lyst right evel to pleye)
> Rather then that y shulde deye
> Thorgh defaute of slepyng thus,
> I wolde yive thilke Morpheus,
> Or hys goddesse, dame Juno,
> Or som wight elles, I ne roghte who—
> "To make me slepe and have som reste
> I wil yive hym the alderbeste
> Yifte that ever he abod hys lyve. . . ." (231–47)

Again, one transaction opens onto another, if only an imagined one. The imagined words bring sleep (270–75), and with sleep, a dream: a dream that, moreover, is laden with transactions between speaker and listener, with the dreamer himself now audience to the man in black. And even within the dream's largest transaction, that between the Knight and the dreamer, there are others: songs, avowals of love, and a dialogue that touches specifically on the reciprocity of discourse.

There is a sense at every juncture of Chaucer's poem that in discourse the role of the listener is as significant as the role of the speaker, and by extension, the reader as significant as the fable read, the interpreter as significant as the dream interpreted. As he introduces the dream that forms the poem's central material, the speaker claims that he

> . . . mette so ynly swete a sweven,
> So wonderful that never yit
> Y trowe no man had the wyt
> To konne wel my sweven rede. (276–79)

In the dream, the speaker is not only the subject of his discourse, but also, and extendedly, an audience, the figure listening and responding to the man in black (445). Compared to the Ceys and Alcyone episode of the *Book of the Duchess,* the dream gives even more pointed emphasis to the processes of listening and responding.

The larger transaction between dreamer and the Black Knight is punctuated along the way by a series of smaller transactions that specifically concern the nature of communication. In the most extended instance of this, the Knight is already deep into his lament when the dreamer, apparently misunderstanding his meaning, cites literary precedents for the response to false lovers and concludes that there is no man alive who "wolde for a fers make this woo!" (740–41). Realizing at once that their communication has not been fully successful—

> "Thou wost ful lytel what thou menest;
> I have lost more than thow wenest . . ." (743–44)—

the Black Knight responds to the dreamer's puzzlement by first exacting from him a promise concerning the quality of his listening. It is noteworthy that Chaucer pauses for this transaction between speaker and listener, especially as the dreamer has already been a most attentive listener, showing sensitivity and asking questions that propel the Knight's narrative forward. The present transaction is much more extended than in Machaut's *Le Jugement dou Roy de Behaingne,* Chaucer's source here.[7] Chaucer's poem creates a situation in which there is direct engagement between the narrative *persona* and the sorrowing lover. Though the Knight in the *Book of the Duchess* poses the condition and the dreamer

---

[7] Chaucer enlarges the role of the speaker, or narrative *persona,* and thus provides an intermediary through which discourse can be experienced. Secondly, he recombines and rearranges material from Machaut's two lovers, the Lady and the Knight, giving the Black Knight extended passages from both, as well as from the *Remede de Fortune.*

swears his "trouthe," speaker and listener are finally mutually engaged and mutually dependent.

Chaucer suggests this mutuality poetically through the interlacement, in the diction, of key terms:

> "Loo, [sey] how that may be?" quod y;
> "Good sir, telle me *al hooly*
> In what wyse, how, why, and wherfore
> That ye have thus youre blysse lore."
>   "Blythely," quod he; "com sytte adoun!
> I telle the upon a condicioun
> *That thou shalt hooly, with al thy wyt,*
> *Doo thyn entent to herkene hit."*
>   "Yis, syr." "*Swere thy trouthe therto.*"
>   "Gladly." "*Do thanne holde hereto!*"
>   "I shal ryght blythely, so God me save,
> *Hooly, with al the wit I have,*
> Here yow as wel as I kan." (745–57; italics mine)

Just how reciprocal the engagement is, is demonstrated in the course of the lament itself. Though the Knight's voice may dominate the dialogue, its content, pace, and tone are predicated on the listener. From the moment in which the dreamer stalks (458) the man in black, his listening is active, like a hunter moving in on the "herte" with indirection and art.[8]

As the questions Chaucer's dreamer asks shape the Knight's revelations, the Knight is artfully brought, as critics have noted,[9] through a psychologically healing process of mourning. One aspect of this healing is certainly—in the dreamer's words—to have been heard "Hooly, with al the wit I have" (756). Though the words may have been *spoken* before

---

[8] For wordplay on "hart/heart," see the studies named in *The Riverside Chaucer*, ed. Larry D. Benson et al., 3rd ed. (Boston: Houghton, 1987) 969; and in the note for lines 344–86 of the *Book of the Duchess*, esp. Helge Kökeritz, *PMLA* 69 (1954) 937–52, esp. 951.

[9] See especially John Lawlor, "The Pattern of Consolation in the *Book of the Duchess*," *Speculum* 31 (1956): 640–48. Recent developments of the topic (with bibliography) include Helen Phillips, "Structure and Consolation in the *Book of the Duchess*," *Chaucer Review* 16 (1981): 107–18; James Dean, "Chaucer's *Book of the Duchess*: A Non-Boethian Interpretation," *Modern Language Quarterly* 46 (1985): 235–49; and Richard Rambuss, " 'Processe of tyme': History, Consolation, and Apocalypse in the *Book of the Duchess*," *Exemplaria* 2 (1990): 659–83.

(and, in fact, they have several times over), they are now truly received. Before he rides homeward, the Black Knight has, finally, been fully heard and fully understood:

> "Allas, sir, how? What may that be?"
> "She ys ded! "Nay!" "Yis, be my trouthe!"
> "Is that youre los? Be God, hyt ys routhe!"
> And with that word ryght anoon
> They gan to strake forth; al was doon,
> For that tyme, the hert-huntyng. (1308–13)

But even this transaction, with its close attention to the engagement between speaker and listener, opens onto another, as the speaker, having fully experienced the Black Knight's loss, now announces his intention to give it poetic expression. Having left the conspicuous transactions of his poem open—the problem of unrequited love, the Ceys and Alcyone story, and the dreamer's experience of the Black Knight's bereavement, which does not end the poem—and having reminded us of the poet's relationship to both the dream and the book, the speaker now initiates a further transaction, this time with the audience itself:

> . . . "Thys ys so queynt a sweven
> That I wol, be processe of tyme,
> Fonde to put this sweven in ryme
> As I kan best, and that anoon." (1330–33)

That the narrative *persona* in Chaucer's *Book of the Duchess* is at once the source of the discourse and the audience to it serves to make all the more emphatic the degree to which these apparently distinct roles, or aspects of discourse, are already, for Chaucer, parts of a continuum.

THE *HOUSE OF FAME*

Keeping in mind that fame "is closely linked with language—that it is, in a certain sense, the personification of this primary function of the human being: speaking, hearing, communicating"[10]—it is not surprising that Chaucer's *House of Fame* typically calls attention to discourse itself.

---

[10] Piero Boitani, *Chaucer and the Imaginary World of Fame* (Totowa, NJ: Barnes, 1984) 19.

It is more self-reflexive than any other of Chaucer's early poems and also more analytical. Chaucer seems especially to feel the power of discourse to amuse, to divert, but also to misinterpret, profane, and obliterate, and he respects this power. The poem touches on all the areas of the humanists' praise of speech[11] and sets their estimate on its head. It is as if he had resolved to reverse every one of their ideas of speech as philosophical inquiry, as community, intelligence, justice, understanding, and morality. We see this not only in the mechanics of the poem—in its many-sided playfulness and in its frequent failure to attend consecutively to its own argument—but also in its explicit statement. The dreamer's early and sharp curse on those who would misjudge or misinterpret the dream itemizes the psychological and social forces, the malicious intent, presumption, hate, scorn, envy, malice, deceit, and churlishness (93–96) that underlie faulty reception. Elsewhere these forces are projected onto the poem itself, to its own lack of resolution and closure and its playful skirting of the issues it raises.

The playfulness is indeed one of the first things we notice as we read through the *House of Fame*.[12] The poem rebels against the conventional expectations of discourse. It is playful in at least five or six different ways. In the first place, it exaggerates, inverts, or otherwise transforms rhetorical tropes and poetic conventions, including, of course, elements of its own sources. The poem's opening *dubitatio* (or "indecision"), a common feature of Chaucer's dream visions, is so extensive and spirited that it seems less to suggest indecision than exuberance.[13] The impressive list of figures—including Demophon, Achilles, Paris, Jason, Hercules, and Theseus (388–426)—invoked to exemplify Aeneas's "untrouthe" is suddenly rendered useless when Aeneas is then promptly and fully excused of all his great trespass (427–32).

Playful as well are the swift changes of tone in the *House of Fame*. The humorous invocation to the god of sleep and the blessing on those

---

[11] See discussion in preceding chapter, especially Boccaccio's estimation of speech.

[12] Wolfgang Clemen, in *Chaucer's Early Poetry,* trans. G. A. M. Sym (New York: Barnes, 1964), long ago pointed out the "note of entertainment" (94) running through the poem's invocations, of which there are six. Clemen comments generally on "Chaucer's serenely playful attitude to even the most revered models" (76). In the *House of Fame,* at least one element of those models, the journey, that "sublime translation into unknown spheres," in Clemen's words, becomes, "a diverting trip" (72).

[13] George Lyman Kittredge describes the catalogue of causes, effects, and distinctions concerning dreams as "one long, eager, and breathless sentence." See his *Chaucer and His Poetry* (Cambridge: Harvard UP, 1915; rpt. 1951) 75.

that take the dream well is suddenly transformed into a spirited curse on those that would misinterpret it (97). We find an equally sharp shift in tone at the end of Book 1 where, with the introduction of the eagle—"Me thoughte I sawgh an egle sore" (499ff.)—we are momentarily lifted into the cadences and hyperbolic depictions of nature of the French dream visions only to then be dropped into the plodding verse and comic understatement that open Book 2. This is a starker reality where even language is a skill that must be mastered:

> Now herkeneth every maner man
> That Englissh understonde kan. . . . (509–10)

Similarly, the dreamer's intense philosophical absorption in Marcian, Anteclaudian (985–86), and the heaven's region (988) in the same part of the poem is abruptly broken off by the eagle's "Lat be . . . thy fantasye!" (992).

Yet another kind of playfulness is found in the several self-portraits in the *House of Fame*. The audience's curiosity about autobiographical (and domestic) detail is teased when the eagle's "vois and stevene" are compared to "oon I koude nevene" (561–62).[14] In the more extended self-reference that follows, the eagle provides a rationale for the journey. He promises the tidings as "som disport and game" (664) in compensation for the solitary hours spent by the poem's speaker at labor with his reckonings and at home with his book, sitting "domb as any stoon" (652–57). Chaucer's mixing of genres in the *House of Fame* playfully dislocates the reader's sensibility and draws attention to the discourse itself: he is not like Boccaccio in the *Corbaccio* writing autobiographically, nor is he as in other dream visions simply using a fictive first-person. Projected thus unexpectedly into the narrative, the autobiographical detail introduces "a second level of 'reality' into the imaginative invention" and compels the audience to notice "how forceful is the fiction that can treat even the author as a piece of fiction."[15]

---

[14] A recent treatment of these lines as autobiography is Derek A. Pearsall's *Life of Chaucer: A Critical Biography* (Cambridge, MA: Blackwell, 1992) 98–99.

[15] On this kind of self-reference in literary art, see Rosalie Colie's comments in *Paradoxia Epidemica: The Renaissance Tradition of Paradox* (Princeton: Princeton UP, 1966) 70. Colie argues that autobiographical detail in this context—like paradox itself—forces "consideration of relativity" and draws attention to the power of discourse, a discourse that "can treat even the author as a piece of fiction" (361–62). On Rabelais's use of this technique, Colie observes that he "plays back and forth among the sorts of illusion and

The creation of the eagle is Chaucer at his most playful. He is introduced into the poem at what would seem to be a moment of optimum receptivity (470–79) in the dreamer: looking for any stirring man that can tell him where he is (478–79), the dreamer is instead swooped up by "grymme pawes stronge" (541) and carried by these as easily as if he were a lark (546). The physical inequality between dreamer and eagle cannot but focus humorous attention on the matter of pedagogic authority.[16] The dreamer is literally a captive audience:

> Thus I longe in hys clawes lay,
> Til at the laste he to me spak
> In mannes vois, and seyde, "Awak!" (554–55)

Given its context, the eagle's discourse, especially his learned disquisition on sound's inclination "kyndely to pace / Al up into his kyndely place" (841–42) like all else in nature, is at once entirely logical and entirely ridiculous. It repeatedly asserts and defines its conclusiveness and its authority:

> "Geffrey, thou wost ryght wel this . . ." (729)

> "I preve hyt thus . . ." (787)

> "And whoso seyth of trouthe I varye,
> Bid hym proven the contrarye." (807–8)

The eagle's discourse moves reliably from general principle, the concept of "kyndely" (soon to be repeated eight times in twenty-nine lines)[17]—

> "Geffrey, thou wost ryght wel this,
> That every kyndely thyng that is
> Hath a kyndely stede ther he

---

reality he perceives, fictionalizing himself to force on his readers the realization of how forceful is the fiction that can treat even the author as a piece of fiction, can rearrange even the author by the force of the words in a fictional man's mouth . . ." (70).

[16] D. W. Davenport remarks on "the mockery of the teacher/pupil relationship in Book 2 of the *House of Fame*" in "Patterns in Middle English Dialogue," *Medieval English Studies Presented to George Kane* 137.

[17] *The House of Fame*, lines 823–52.

May best in hyt conserved be . . ." (729–32)—

via analogy,[18] and authority,[19] to the conclusion that

". . . every speche of every man,
As y the telle first began,
Moveth up on high to pace
Kyndely to Fames place." (849–52)

What might in another context be standard discourse in natural philosophy,[20] is playfully undermined as the *House of Fame* mixes perspectives and promotes the sense of interacting fictions. Like Abelard, the eagle is concerned with the relation of sound and speech:

"Soun ys noght but eyr ybroken;
And every speche that ys spoken,
Lowd or pryvee, foul or fair,
In his substaunce ys but air." (765–68)

His definition recalls Abelard's description of a spoken sentence (*vocalis oratio*) as merely air; but unlike the eagle, Abelard takes issue with the view that "meaningful sound is nothing but the striking of the air" and argues that "sound is significant whenever the waves which are sustained through the air reach the ear and create understanding."[21] We are also reminded in Chaucer's poem that it is a bird who holds the dreamer both with his hierarchical discourse and his feet. The rather grand con-

---

[18] "Ryght so" (770); "And ryght anoon" (793); "And thus" (798); and so on.

[19] See the *House of Fame,* lines 757ff.

[20] Derek Pearsall observes that the eagle's disquisition "is all solid science, and the eagle is neither garrulous nor pedantic in any ordinary sense; he is simply overwhelmed by the pedagogic opportunity of communicating what he knows to someone who does not know what he knows." Pearsall also notes the eagle's methodology, pointing out that "he is constantly insistent upon the value of empirical proof, demonstration and experience (707, 727, 737, 787, 814, 826, 839, 854, 878)" and that this was "fashionably up to the minute in the late fourteenth century" (*The Life of Chaucer* 115).

[21] This issue, as discussed by Abelard, is found in Brian Stock, *The Implications of Literacy: Written Language and Models of Interpretation in the Eleventh and Twelfth Centuries* (Princeton: Princeton UP, 1983) 372–76. Stock cites Abelard's *Glossae in Categorias, Super Aristotelem De Interpretatione. De divisionibus. Super Topica glossae,* ed. M. del Pra, Nuova Biblioteca Filosofica, 2d ser., vol. 3 (Milan, 1954) 33–34 and 65.

clusiveness of the eagle's discourse is undercut as bird-like qualities are
projected on it—

> "A ha," quod he, "lo, so I can
> Lewedly to a lewed man
> Speke, and shewe hym swyche skiles
> That he may shake hem be the biles,
> So palpable they shulden be . . . ." (865–69)—

and on the listener:

> "And with thyne eres heren wel,
> Top and tayl and everydel. . . ." (879–80)

The instance of the eagle is, of course, only one and the most amus-
ing in the *House of Fame* where the weight of authority is undermined.
Most notably, the voice of great authority (2158) at the poem's "end,"
by whatever accident, gets cut off just when that voice promises to be
most meaningful. Additionally, the poem teases its audience at every
thematic and stylistic level with the expectation of the resonant conclusion, the authoritative inspiration, only to deflate that expectation. As
we have noted, in Book 1, Aeneas's "untrouthe" (384–426) is rather
suddenly excused (427–28). In Book 2, the implication of the eagle's
long catalogue describing the tidings that he will hear (672–98), full of
the large and small wretchednesses of love, is essentially passed over
when the dreamer turns, instead, to more limited and specific questions
of mechanics (701–6). He wants to know, not about the nature of tidings, but how it is possible, even with all the magpies and all the spies
(704) in the entire realm—for Fame to hear all this (705).

When "Geffrey" is borne aloft by the eagle, the dreamer quotes
Boethius, but in the midst of Boethius's movement toward a resonant
conclusion in "the verray knowleche of God" (*De musica* 1.14), he suddenly stops, cuts Boethius off in mid-sentence,[22] and palpably wrests
attention away from the thought's flight upward:

> And thoo thoughte y upon Boece,
> That writ, "A thought may flee so hye

---

[22] See John Fyler, *Chaucer and Ovid* (New Haven: Yale UP, 1979) 46.

With fetheres of Philosophye,
To passen everych element,
And when he hath so fer ywent,
Than may be seen behynde hys bak
Cloude. . . ." (973–79)

Later in the same book, the eagle's offer to "Geffrey" of instruction of
the highest sort is similarly inconclusive, even deflating. To his "Wilt
thou lere of sterres aught?" the dreamer's response is simply, "Nay, cer-
teynly . . . ryght naught" (993–94). And in Book 3, when the dreamer
arrives at the rock of ice (1130) noting the many famous peoples' names
engraved on it (1137), he disappoints the promised revelation: instead,
he simply announces that one or two of the letters of every name had
melted away (1144–45).[23]

Chaucer's description of the poets on their pillars (1419–1515) fit-
tingly suggests that culture can be analyzed through discourse, but also
implies that this authority, like others, is inconclusive. As he flushes out
the ramifications of discourse—in history, poetry, art, and learning—
Chaucer indicates that here, too, there are undermining forces.[24] The
narrator beholding the pillar of iron housing Homer and others who
contributed to the story of Troy (Dares and Dictys, Lollius, Guido delle
Colonne, and Geoffrey of Monmouth) remarks:

So hevy therof was the fame
That for to bere hyt was no game.

---

[23] On the effects of time see also Boccaccio, *De casibus*, I.V.3–4: "Quot iam dudum
imperatores incliti, quot illustres phylosophi, quot insignes poete, quot etiam plurimi
summa cum difficultate suis seculis meruere laudes, quorum—ne reliqua dicam—nomen
etiam in tempore consumptum est adeo ut nulla penitus ex eis sit memoria apud nostros?
Innumerabiles, arbitror! Inter quos non erit absurdum credere fere omnes evanuisse
priores. . . ."
[How many emperors once famous, how many illustrious philosophers, how many worthy poets, how many others who in their time earned praise through supreme effort,
not to mention others, how many are there whose names have been consumed by time,
so that among us there is no memory of them at all? I believe these forgotten ones are
without number; and among them almost all before this time in history have vanished,
it is not unreasonable to think.] *The Fates of Illustrious Men*, trans. Louis Brewer Hall
(New York: Ungar, 1965) 6.

[24] See the poem's beginning, particularly lines 93–96, where Chaucer's dreamer refers to the psychological and social forces that can hinder in the understanding of his
dream.

41

> But yet I gan ful wel espie,
> Betwene hem was a litil envye.
> Oon seyde that Omer made lyes,
> Feynynge in hys poetries,
> And was to Grekes favorable;
> Therfor held he hyt but fable. (1473–80)

Another hub of inconclusiveness—of things not fitting—is in Chaucer's lengthy treatment of the nine groups of petitioners to Fame (1553–1838), a magnified vision of society's injustice vis-à-vis reputation.[25] In this imaginary house of fame, there is no logical correspondence between action, speech, and consequence. Speech as intelligent understanding and as justice—as the human instrument for praising virtue, and deprecating vice—is repeatedly thwarted. So, for example, the first group asks for renown as full compensation for good works and is given, instead, anonymity: "No wyght shal speke of yow, ywis, / Good ne harm, ne that ne this" (1565–66). A similar request by a second group earns slander (1609–30). The third group wins fame far beyond what it deserves (1665–68). The fourth, arguing that it acted for goodness and "no maner other thing" (1697–99), is given anonymity, while the fifth, asking the same, has the golden trumpets blown for it (1713–26). The golden trumpets are blown, as well, for the life of idleness announced by the sixth group. The seventh, asking for the treatment just received by the sixth (1771–75), is rewarded, rather, with a barrage of insult that compares them finally to the cat who wants fish but is too lazy to wet its claws (1776–85). Demanding good fame for its treachery and wickedness, the eighth group is denied this with words that mix the rational and the capricious, the truth and the lie:

> "Nay, wis," quod she, "hyt were a vice.
> Al be ther in me no justice,
> Me lyste not to doo hyt now,
> Ne this nyl I not graunte yow." (1819–21)

The ninth group, "lepynge in a route" (1823), requests fame for wicked deeds and promptly receives it (1838).

---

[25] These lines, like the opening passus of *Piers Plowman,* surely point to prevailing and troubling social issues. On contemporary attitudes toward the judiciary, see particularly Alan Harding, "The Revolt against the Justices," in *The English Rising of 1381,* ed. R. H. Hilton and T. H. Aston (New York: Cambridge UP, 1984) 165–93.

When the narrator is now asked by someone who "stood ryght at my bak" (1869) what his name is and whether he, too, has come here to receive fame, his answer is an emphatic no. But his response is also a reminder that identity in a predominantly oral culture is necessarily a construct of the opinions of others. Though the narrator may assert his independence from that construct, he does so in the context of a poem about communication and reputation, a poem that describes most vividly and satirically the extent to which culture is discourse. The expressed assertion of individuality—like other moments in the *House of Fame*—tweaks the authority of that discursive culture. His words—as narrator and, more importantly, as poet—propose an emphasis on experience and self-knowledge that can loosen the hold of authority:

> "I cam noght hyder, graunt mercy,
> For no such cause, by my hed!
> Sufficeth me, as I werre ded,
> That no wight have my name in honde.
> I wot myself best how y stonde;
> For what I drye, or what I thynke,
> I wil myselven al hyt drynke,
> Certeyn, for the more part,
> As fer forth as I kan myn art." (1874–82)

The description of the House of Daedalus, especially Chaucer's comment that there is no porter to prevent any kind of tiding from entering (1955–56), recalls Boccaccio's comment in *De casibus* that princes have guards at their doors who examine everyone for weapons, and food tasters who test for poisons, but no one to guard them from what is much more threatening to them, speech itself.[26] In the more specific treatment of discourse and the tidings in the House of Daedalus that follows (1916ff.), we find that what was offered at the journey's start as compensation for the poet's labor and devotion to Love (665–68) is instead something wholly unsettling. Chaucer's catalogue of tidings, the "rounynges" and "jangles" that fill the house, begins and ends with items that mark civic life and the commonwealth. It is a copia of tidings, a remarkable mixture of offerings:

---

[26] For the full quotation, see chap. 1, pp. 10–11, above.

And over alle the houses angles
Ys ful of rounynges and of jangles
Of werres, of pes, of mariages,
Of reste, of labour, of viages,
Of abood, of deeth, of lyf,
Of love, of hate, acord, of stryf,
Of loos, of lore, and of wynnynges,
Of hele, of seknesse, of bildynges,
Of faire wyndes, and of tempestes,
Of qwalm of folk, and eke of bestes;
Of dyvers transmutaciouns
Of estats, and eke of regions;
Of trust, of drede, of jelousye,
Of wit, of wynnynge, of folye;
Of plente, and of gret famyne,
Of chepe, of derthe, and of ruyne;
Of good or mys governement,
Of fyr, and of dyvers accident. (1959–76)

The congregation roaming about both inside and outside the house dra-
matizes the human propensity not only for speech itself (2043ff.), however debased, but also for assertion and closure:

And than he tolde hym this and that,
And swor therto that hit was soth—
"Thus hath he sayd," and "Thus he doth,"
"Thus shal hit be," "Thus herde y seye,"
"That shal be founde," "That dar I leye. . . ." (2050–54)

Though they were playfully introduced at the poem's beginning,
the tidings now have remarkable and conclusive powers of destruction:

Were the tydynge soth or fals,
Yit wolde he telle hyt natheles,
And evermo with more encres
Than yt was erst. Thus north and south
Wente every tydyng fro mouth to mouth,
And that encresing ever moo,
As fyr ys wont to quyke and goo

> From a sparke spronge amys,
> Til al a citee brent up ys. (2072–80)

The comparison of the movement (and transmission) of tidings to a city destroyed by fire is itself powerful; the present image also recalls the opening reference to Synon's perjury (153–54) and the destruction of Troy by fire (163ff.) and thus perhaps to a London similarly imperiled.[27] The volatile nature of this kind of discourse and the fact that tidings move as rapidly as fire through a city, lend urgency to Chaucer's subject.

In the *Liber Albus,* the entry immediately preceding a reference to London's illustrious past concerns the nature of tidings "in a city so populous as this." As it sets forth the distinction between the course of justice outside the city and in London, especially as this concerns who "are the presenters and finders of homicides, murders, or other misadventures," the *Liber Albus* asserts that London perforce relies on the common people for tidings. The fact that there is no way to prevent the spread of such information saves hiring someone specifically for doing so:

> For that in a city so populous as this, occurrences of such a nature can by no possibility be concealed; seeing that, before intimation therof could be given to the bailiffs, tidings of such matters would be spread far and wide from end to end of the city. And that therefore there is no such person kept in the City, nor of usage has been wont to be; but the only mode of gaining such information is through the common people of the city.[28]

---

[27] An entry in the *Liber Albus: The White Book of the City of London*, ed. and trans. Henry Thomas Riley (London: Richard Griffin, 1861), suggests that the association between London and Troy was of long standing:

> Among the noble cities of the world which fame has rendered illustrious, the City of London is the one principal seat of the realm of England which diffuses far and wide the celebrity of its name. It is happy in the salubrity of its climate, in the enjoyment of the Christian religion, in its liberties so well deserved, and in its foundation at a most ancient date. Indeed, according to the testimony of the chronicles, it is much older than the City of Rome; for springing from the same more ancient Trojans, London was founded by Brut, in imitation of great Troy, before the foundation of Rome by Remus and Romulus; whence it is that, even to this day, it possesses the liberties, rights, and customs of that ancient city of Troy, and enjoys its institutions. . . . (54–55)

[28] *Liber Albus* 54.

In June of 1381, the "Injunctions issued by the Mayor, for keeping peace within the City" direct "the Aldermen, and other persons in great numbers, men of good heart, of every Ward in the City and from without . . . to meet all rumours imagined within the said city, or without, against the honour of our said Lord and of the City." Arrest and punishment are ordered, "if you shall find any persons rebellious in conforming to all the points aforesaid"—"unless he be a gentleman, or else an archer, who will say upon his faith that he has now come unto our said Lord the King, to go forth with him against his rebels."[29]

Expectably, the Letter-Books of the early 1380s suggest a spirited concern with the dangers of rumor and lying. More than appears to be customary of other crimes recorded in this period, those involving "lies" or "spreading false rumours" contain—along with the description of the punishment—an attempt to explain the reasoning behind the particular penalty exacted.[30] So, for example, in the entry of the 29 November, in the fifth year of Richard's reign, after a brief comment concerning the mayor's accusation that Simon Figge "had falsely lied therein" and that he now "could say nothing" in response, "but put himself upon the favour of the court," a rationale follows:

> And because that the said Mayor and Aldermen had the King's commands to keep in peace the said City, and the suburbs thereof, so as to have no strife or affray therein, and especially at this time of the present Parliament; and so, if that lie should reach the ears of him, our Lord the King, the whole city might easily be damnified thereby; and also, because that through the same lie dissensions might easily—and might such not be the case—arise between the nobles of the realm etc., it was adjudged that the said Simon should be put upon the pillory, there to remain for one hour of the day, with a whetstone hung from his neck.[31]

If it is discourse in all its manifestations that defines the social order, a degraded discourse in which truth and falsehood are irretrievably

---

[29] *Memorials of London and London Life in the XIIIth, XIVth and XVth Centuries,* A.D. 1276–1419, ed. and trans. Henry Thomas Riley (London: Longmans, 1868) 451–52.

[30] See *Memorials of London* 454, 460, 471, 475, 477, 479, 482, 507. What stands out in these reports of the punishment accorded the lie is the clear need to justify the severity of the punishment. Such justification is not found in the same degree in most of the reports on other crimes.

[31] *Memorials of London* 454.

mixed[32] can also destroy it. The playfulness of the *House of Fame* and its pervasive lack of closure are surely a profound comment on the instability of discourse. But the same indirection and playfulness may also provide Chaucer a protected way of raising serious issues close to home. The *House of Fame* at once describes the expanse and power of language and sounds a note of local alarm.

THE *PARLIAMENT OF FOWLS*

Though the *Parliament of Fowls* charts a movement between two distinct kinds of discourse—the ideal prescription of the Dream of Scipio and the realistic discourse of the parliament of birds—none of the critical formulations of the way the poem is structured sees it as turning on the axis of discourse itself. Critics have interpreted the relationship between the successive parts of the poem in a number of different ways. J. A. W. Bennett, for example, comments on Chaucer's "speculative freedom" in the *Parliament of Fowls* and suggests that his movement in the poem "from the doctrines of Macrobius to the goings-on of birds" may well reflect a similar "turning away from metaphysics to study the actual behavior of things" in contemporary philosophical thought.[33] Robert O. Payne finds in the *Parliament* "a content of paradox and contradiction . . . distributed through a highly stable, almost ritualized form" and argues that Chaucer turns "the form and the substance" of the *Parliament of Fowls* "into a mutual critique," making of "the whole an essay in poetics as well as a poem about its subject."[34] Paul A. Olson, who considers the *Parliament* "a very great civic poem," sees its segments as all concerning "the nature of the social and social love in general" with the parliament itself "a representation of that vehicle through which late medieval man found it most possible to develop his sense of sociability and conviviality."[35] A. C. Spearing has asserted that in its "texture" and "feel," the *Parliament* "is genuinely like a dream": the poem "may make use of conceptual thought, but it does so in the most tentative way, with

---

[32] Chaucer gives repeated emphasis in the poem's final section to the mixing of "soth" and "fals" through repetition and variation: see lines 2059ff., esp. 2060–67, 2072–75, 2081–83, 2088–109, and 2121–24.

[33] J. A. W. Bennett, *"The Parlement of Foules": An Interpretation* (Oxford: Clarendon, 1957) 14–15.

[34] Robert O. Payne, *Chaucer and the Key of Remembrance: A Study of Chaucer's Poetics* (New Haven: Yale UP, 1963) 144–45.

[35] Paul A. Olson, "*The Parlement of Foules*: Aristotle's *Politics* and the Foundations of Human Society," *Studies in the Age of Chaucer* 2 (1980): 69, 53.

conceptual oppositions largely replaced by concrete contrast, and one contrast merging dreamlike into another.''[36]

Might not the *Parliament of Fowls,* by setting the squabbling birds up against the measured and philosophical device of the Dream of Scipio, be telling us something about the role of discourse in society? It has not been remarked that the discursive segments of the *Parliament of Fowls* can be seen as representing polar attitudes (or strategies) towards a perceived reality. Or, differently put, the opening and closing episodes represent discourse at the extremes of its relationship to order and certainty. Thus, while discourse is an ordering principle in the Dream of Scipio, it is the vehicle of disorder in the debate of the birds.

The Dream of Scipio, the "old bok totorn" (110), constitutes a measured and abstract discourse on the perfection of the common-wealth.[37] Its knowledge is (literally) contained and it is cosmically or-dered:

> This bok of which I make mencioun
> Entitled was al ther, as I shal telle:
> "Tullyus of the Drem of Scipioun."
> Chapitres sevene it hadde, of hevene and helle
> And erthe. . . . (29–33)

Scipio's dream, as Chaucer's speaker treats it here, is self-contained and self-referential; and it promotes its own authority.[38] As such it can be

---

[36] A. C. Spearing, *Medieval Dream-Poetry* (Cambridge: Cambridge UP, 1976) 100–1.

[37] The civic emphasis of Cicero's *De republica* (of which *The Dream of Scipio* is a fragment) is downplayed in the twelfth and thirteenth centuries, with Macrobius's fourth-century commentary on the dream being "one of the major sources of inspira-tion" for urging the superiority of the spiritual life. Hans Baron, *In Search of Florentine Civic Humanism,* 2 vols. (Princeton: Princeton UP, 1988), comments that "Macrobius' intention in presenting the Roman classic to a new audience was to prove that, despite his championship of the active political life, Cicero had been aware that religious con-templation was on a higher plane" (1: 102). Baron considers that the changing percep-tion of Cicero as predominantly civic-minded provides a "framework for the history of Humanism" (1: 96–97). I would suggest that Chaucer's drawing attention to discourse puts him among those "humanistic readers" who, in Baron's words, "began to sense the true Ciceronian attitude behind Macrobius' commentary and to free the Roman core from its Neoplatonic shell" (1: 104).

[38] This is not to say that Chaucer, or even the poem's speaker, is promoting the stated philosophy. We recall that the speaker introduces the Dream of Scipio with the tantaliz-ing comment that he was reading it "a certeyn thing to lerne" (20); equally tantalizing, of course, is his Boethian comment (see Chaucer's *Boece* 3.3.33–36) after he transmits

transmitted directly to the audience: "as shortly as I can it trete, / Of his sentence I wol yow seyn the greete" (34–35). In conveying the Ceys and Alcyone story in the *Book of the Duchess,* Chaucer emphasizes the speaker's emotional involvement with it; here, by contrast, the emphasis is on effectively transmitting closely argued philosophical truth.

As the poem relates the dialogue between Scipion and Affrycan, its consistent syntax and logical progression from point to point—"First telleth it . . ." (36); "Thanne telleth it . . ." (39); "Thanne shewed he hym . . ." (57)—accords with the order and certainty of its views. The authoritativeness of the discourse is everywhere suggested: the discourse reaches into and enriches itself. It is replete with modifiers and interpretations. It reminds us of the authoritative source and provides moral explanation:

> Thanne shewede he hym the lytel erthe that here is,
> At regard of the hevenes quantite;
> And after shewede he hym the nyne speres;
> And after that the melodye herde he
> That cometh of thilke speres thryes thre,
> That welle is of musik and melodye
> In this world here, and cause of armonye.
>
> Than bad he hym, syn erthe was so lyte,
> And dissevable and ful of harde grace,
> That he ne shulde hym in the world delyte. . . . (57–66)

Particularly in the matter of justice, cause and effect are reassuringly related. All is argued in the context of eternity:

> . . . oure present worldes lyves space
> Nis but a maner deth, what wey we trace;
> And rightful folk shul gon, after they dye,
> To hevene; and shewede hym the Galaxye. (53–56)

And there are clear distinctions between "rightful folk," those that "werche and wysse / To commune profit" (74–75), and "Brekers of the

---

the fragment's discourse: "For bothe I hadde thyng which that I nolde, / And ek I ne hadde thyng that I wolde" (90–91). Might Chaucer be saying that this kind of abstract construct has always been available to philosophy? What is wanted is a way of dealing with the events around you.

lawe . . . / And likerous folk" (78–79). Especially when we recall the skewed sense of justice in Book 3 of the *House of Fame* (1549ff.), we appreciate the degree to which the justice described in the Dream of Scipio is anchored in an ideal moral universe, with an eye "to that place deere / That ful of blysse is and of soules cleere" (76–77).

In the Dream of Scipio, discourse is implicitly a vehicle of order and of an ideal universe; in Nature's garden, by contrast, speech threatens order. Nature's garden is defined by its emphasis on speaking and listening. Indeed, discourse is the reason for being there on Saint Valentine's Day:

> Ne there nas foul that cometh of engendrure
> That they ne were prest in here presence
> To take hire dom and yeve hire audyence. (306–8)

Though the original plan may be a perfectly authoritative discourse, it is "noyse" that characterizes the plenitude of Nature's garden. The dreamer is immediately struck by this:

> . . . so huge a noyse gan they make
> That erthe, and eyr, and tre, and every lake
> So ful was that unethe was there space
> For me to stonde, so ful was al the place. (312–15)

The catalogue of birds that opens this section of the poem (330ff.) looks forward to the garrulous disorder of the poem's final segment. For the distinguishing traits of many of the birds are directly related to speech, especially to speech in the political arena—"the janglynge pye," "the skornynge jay," "the false lapwynge, ful of trecherye; / The stare, that the conseyl can bewrye" (345–48)—and suggest the discursive conflict that will soon erupt among them.[39] This fascination with talk—and especially with talk as it impacts the social body—will, of course, be more fully developed in the *General Prologue* of the *Canterbury Tales,* where speech is a distinctive aspect of many of the pilgrims.

Nature emphasizes order and hierarchy: the birds are there "To take hire dom and yeve hire audyence" (308); she reminds them of her

---

[39] Alain de Lille's *De planctu Naturae* (2.145–95), one of the sources for Chaucer's catalogue of birds here (lines 343–57), does not include the birds' discursive presence.

"ryghtful ordenaunce" (390), and of the fact that "he that most is worthi shal begynne" (392) and "after hym by ordre shul ye chese" (400). But the fowls will disrupt that order in their eagerness to speak.[40] There is the general impatience among the lower birds with the formality of the tercel eagles—"Have don, and lat us wende!" (492); " 'Com of!' they criede, 'allas, ye wol us shende!' " (493). What the dreamer characterized as "gentil ple in love" (485), they see as "cursede pletynge" (494) that threatens to be useless:

> "Whan shal youre cursede pletynge have an ende?
> How sholde a juge eyther parti leve
> For ye or nay withouten any preve?" (495–97)

The most salient feature of the avian squabble is its participants' disinclination to complete it. The tercel eagles convey a sense of the necessity for expression:

> And from the morwe gan this speche laste
> Tyl dounward went the sonne wonder faste. (489–90)

This eagerness is yet more graphic in the subsequent dispute among the lower birds. The goose is picked to represent the waterfowl, to "telle oure tale" because she "so *desyreth* to pronounce oure nede" (558–60; italics mine). Like the eagle in the *House of Fame,* these birds suggest a love of speech for its own sake. Indeed, in the *Parliament,* the desire to speak defines the species: "a fol can not be stille" (574).

Here, the birds allow Chaucer to draw attention to the mechanics of discourse and to delight in the potentiality for satire. The birds demonstrate that there is small relation between garrulousness and knowledge, and that consultation does not necessarily bring enlightenment. Legal procedures and terms are juxtaposed with flat-out bird talk:

> "How sholde a juge eyther parti leve
> For ye or nay withouten any preve?"

---

[40] Notice the wordplay on "foule" (fool/fowl) throughout; also the couplet spoken by Nature, in which "men" and "foules" are juxtaposed, one line referring to "of every folk men shul oon calle," the next to "yow foules alle" (524–25). See also line 574 (the last line of a stanza), "a fol can not be stille," and line 575 (the first of the next stanza), "The laughter aros of gentil foules alle."

> The goos, the cokkow, and the doke also
> So cryede, "Kek kek! kokkow! quek quek!" hye. . . . (496–99)

And a brief deliberation ("a short avysement") is the result of many large mouthfuls: "Whan everych hadde his large golee seyd" (555–56).

The initial formality of the tercel eagle's "gentil ple in love," Nature's emphasis on governance and order, and the parliamentary terms throughout,[41] all draw attention to the disorderly reality of communication. The discourse breaks into technicolor. The birds explode with their conflicting viewpoints and rebuttals. Colloquialisms, proverbs, and witticisms fly and each suggests world views invariably in conflict with one another: "God forbede a lovere shulde chaunge!" (582); "There been mo sterres, God wot, than a payre!" (595); "Thow farst by love as oules don by lyght: / The day hem blent, ful wel they se by nyght" (599–600); "Ye, have the glotoun fild inow his paunche, / Thanne are we wel!" (610–11).

The Valentine's Day setting of the action may occasion a certain eagerness to be done with speaking—

> The noyse of foules for to ben delyvered
> So loude rong, "Have don, and lat us wende!" (491–92)—

but the *Parliament of Fowls* revels in the discursive world the birds create. The birds are constitutionally unable to keep quiet; they repeatedly cut in on one another: "ye don me wrong, my tale is not ido!" (542). At one point, Nature has to shut them up: "Holde youre tonges there!" (521). Once loosed, speech creates a *place*, a landscape that is infinitely varied and unpredictable. There are as many words for conclusiveness as there are species of birds, among them, "remedie" (502); "verdit" (503); "termyne" (530); "the juges dom" (547); "the sothe sadde" (578). Para-

---

[41] Derek Brewer's list of words with "a Parliamentary flavour" include "statute" and "ordenaunce" (lines 387 and 390), "delyvered" (491), "presente" and "accepteth" (531–32), "remedie" (502), and "common profit" (47 and 75). Brewer also points out that "assentuz et accordez" (cf. lines 526, 608) occur frequently in the "Parliamentary jargon of the period." See *The Parlement of Foulys,* ed. Brewer (Manchester: Manchester UP, 1960) 37–38 and 119, note for lines 387 and 390. Notes and bibliography for parliamentary terms are also found in Bennett, *"The Parlement of Foules": An Interpretation.* On parliamentary debate in England and its possible influence on *The Parliament of Fowls,* see esp. Thomas L. Reed, Jr., *Middle English Debate Poetry and the Aesthetics of Irresolution* (Columbia: U of Missouri P, 1990) 88–96.

doxically, Chaucer shows, the desire to assert authority, to make the definitive statement, is itself a signal part of the forces of disorder unleashed by speech.

Closure seems all but impossible. One speaker's sense of authority and resolution is inevitably the opening for another's equally authoritative stance. The goose may promise closure, but such closure will irritate the cuckoo, whose closure in turn will be unacceptable to the turtledove:

> The goos seyde, "Al this nys not worth a flye!
> But I can shape herof a remedie,
> And I wol seye my verdit fayre and swythe
> For water-foul, whoso be wroth or blythe!"
>
> "And I for worm-foul," seyde the fol kokkow,
> "For I wol of myn owene autorite,
> For comune spede, take on the charge now,
> For to delyvere us is gret charite."
> "Ye may abyde a while yit, parde!"
> Quod the turtel, "If it be youre wille
> A wight may speke, hym were as fayr be stylle." (501–11)

Every posture, particularly an extreme one, suggests its opposite. And each will come complete with its own rationale. Rhetorical assertions of modesty simply contribute to the sense of an irrepressible, even incurable penchant for having the last word, for making the authoritative statement. To the "fol" cuckoo's questionable assertion that he will

> ". . . of myn owene autorite,
> For comune spede take on the charge now . . ." (506–7)

there is the turtledove's wordy advice (with its final proverbial wisdom) against unsolicited interference:

> "I am a sed-foul, oon the unworthieste,
> That wot I wel, and litel of connynge.
> But bet is that a wyghtes tonge reste
> Than entermeten hym of such doinge,
> Of which he neyther rede can ne synge;

And whoso hit doth ful foule hymself acloyeth,
For office uncommytted ofte anoyeth." (512–18)

In their several responses to one another, the fowls convey the psychological postures, social tensions, and barely masked self-interest that characterize practical communication. Substitute regionalism or guilds for species of birds, and you have the political reality most effectively portrayed by the debate of the birds.

Though offered as a "conclusioun" (620), Nature's decree is, in fact, inconclusive. Her offer to give the formel eagle "eleccioun / Of whom hire lest" (621–22) results in the suspension of choice—the formel's eagle's request for

. . . respit for to avise me,
And after that to have my choys al fre." (648–49)

Seen against the ideal order of Scipio's dream, the discourse of Nature's garden is most striking for its garrulous disorder: Nature calls an assembly and discourse threatens to rip it apart. Here, in a quasi-political setting, the debate of the birds satirically reenacts the Dream of Scipio. The definitive statement of ideal political order dissolves into a chaos of discourse and ambiguous suspension.

3

Speche in *Troilus and Criseyde*

As we have seen, speech is one of the chief subjects of Chaucer's attention in the *Book of the Duchess,* the *House of Fame,* and the *Parliament of Fowls.* In each of these early poems, Chaucer is deeply interested in the social and political implications of discourse—in its reciprocity, its potential for good or for ill, and its challenge to ideal political order. The political reverberations of *Troilus and Criseyde,* especially as they concern the complex miscommunications of speech, are profound. The poem may be Chaucer's most extended attempt not only to celebrate the variousness of human discourse, but also to realize the humanist sense that the study of speech is a kind of sociology, a way of understanding human behavior and human interaction. At least three times in the poem Chaucer draws our attention specifically to the changing nature of *speche* through time and across cultures. In these overt references to *speche,* Chaucer reminds us of our tongues' difference (1.393–98). He insists, should one wonder about Troilus's speech or his behavior, that speech changes over time (2.22–49), and urges in his ending that what we are witnessing be understood in the context of the form, or style, of "olde clerkis speche" in poetry (5.1854–55).

Only partially masked by these references to the relative nature of *speche* in history is the related and more immediate concern with *speche* as it is exhibited in society, in persons ranging from the treasonous Calchas, respected for his advice (1.83), to the brilliantly agile communicator,

Pandarus ("And in he lepte, and seyde hym in his ere" (2.1637), to Diomede, who in courting Criseyde, "shal namore lesen but my speche" (5.798). A sense of the power of words pervades every aspect of *Troilus and Criseyde,* and not just as it relates specifically to love— where, as Pandarus reminds Criseyde, "with o word ye may his herte stere" (3.910). There are, moreover, no two speakers in *Troilus and Criseyde* for whom speech implies the same premises or set of assumptions. This is apparent both in the ways each of them uses speech and in their comments about it. Communication, if not the subject of the poem, is its universally functioning mechanism.

But given the reality of a world in which the underlying assumptions of speech are as varied as they are in *Troilus and Criseyde,* the poem is expectably rich in references to the misperceptions and distortions of speech. The communicative transaction is never simply assumed; it is repeatedly subjected to aggressive scrutiny. More than any other of Chaucer's poems, the *Troilus* is pervaded by questions of intention,[1] and of what something means. Deceit, already an issue in the dream visions, and especially in the Dido and Aeneas episode of the *House of Fame,* is explored here in all its nuances. To this end, Chaucer's *Troilus* sharpens the contrasts between the speech of the characters found in Boccaccio's *Filostrato,*[2] enlarges the sense of narrative ambiguity, and ends the poem by drawing further attention to the problematic nature of communica-

---

[1] "Entente" occurs thirty-five times in *Troilus and Criseyde*; "entencioun" seven times, as well as in several other forms, including "entende." See John S. P. Tatlock and Arthur G. Kennedy, *A Concordance to the Complete Works of Geoffrey Chaucer and to "The Romaunt of the Rose"* (Washington, DC: Carnegie Institution, 1927). In her study of the relationship of meaning to ending in *Troilus and Criseyde,* Rosemarie P. McGerr remarks on the frequency of words relating to meaning and ending: "On the most basic level, the poem practically teems with various forms of the words *mene* and *ende* and synonyms such as *purpos, entende, entencioun, fyn, signifye, stynte, cesse, determyne,* and *diffyne.*" See McGerr, "Meaning and Ending in a 'Paynted Proces': Resistance to Closure in *Troilus and Criseyde,*" in *Chaucer's "Troilus and Criseyde": "Subgit to Alle Poesye": Essays in Criticism,* ed. R. A. Shoaf (Binghamton, NY: Medieval and Renaissance Texts and Studies, 1992) 181 and n2. See also Richard H. Osberg, "Between the Motion and the Act: Intentions and Ends in Chaucer's *Troilus,*" *English Literary History* 48 (1981) 257–70.

[2] Chaucer's innovations in the area of characterization (which in this poem means dialogue) are considerable. C. David Benson, *Chaucer's Troilus and Criseyde* (London: Unwin Hyman, Ltd., 1990), reminds us that Boccaccio's Troilo is "experienced," "active," and "capable of immediate practical action in his own cause"; Pandaro "little more than an extension of the prince"; Criseida "not very different from the male characters"; and Diomede "another double of Troilo" (20–21).

tion and closure.[3] Even the apparently disproportionate space given Criseyde's discourse in Book 4 on the verbal deceit she intends for Calchas once she is in the Greek camp (4.1366–1421) and Troilus's response to this (1450–63),[4] gains new meaning if understood thematically, rather than as usually, in terms of character or plot development.[5]

It is a matter of common knowledge that for the *Troilus* Chaucer is reading both Boccaccio and the *Roman de la Rose.* Scholarship has established that Chaucer works closely with Boccaccio's *Filostrato,* that he

---

[3] David Wallace has noted Boccaccio's "fewer personal incursions into the narrative." See Wallace, "Troilus and the Filostrato: Chaucer as Translator of Boccaccio," in *Chaucer's "Troilus and Criseyde": "Subgit to Alle Poesye": Essays in Criticism,* ed. R. A. Shoaf (Binghamton, NY: Medieval and Renaissance Texts and Studies, 1992) 260. The resistance to closure in *Troilus* has also been remarked by McGerr, who notes the "unusual emphasis on means and ends" and argues that "the poem illustrates the difficulty of determining or closing meaning . . . of harmonizing the means and ends of language" ("Meaning and Ending in a 'Paynted Proces,' " 182 and n9).

[4] In general, this considerably greater attention to deceit and intention in *Troilus and Criseyde* is Chaucer's own. The scene (in Book 2) at Deiphebus's house and involving Pandarus's extravagant deceptions is not, for example, in the *Filostrato* at all. In Boccaccio's *Filostrato,* Criseida's intention to deceive her father is presented in summary fashion only (Chaucer's poem and Boccaccio's *Filostrato* [in Italian] are provided side by side with extensive notes for each in B. A. Windeatt, ed., *Troilus and Criseyde: A New Edition of "The Book of Troilus"* [New York: Longman, 1984]. My citations from the *Filostrato* are from this edition):

> Egli e, come tu sai, vecchio ed avaro,
> e qui ha cio che el puo fare o dire;
> il che io gli diro, se el l'ha caro
> per lo miglior mi ci facci reddire,
> mostrandogli com'io possa riparo,
> ad ogni caso che sopravvenire
> potesse, porre, ed el, per avarizia,
> della mia ritornata avra letizia. (4.136)

Neither does Troilo's response to Criseida touch on the problem of outwitting a deceiver.

[5] The centrality of character in the criticism of *Troilus and Criseyde* is noted by C. David Benson, *Chaucer's Troilus and Criseyde,* who remarks that "Chaucerians as diverse as Aers, Bishop, McAlpine and Wetherbee—like Donaldson, Muscatine and Robertson before them, and Kittredge and Lewis before *them*—pay special attention to the people in Chaucer's poem" (84). A notable exception to this critical trend is Eugene Vance, who comments that "the axis of intertexuality cuts across all of the different levels of fiction in the *Troilus,* making apparent to what extent the conventional nature of verbal signs preempts the 'reality' of the instance of discourse in the speaking subject." Or, as Vance also puts it, "the speaking individual does not appropriate courtly discourse; rather it appropriates him." See Vance, "Marvelous Signals: Poetics, Sign Theory, and Politics in Chaucer's *Troilus,*" *New Literary History* 10 (1979): 293–337, esp. 306–7.

"transforms but never ignores" the matter and the style of his Italian source.[6] It has also been demonstrated that Chaucer's *Troilus* "bears the stains of its happy contagion by Jean's poem on its every page"[7] and that its meaning "depends as fully on the style and ethos represented by Jean de Meun as on the values of Chrétien and Guillaume de Lorris."[8] Chaucer's sense of the range of speech and its potential to reveal the conflicts that underlie the social order—owes much to the humanism not only of Boccaccio but also of Jean de Meun.[9] Before looking more closely at these issues of speech in Chaucer's *Troilus,* it is important to note that there are profound contrasts both in the nature and the stature of speech in Chaucer's sources—particularly in Guillaume and Jean de Meun— that can illuminate Chaucer's treatment of speech in the *Troilus.*

Characterized as "pure in attitude" and "linear in design,"[10] Guillaume's *Roman* defines one register of Chaucer's sense of the range of speech, providing him in the *Troilus* with conventions of courtly love in their unalloyed form. Like the Lover in Guillaume, Troilus is initiated into "observaunces" that are closely associated, if not directly related, to speech. We may remember that having locked the lover's heart, Guillaume's God of Love charges him, "word by word, with his commandments" (2055–56).[11] Among these, those that specifically address discourse precede others concerning the lover's pride, elegance, attire, and cleanliness, and his states of mind. Notably, the commandments regarding speech all counsel restrictions on it. So, for example, Guillaume's Lover is to avoid Vilenie, allegorically presented in the *Roman*

---

[6] C. David Benson, *Chaucer's Troilus and Criseyde* 14. On the relationship between Boccaccio's *Filostrato* and Chaucer's *Troilus,* see esp. Barry A. Windeatt, "Chaucer and the *Filostrato,*" in *Chaucer and the Italian Trecento,* ed. Piero Boitani (Cambridge: Cambridge UP, 1983); David Wallace, "Chaucer and Boccaccio's Early Writings," in *Chaucer and the Italian Trecento* 141–67; and Wallace, *Chaucer and the Early Writings of Boccaccio* (Dover, NH: Brewer, 1985).

[7] John V. Fleming, "Jean de Meun and the Ancient Poets," in *Rethinking "The Romance of the Rose": Text, Image, Reception,* ed. Kevin Brownlee and Sylvia Huot (Philadelphia: U of Pennsylvania P, 1992) 85.

[8] Charles Muscatine, *Chaucer and the French Tradition* (Berkeley: U of California P, 1957) 131.

[9] In Fleming's estimation, "Jean deserves not only a place but a place of pride" among "the great Christian humanist poets of the Middle Ages" ("Jean de Meun and the Ancient Poets," in *Rethinking "The Romance of the Rose"* 85).

[10] Muscatine, *Chaucer and the French Tradition* 30–31.

[11] Citations are by verse to Guillaume de Lorris and Jean de Meung, *Le Roman de la Rose,* ed. Felix Lecoy, 3 vols. (Paris: H. Champion, 1965–70). Translations are my own.

de la Rose as a "wicked creature, mad, cruel, and outrageous, ill-speaking and insolent" (160–62). The Lover is commanded to refrain from gossip and slander (2075–77). He is further commanded:

> Soies cortois et acointables,
> de paroles douz et resnables
> et au granz genz et aus menues. (2087–89)

> [Be courteous and easy to meet, a person of mild and reasonable speech, both to important people and to plain folks.]

He is to be the first to greet people, but if greeted first, he is to return the greeting promptly. He is to avoid dirty or bawdy words:

> ja por nomer vilainne chose
> ne doit ta bouche estre desclouse.
> Je ne tien pas a cortois home
> qui orde chose et laide nome. (2099–2102)

> [Your mouth should never be opened to mention a vulgar thing. I don't consider a man courteous who names vile or ugly things.]

Not only is the Lover to avoid speaking slanderously himself, but if he hears anyone slandering women, "he should put him in his place and tell him to keep quiet" (2105–7). For Guillaume's Lover, as will be true also of Troilus, the extreme modification of discourse in the public realm is accompanied by a conspicuously isolated discourse in the private realm. The Lover is warned that often when he is thinking of his beloved, he will be forced to leave other people so that they will not notice the anguish that he is suffering. For Guillaume, a lover burns for his beloved, but seeing her, he will forget himself and stand motionless and mute (2272–78). His self-consciousness is extreme; thoughts and words fail him when he tries to converse with "la bele" (2359). Indeed, the lack of discursive transaction provides the image of the lover's condition generally:

> S'il avient chose que tu troves
> la bele ou point que tu la doives

araisoner ne saluer, / lors t'estovra color muer,
si te fremira tot li sans, / parole te faudra et sens
quant tu cuideras comancier;
et se tant te puez avancier
que ta resson comencier oses, / quant tu devras dire .III. choses,
tu n'en diras mie les .ii.,
tant seras vers li vergondeus. . . .

Quant ta reison avras fenie
sanz dire mot de vilenie,
mout te tendras a conchié
quant tu avras rien oublié
qui te fust avenant a dire.
Lores seras en grant martire:
c'est la bataille, c'est l'ardure,
c'est li contanz qui tot jors dure;
amanz n'avra ja ce qu'i quiert,
tot jors i faut, ja em pais n'iert. (2379–90, 2399–2408)

[If it should happen that you find the beauty where you must
greet her and speak to her, then your color will have to
change and your pulse will flutter. Just as you want to begin,
words and ideas will fail you; if you can get yourself together
enough to dare to begin your speech, you'll be so embar-
rassed before her that when you want to say three things, you
won't be able to say two of them. . . .

When you've finished your talk without saying a single vul-
gar word, you will still think yourself tricked because you
will have forgotten something that you should have said.
Then you'll be in great martyrdom. This is the battle, this is
the anguish, this is the struggle that lasts forever; a lover will
never enjoy what he seeks, there is something always lacking,
he is never at peace.]

The Lover is told more than once that he will spend hours in his chamber and in his bed. His lyrical utterances require no audience. Here he
laments his condition, makes complaints, and offers songs to his beloved;

he builds castles in the air and fools himself, taking joy in deluding himself with "delectable thought that is nothing but lies and fables" (2433–34).

Although the Lover is often a victim of self-deception, there are also occasions when he must deceive others. So, for example, the God of Love advises him to seek out the house of the beloved, but adds that he should hide this from others and invent some excuse for being there: find an alibi for having to go to that neighborhood (2365–77). Later in the poem, Ami (Friend) counsels the Lover to use flattery to overcome Dangier (Disdain), for he is greatly to be pacified by sweet talk and flattery (3127–29). The Lover follows his advise, but there is a great difference between the true lover's innocent deceptions[12] and the wickedness of false lovers.

Guillaume briefly evokes salient traits of false lovers when he describes the true lover's proneness to confusion and shame. The true lover is susceptible to shame and embarrassment; false lovers, on the other hand, are recognized by speech that is assured, active, and based in deception:

> Mes faus amanz content lor verve
> si come il veulent, sanz peor;
> icil sont fort losengeor;
> il dient un et pensent el,
> li traïtres felon mortel. (2394–98)

[But false lovers recite their big talk as they will, without compunctions; they are great liars; they say one thing and think another, the murderous traitors.]

As though sketched in cameo, Guillaume's false lovers (and elsewhere his churls) give us a momentary glimpse of the political reality of speech that dominates Jean's *Roman*.

Jean's poem supplies us with (among other things) the blueprint for

---

[12] An aspect of courtly as well as of pragmatic speech, deception is found in Troilus's concern early in the poem to conceal his lovesickness, as well as in Pandarus's masterly ability to arrange a dinner in such a way that no one knows its import. On courtly love and deception (Pandarus refers to "engyn" at least twice: 2.565, 3.274), see Robert W. Hanning's discussion in *The Individual in Twelfth-Century Romance* (New Haven: Yale UP, 1977) 105–38.

such discourse. Both in its specific references to Guillaume's commandments (Jean refers to these quite specifically, once having the lover recap them) and in its treatment of speech generally, Jean's *Roman* will break down Guillaume's set injunctions favoring self-control and moderation, and counsel the lover toward energetic initiatives that suggest an entirely different attitude towards discourse. Jean's Lover is instructed to master the discourse Guillaume specifically attributes to false lovers. What Jean's lover must hide are not his real feelings, as in Guillaume, but his fraud. The sense of control and containment in a lover's speech gives way, in Jean's *Roman,* to instruction in a wily many-sidedness that celebrates the potentialities of speech.

Jean's break with the authority implicit in Guillaume's commandments regarding speech and his urging of greater discursive freedom[13] is particularly evident in his early discussion of so-called bawdy speech. He begins by undermining Guillaume's clear-cut distinction between what is courteous and what is bawdy, having Raison urge that the Lover question the underlying assumptions of a commandment against bawdy speech. Raison's response to the Lover's objection to her own bawdy speech—"parleüre baude" (6951)—is to remind the lover that she was created and nourished by God, the origin of all courtesy, and that with God's permission she customarily speaks without gloss—"sanz metre gloses" (7050). She concedes that though God *might* have named things, He did not, choosing to let her do so at her pleasure—to increase our understanding, individually and communally:

> Et la parole me dona,
> ou mout tres precieus don a.
> Et ce que ci t'ai recité
> peuz trover en auctorité,
> car Platon lisoit en s'escole
> que donee nous fu parole

---

[13] Per Nykrog reminds us of the social and political context of Jean's work, of the repression and censorship in Paris in the late thirteenth century. He observes the effects of this on Jean and others: "La severité rigoureuse qu'il abhorrait s'est installée pour dominer la vie intellectuelle pendant des siècles. Les écrits de Christine de Pisan et surtout de Jean Gerson, un siècle plus tard, montrent à quel point son texte était fait pour inspirer de l'horreur aux bien-pensants" (*L'Amour et la Rose: Le Grand Dessein de Jean de Meun,* Harvard Studies in Romance Languages 41 [Lexington, KY: French Forum Publishers, Inc., 1986] 87). Jean's treatment of particular aspects of Guillaume's commandments concerning speech argue against repression of any kind.

por fere noz volairs entendre,
por enseignier et por aprendre. (7065–72)

[He gave me speech, wherein is a very precious gift. And you can find what I've said in the authorities, for Plato taught at his school that speech was given us to make our wishes understood, to teach and to learn.]

In citing Plato's *Timaeus* and the view of discourse itself as a precious gift given by God for purposes of exploration and understanding, Raison complicates, if not makes moot, Guillaume's specific distinction between ribald and courteous speech.[14] Here, in the discussion of bawdy speech (as is true also of Chaucer's defense of "villainous" speech in the *General Prologue* and in the *Miller's Prologue*) the reference to Plato's comments on language suggest (and urge) a broader, more open view of discourse.[15]

In Jean's *Roman,* speech explores the world, as well as defines it; in addition to directly referring to them, Jean subjects Guillaume's restrictive commandments to a rich and provocative dialectic. The poem, in the words of one critic, is a "grand debate."[16] Jean engages us in multiple and often conflicting discursive realities, each with what one might call a completely rational grammar of its own. Speech gains a stature and freedom here that is wholly unlike its role in Guillaume's *Roman.*[17] As

---

[14] The tradition of speech here evoked by Jean de Meun is, of course, the same one that Boccaccio draws on in Book VI of his *De casibus* (see chapter 1, pp. 5–6 and n.17 above).

[15] On this passage in Jean and its relation to similar issues in the fabliaux, see Charles Muscatine, "Sexuality and Obscenity" in *The Old French Fabliaux* (New Haven: Yale UP, 1986), esp. 146–49.

[16] E. K. Rand, cited in Alan M. F. Gunn, *The Mirror of Love: A Reinterpretation of "The Romance of the Rose"* (Lubbock: Texas Tech P, 1952) 65. Gunn also refers to the poem as a "disputation" (65) and as a "symposium" (474). See particularly his discussion on "The Medieval Conflictus" (475–80). More recently, David F. Hult has also drawn attention to the debate structure of the *Roman* and pointed us to Bakhtin's definition of "dialogism": "What I have termed the romance's debate structure is only the most superficial formal indication of the stylistic phenomenon that Bakhtin has termed 'dialogism,' which is to say the interpenetration within a single discourse (not necessarily an actual dialogue) of two or more socially or ideologically charged codes" ("Language and Dismemberment," *Rethinking "The Romance of the Rose"* 106). See Bakhtin's "Discourse in the Novel," in *The Dialogic Imagination,* ed. Michael Holquist, trans. Caryl Emerson and Michael Holquist (Austin: U of Texas P, 1981) 259–422.

[17] Gunn (and G. M. Paré before him) notes "the influence of the scholastic method of disputation and reasoning" in Jean's writing. See Gunn, *The Mirror of Love* 441–42;

one discourse opens onto another in Jean's dialectic, there is hardly the possibility of resolution. The emphasis in Guillaume's *Roman* on discourse restricting discourse (on commandments to which the lover must submit) is replaced in Jean's *Roman* by an emphasis on discourse ("parole") as a tool of exploration and understanding. With magnificent understatement, Jean says of his own poem that it does nothing but recite what other poets have done (si con font antr'eus li poete), that he has only added "quelque parole" (15206–7); his comment is made more complex considering the stature of "parole" in Jean's humanism.[18]

Astonishingly many-sided, discourse in Jean's view (and here we think of Pandarus) is a skill that can be learned. Indeed, seen one way, the Lover's progress toward the Rose in Jean is instruction in the potentialities of speech. Thus can Jean's Lover learn from the trickster, if only to be able to combat his talk. So, for example, the Lover is told to avoid Male Bouche, but if he cannot be avoided, then he is to be dealt with in his own terms: Jean urges that it is simply sensible to use fraud to deal with fraud. Both folk wisdom and the proverb amply support such deception: "A wise man covers up his ill will" (7311); "A cunning man against a wily one" (7322); "it's smart to pat a dog until you've passed him" (7362–63). Assured, active, and thoroughly trained in deception, the discourse described (and enacted) for Jean's Lover could not be more unlike that of Guillaume's. However satirically intended,[19] Jean's treatment of Guillaume's commandments instructs in a discourse that is pragmatic, canny, and attuned to political reality.

Chaucer embraced fully the *Roman*'s great range of views of speech and found in Jean de Meun an attitude highly congenial to his own sympathy with humanism. In Chaucer's hands, the *Roman* will account for all the speakers in the *Troilus,* and also, of course, for any number of speakers in the *Canterbury Tales*.

Gerard Marie Paré, *Le Roman de la Rose et la Scolastique Courtoise* (Paris: J. Vrin, 1941), and *Les Idées et les lettres au XIIIe siècle: le Roman de la Rose* (Montreal: Centre de psychologie et de philosophie, 1, 1947).

[18] Jean's understatement here (15206–7) is in keeping with what John V. Fleming describes as Jean's first "modification" or "anti-assumption" concerning his relation to the ancient poets. Fleming asserts "that Jean considers himself to a considerable and quite self-conscious degree to be a translator working in the classical tradition rather than a romance *poet* augmenting a vernacular corpus" ("Jean de Meun and the Ancient Poets," *Rethinking ''The Romance of the Rose''* 84).

[19] Ovid's influence, particularly with respect to tone, is, of course, considerable.

In *Troilus and Criseyde,* Troilus's entry into Love's service (1.912) is much like that of Guillaume's lover;[20] it involves a complete conversion and, not surprisingly, repentance "If I mysspak" (1.934–35). Troilus's first impulse upon being "hitte" by the God of Love (1.208) is to dissimulate (1.279–80, 321–22, 326–29) and to weigh the relationship between the private and the public self, especially in the area of speech (1.379–85):

> And over al this, yet muchel more he thoughte
> What for to speke, and what to holden inne. . . . (1.386–87)

Chaucer's poetry describes a human being leveled, subjugated, and increasingly isolated by the effects of love: Troilus speaks with piteous voice (422). The lack of an audience to his laments, complaints, and song is emphasized by the narrative observation: "Al was for nought: she herde nat his pleynte" (544). It is, of course, in his chamber bewailing thus alone (546) that Pandarus finds him and comments on fools who beweep their woe, without bothering to seek a remedy (762–63). And it is in bed that Troilus plans the speech that he will, predictably, be unable to deliver successfully:

> Lay al this mene while Troilus,
> Recordynge his lesson in this manere:
> "Mafay," thoughte he, "thus wol I sey, and thus;
> Thus wol I pleyne unto my lady dere;
> That word is good, and this shal be my cheere. . . ." (3.50–54)

Whether in public or in private, Troilus's discourse is progressively less communicative. Were it not for Pandarus, there would be no discursive transaction at all.[21]

---

[20] C. S. Lewis, *The Allegory of Love: A Study in Medieval Tradition* (New York: Oxford UP, 1936), points out that though Chaucer does not recount the god of love's commandments, we see Chaucer's Troilus "actually obeying them" (180). It is Lewis, of course, who calls the *Troilus* "a great poem in praise of love" (197).

[21] Pandarus more than once urges speech on Troilus. For example, having made the arrangements for the dinner at Deiphebus's house, he exhorts him:

> "Now spek, now prey, now pitously compleyne;
> Lat nought for nyce shame, or drede, or slouthe!
> Somtyme a man mot telle his owen peyne.
> Bileve it, and she shal han on the routhe:

A limited way of understanding experience, courtly love is an authoritative discourse that supplies Troilus with stock alternatives and stock postures. Troilus repeatedly transmutes the realistic world into the discourse of courtly idealism. He invokes the authority of that courtly idealism, its conventions, its loyalty to "trouthe," its suffering, its lyricism, and its hyperbolical extremes. In the rather extended exchange about the name to be given Pandarus's activities on Troilus's behalf (3.239–413), Troilus asserts the authority of the discourse over experience itself, reassuring Pandarus (who has raised the issue) that diversity is required between like things and that what he is doing for him is called "gentillesse," not "bauderye" (3.395–406). Especially in Book 5, he shows a marked inability to respond to the evidence of his senses. Thinking he has miscounted the days until Criseyde's return (5.1185), Troilus walks the walls, blinded by his hope (1195). His response to Criseyde's continued failure to return is an increasingly isolated discourse. He tells all his sorrow to the moon (5.649). Indeed, he creates a private mythology in which the wind blowing in his face "Is of my ladys depe sikes soore" (5.675).

But as though to remind us that Chaucer's thematic interests in a poem often outweigh consistency of character, there are notable instances where Troilus himself breaks out of the passivity of courtly speech, at least twice commenting astutely on speech itself. We recall his response in Book 4 to Pandarus's innumerable arguments (386–427) that Troilus should love another all freshly new and let Criseyde go (456–57):

> "O, where hastow ben hid so longe in muwe,
> That kanst so wel and formely arguwe?" (496–97)

Similarly shrewd is Troilus's response to Criseyde's argument in Book 4 concerning her ability to betray her father and thus to return to Troy.

In order to return to Troilus, Criseyde intends to outdo Calchas in the art of deception. The poem's main plot, the love affair between Criseyde and Troilus, is momentarily, but starkly, infused with its over-

---

Thow shalt be saved by thi feyth, in trouthe." (2.1498–1503)

The narrator's "And was the firste tyme he shulde hire preye / Of love; O myghty God, what shal he seye?" at the conclusion of the Book 2 (1756–57) draws further attention to Troilus's difficulty and challenge.

plot, Calchas's treason and the political reality of war between Troy and Greece. In a scheme that involves material possessions in huge quantity and counts on Calchas's thrice-invoked greed (1369, 1377–78, 1399), Criseyde claims that she will convince Calchas that it was his cowardice that caused him to misgloss "goddes text" (1409–11). She urges that she will enchant him with her "sawes" (4.1394–96) and use all her powers to convince him:[22]

> "And yf he wolde ought by hys sort it preve
> If that I lye, in certayn I shal fonde
> Distorben hym and plukke hym by the sleve,
> Makynge his sort, and beren hym on honde
> He hath not wel the goddes understonde;
> For goddes speken in amphibologies,
> And for o soth they tellen twenty lyes." (4.1401–7)

When the narrator subsequently insists that Criseyde really means what she says, that all this thing was said with good intent and that her heart was true and kind (4.1415–18), he cannot but draw our attention to the paradox that she is simultaneously promising to lie and vowing to be true.

Criseyde's unfaithfulness (which has already been promised) would seem to give way to the more urgent problem of the unfaithfulness of speech itself. In Troilus's response, Chaucer drops Troilus's ingenuousness to make him temporarily the vehicle of practical comment on Criseyde's projected deceitfulness. Troilus begs the question of Criseyde's attitude toward speech and focuses, instead, on Calchas's expertise:

---

[22] Robert W. Hanning comments more generally on Criseyde's assertions of deception in Book 4: she "becomes an emblem of the use of language ostensibly as an instrument of clarification and comfort but actually to persuade, manipulate, and impose our will upon other people, even as a scholar uses glossing to impose his meaning on other texts." See Hanning, "I Shal Finde It in a Maner Glose," in *Medieval Texts and Contemporary Readers,* ed. Laurie A. Finke and Martin B. Shichtman (Ithaca: Cornell UP, 1987) 44. For an interpretation of this kind of assertion of deceptive speech (especially that of the Wife of Bath) in terms of the "speech act," see George R. Petty, Jr., "Power, Deceit, and Misinterpretation: Uncooperative Speech in the *Canterbury Tales,*" *Chaucer Review* 27 (1993): 413–23. Petty argues quite persuasively that such assertions are useful "against (or on behalf of) ideological language" (413); in terms of speech act theory, they are "violations" of the "cooperative principle" upon which successful communication depends (414).

"It is ful hard to halten unespied
Byfore a crepel, for he kan the craft;
Youre fader is in sleght as Argus eyed;
For al be that his moeble is hym biraft,
His olde sleighte is yet so with hym laft
Ye shal nat blende hym for youre wommanhede,
Ne feyne aright; and that is al my drede." (4.1457–63)

No matter how expert, Criseyde will not deceive Calchas at his own
craft. The formulations given to Troilus alert us to the psychological and
social forces that drive speaker as well as listener: to counter Criseyde's
bold comment that her father's "coward herte / Made hym amys the
goddes text to glose," we have Troilus's equally blunt "youre fader shal
yow glose / To ben a wif" and his intuition that Calchas will so praise
and commend some Greek that "ravysshen he shal yow with his speche"
(4.1410–11, 1471–74). The disproportionate space given here to the
verbal deceit Criseyde intends once she is in the Greek camp cannot but
focus attention on one of the extreme reaches of speech, speech as an
instrument divorced from truth or content. Indeed this implication is
underlined by Troilus's unusual use of the word "ravysshen," which,
elsewhere in the poem has exclusively physical connotations (1.62;
4.530 and 548).

But if, with these notable exceptions, Troilus's discourse is largely
one-dimensional, defined by the forms of courtly love and finally para-
lyzed by them, the speech of Pandarus, Criseyde, and Diomede (though
there are also, as we shall see, distinctions among them) is, by contrast,
multi-layered, responsive to a changing context, and pragmatic.

Pandarus's physical agility and his hurry to communicate emphasize
his love of speech for its own sake: we are reminded of the eagle's seem-
ingly unquenchable garrulousness in the *House of Fame,* the birds' quar-
reling in the *Parliament,* the Wife of Bath's love of talk, and of the
Pardoner.[23] Pandarus looks for talk. And when he finds it, he probes his
subjects, plots his course, and adjusts his methods to the particular listener and circumstance. His style can be colored or plain, copious or

---

[23] The descriptions of Pandarus and the Pardoner—"This Pandarus gan newe his
tong affile" (2.1681), and "For wel he wiste, whan that song was songe, / He moste
preche and wel affile his tonge" (I [A] 711–12)—both suggest Cicero's "prava virtutis
imitatrix," discussed briefly in chap. 1, above. Chaucer's play with all the nuances of
deception is, of course, another matter.

brief, and his subject matter infinitely varied and contradictory. He draws on every available kind of discursive material and rhetorical stance: exhortation, humor, anger, proverbs, and philosophical disquisition. Asked how he—who could "nevere in love thiselven wisse" (1.622)—could possibly bring Troilus to bliss, Pandarus responds that counsel can be employed beneficially by anyone, even a fool. He invokes the theory of contraries (1.637)[24] and compares discourse to a whetstone which, though not itself sharp, can sharpen tools (see 1.624–36). Pandarus's *speche* has an eye to the "remedye" or "cure"; he is interested in making things happen. Or, as Muscatine has put it, "Pandarus operates in a naturalistic world where speech is action."[25] He announces that pragmatism—that eye to a cure—even in his final "I kan namore seye" (5.1742), once Criseyde's unfaithfulness—"tresoun," he calls it (5.1738)—is undeniable, even to Troilus.

Particularly in his interactions with Criseyde, Pandarus's speech is finely attuned to the sense of what lurks beneath words and conventional conversation. The disparity between Pandarus's wise speech and the symptoms of love's sharp arrows announced at the opening of Book 2 (57–60) hardly prepares us for the oblique dynamics of the talk between Pandarus and Criseyde that follows. The conversational subtleties that Chaucer conveys in this scene, subtleties that announce the essential unity of speaker and listener, may well be a historical landmark in the representation of speech.

---

[24] The theory of contraries described by Jean de Meun (and quoted immediately below) is discussed as a central poetic principle in the *Roman* by Nancy Regalado in " 'Des contraires choses': la fonction poétique de la citation et des exempla dans le 'Roman de la Rose' de Jean de Meun," *Litterature* 41 (Feb. 1981): 62–81.

> "Ainsinc va des contreres choses,
> les unes sunt des autres gloses;
> et qui l'une an veust defenir,
> de l'autre li doit souvenir,
> ou ja, par nule antancion,
> n'i metra diffinicion;
> car qui des .ii. n'a connoissance,
> ja n'i connoistra differance,
> san quoi ne peut venir en place
> diffinicion que l'an face." (21543–52)

[Thus things go by contraries; one is the gloss of the other. If one wants to define one of the pair, he must remember the other, or he will never, by any intention, assign a definition to it; for he who has no understanding of the two will never understand the difference between them, and without this difference no definition that one can make can come to anything.]

[25] Muscatine, *Chaucer and the French Tradition* 145.

Oblique, but totally congenial to both, the dialogue between Pandarus and Criseyde in Book 2 becomes a kind of dance in which both parties are fully attuned to the levels of meaning that lurk just beneath the script. As they read one another, responding not only to the words they hear but also to the complex psychology and social awareness that motivates their words, Criseyde proves herself a worthy partner in a process that Pandarus nonetheless dominates. Not only words but also the objects at hand cooperate in the creation and reading of second and third levels of meaning. So, for example, the book—the tale of the siege of Thebes (2.83–34)—that Pandarus finds Criseyde reading with her ladies becomes the implement with which Pandarus can easily direct the conversation in his great "emprise" (73):

> "But I am sory that I have yow let
> To herken of youre book ye preysen thus.
> For Goddes love, what seith it? telle it us!
> Is it of love? O, som good ye me leere!" (2.94–97)

Criseyde will provide him (unnecessarily, it seems—"Al this knowe I myselve" [2.106]) with details concerning the book, but only after first responding to him at the next level—" 'Uncle,' quod she, 'youre maistresse is nat here' " (98)—and thus bringing them together into the intimacy of shared laughter (99). Pandarus, in turn, uses the details of the romance to deny interest in the book at all. But when he suggests that she trade wimple and book for "face bare" and dance (109–12), Criseyde momentarily retreats into an excited denial which Pandarus appropriately reads as a challenge:

> "I! God forbede!" quod she. "Be ye mad?
> Is that a widewes lif, so God yow save?
> By God, ye maken me ryght soore adrad!
> Ye ben so wylde, it semeth as ye rave.
> It satte me wel bet ay in a cave
> To bidde and rede on holy seyntes lyves;
> Lat maydens gon to daunce, and yonge wyves."
>
> "As evere thrive I," quod this Pandarus,
> "Yet koude I telle a thyng to doon yow pleye." (2.113–21)

Both Pandarus and Criseyde are adept at acknowledging the sexual reality just beneath the veneer of social discourse, but Criseyde is out-maneuvered, brought by Pandarus to an almost abject curiosity, an eagerness to know that he delights in teasing and stretching:

> "Now, uncle deere," quod she, "telle it us
> For Goddes love; is than th'assege aweye?
> I am of Grekes so fered that I deye."
> "Nay, nay," quod he, "as evere mote I thryve,
> It is a thing wel bet than swyche fyve."
>
> "Ye, holy God," quod she, "what thyng is that?
> What! Bet than swyche fyve? I! Nay, ywys!
> For al this world ne kan I reden what
> It sholde ben; some jape I trowe is this;
> And but youreselven telle us what it is,
> My wit is for t'arede it al to leene.
> As help me God, I not nat what ye meene." (2.122–33)

Promising in quick succession not to tell her (2.134–35) and to tell her (137–38), Pandarus finally brings Criseyde to complete subjection: the narrative now hyperbolically describes her as a thousand times more curious than before, as never before so curious to know something, "sith the tyme that she was born" (2.143), and finally, to agreeing to ask no more, lest it displease:

> And with a syk she seyde hym atte laste,
> "Now, uncle myn, I nyl yow nought displese,
> Nor axen more that may do yow disese." (2.145–47)

Stage one of Pandarus's "grete emprise" (73) is here almost complete—its completion, oddly enough, signaled by Criseyde's stated acceptance that Pandarus has information that he has yet to communicate.

In stage two, in the extended conversation now described,

> . . . with many wordes glade,
> And frendly tales, and with merie chiere,
> Of this and that they pleide, and gonnen wade
> In many an unkouth, glad, and dep matere . . . (2.148–51)

with Pandarus still withholding information, still preparing a nest for his revelations, Criseyde again shows herself equal to the dance—a dance now more emphatically choreographed by Pandarus. Not more than gently coached, Criseyde joins in praises of Hector as well as of Troilus. When Pandarus signals a departure immediately upon an extended praise of Troilus (2.190–207), the moment is perfect, not only for Criseyde's pressing him to stay on, but—as becomes clear—for greater intimacy.[26] Criseyde's request at once successfully detains him and signals her ladies a desire for privacy:

> "Nay, sitteth down; by God, I have to doone
> With yow, to speke of wisdom er ye go." (2.213–14)

In a further round of oblique talk, Pandarus again masterfully builds up Criseyde's curiosity. Her earlier coyness is replaced now by downright inquisitiveness: "A, wel bithought! For love of God . . . / Shal I nat witen what ye meene of this?" (225–26). And Pandarus is still teasing, "No, this thing axeth leyser" (227). Though he does not say so until a few moments later, what he means by "this thing" is the subtle art of talk itself.[27]

What we have here is a kind of essay on the reciprocity of speech. Like lovemaking, language involves the readiness of two, speaker and listener. Pandarus is seducing Criseyde with language. When she urges revelation (climax), he heightens her curiosity (desire) in any number of ways—by changing the rhythm of conversation, announcing that it is time for him to leave, suggesting a dance, or by pretending extreme consideration in the area of speech:

> "Yet were it bet my tonge for to stille
> Than seye a soth that were ayeyns youre wille." (2.230–31)

As these virtuosi read each other, they move into increasingly complex indirection. Criseyde's "Lat be to me youre fremde manere speche"

---

[26] This is a scene not found in the *Filostrato,* where Pandaro immediately moves to a private conversation with Criseida (see *Filostrato* 2.34ff.)

[27] Infinitely various in his discursive poses, Pandarus will contradict himself at least once on this subject of art: he urges that though some might take delight in composing with "subtyl art," the object is "al for som conclusioun"; he will concentrate on conclusions and shun art (2.253–63). This, too, is a discursive pose that Criseyde understands (2.421–25).

(248) in response to Pandarus's elevated declaration of friendship (232–38) is followed by what appears to be an entirely straightforward statement of discursive strategy, belied, of course, by all that precedes and follows it in Pandarus's great enterprise. Chaucer typically gives the moment dramatic presence, thus heightening the sense of a seduction. Here, Criseyde casts her eyes downward, and Pandarus coughs a little and says:

> . . . "Nece, alwey—lo!—to the laste,
> How so it be that som men hem delite
> With subtyl art hire tales for to endite,
> Yet for al that, in hire entencioun
> Hire tale is al for som conclusioun.
>
> "And sithe th'ende is every tales strengthe,
> And this matere is so bihovely,
> What sholde I peynte or drawen it on lengthe
> To yow, that ben my frend so feythfully?" (2.255–63)

In spite of his denial, Pandarus is, of course, neither plain nor brief: he set out to commend Troilus to Criseyde some twenty-six stanzas earlier (1.1055–57). He will finally reveal Troilus's name eight stanzas after the present denial of time and art, and even then, his task is by no means complete.

In truth, Pandarus's apparent straightforwardness, his emphasis here on the end rather than the means, is also part of his discursive strategy. Aloud, Pandarus emphasizes the formal requirements of speech; he looks at speech as a phenomenon, as though from the outside, and observes that however subtly crafted it is (and this because it gives pleasure to the teller), it is intended for a specific conclusion. When thinking to himself (in lines which Chaucer immediately juxtaposes with those containing Pandarus's vocalized words),[28] Pandarus's perspective is entirely different; his comments on speech are now made from the point of view of the speaker, of someone assessing the effect of his words on a listener. Pandarus thus indicates, more than any other speaker in Chaucer's poetry (with the Pardoner in his tale a close second) that the art of speech and rhetoric concerns both speaker and listener, that indeed it provides a psychology of the listener, a way of reading the audience.

---

[28] Pandarus's thoughts (267–73), interjected in the midst of his gazing on Criseyde's face (264–66, 274), are not in the *Filostrato*.

Here, more true to the Pandarus we observe in action, he stresses, not the conclusion or the formal aspects of speech at all, but rather the method and particularly the fit between material and listener:

> Than thought he thus: "If I my tale endite
> Aught harde, or make a proces any whyle,
> She shal no savour have therin but lite,
> And trowe I wolde hire in my wil bigyle;
> For tendre wittes wenen al be wyle
> Theras thei kan nought pleynly understonde;
> Forthi hire wit to serven wol I fonde. . . ." (2.267–73)

Pandarus's discourse must appear to be plain; otherwise, he will arouse the suspicion of trickery. Here, *lack* of artful elaboration is being espoused in order, in fact, to "bigyle."[29] Making a longer "proces"[30] nonetheless—and now drawing attention to it aloud to Criseyde: "What sholde I lenger proces of it make?" (2.292)—Pandarus finally brings his audience to emphatic curiosity. Criseyde begs for the information Pandarus has been holding back:

> "Now, good em, for Goddes love, I preye,"
> Quod she, "come of, and telle me what it is!
> For both I am agast what ye wol seye,
> And ek me longeth it to wite, ywys. . . ." (2.309–12)

And yet Pandarus is still not finished. In the next round of discourse, even after he has revealed Troilus's identity and love (2.319–22), Panda-

---

[29] Here one thinks of the Pardoner, who at the end of his tale turns to the audience present and disarmingly asserts, "And Jhesu Crist, that is oure soules leche, / So graunte yow his pardoun to receyve, / For that is best; I wol yow nat deceyve" (VI [C] 916–18). Like Pandarus, the Pardoner realizes the artfulness of simplicity—that it can, like any other guise, disguise. For a succinct statement of this in Shakespeare, see *King Lear*, II.ii.101–4, where Cornwall says: "These kind of knaves I know, which in this plainness / Harbor more craft and more corrupter ends / Than twenty silly-ducking observants / That stretch their duties nicely."

[30] On "proces" (line 424, "this paynted proces," and lines 268, 292, and 485), see Siegfried Wenzel, "Chaucer and the Language of Contemporary Preaching," *Studies in Philology* 73 (1976): 138–61. "In fourteenth-century Latin, French, and English," Wenzel writes, "the noun *proces* had more specific technical sense referring to the ordered development of a sermon or of its parts after the division of the theme. . . . Robert of Basevorn in his *Forma praedicandi* uses *processus* again and again for 'development' " (154).

rus must bring Criseyde to agree to an arrangement to "make hym bettre chiere / Than ye han doon er this" (3.360–61). The oblique discourse continues, the playfulness between them now interspersed with greater risks—like Pandarus's seeking Criseyde's agreement to love Troilus while denying that he is bawd between them (2.351–57), and Criseyde's denying the sexual bond with Troilus that she and Pandarus land on almost simultaneously, he in speaking, she in listening:

> "And right good thrift, I prey to God, have ye,
> That han swich oon ykaught withouten net!
> And be ye wis as ye be fair to see,
> Wel in the ryng than is the ruby set.
> Ther were nevere two so wel ymet,
> When ye ben his al hool as he is youre;
> Ther myghty God graunte us see that houre!"
>
> "Nay, therof spak I nought, ha, ha!" quod she;
> "As helpe me God, ye shenden every deel!" (2.582–90)

Criseyde's speech, like her uncle's, is versatile, capable both of Troilus's courtly lyricism and Pandarus's immediacy.[31] Indeed, in what the narrator describes in Book 3 as "al that souneth into gentilesse" (3.1414), Criseyde's speech is hardly distinguishable from Troilus's. But she is clearly at ease with more than one level of speech. As is evident in her response when she takes in the full meaning of Pandarus's revelations in Book 2, Criseyde harbors no illusions regarding discursive simplicity:

> "Is al this paynted proces seyd—allas!—
> Right for this fyn? . . ." (424–25)

She is, as we have already seen, adept at moving from level to level in conversation and hiding these as needed (see 2.386–87). But Chaucer makes Criseyde's discursive tactics more transparent than Pandarus's. We are allowed to see her looking behind words, assessing them for their motivation and meaning. So, for example, after Criseyde has heard

---

[31] Close attention to *speche* in the poem throws into doubt C. S. Lewis's comment that "Pandarus is exactly the opposite of his niece" (*The Allegory of Love* 190).

about Troilus's "woo" (2.383), she decides to pursue Pandarus's meaning:[32]

> "I shal felen what he meneth, ywis."
> "Now em," quod she, "what wolde ye devise?
> What is youre reed I sholde don of this" (2.387–89)

She considers the situation—with feeling as well as with some practical cunning— and concludes:

> "It nedeth me ful sleighly for to pleie." (2.462)

Similarly, with a roomful of conversation (at Deiphebus's house),

> Herde al this thyng Criseyde wel inough,
> And every word gan for to notifie. (2.1590–91).

Having had Troilus (in a scene added by Chaucer to Book 3) restate his "entente" (3.127–47), Criseyde studies him and thoughtfully measures her words:

> With that she gan hire eyen on hym caste
> Ful esily and ful debonairly,
> Avysyng hire, and hied nought to faste
> With nevere a word. . . . (3.155–58)

After the lovers' first consummation and reluctant dawn parting, once he is back in his palace and in his own bed, instead of sleeping, Troilus reviews "Hire wordes alle" (3.1542). Criseyde, for her part, is briefly described as having similar thoughts, but in her meeting with Pandarus the following morning, she can view the courtly speech of the consummation scene in another perspective:[33]

---

[32] Windeatt notes Criseyde's "inward response" to Pandarus's speech (*Troilus and Criseyde: A New Edition of "The Book of Troilus"* 171). Criseyde's discursive "tactics" here (and in the subsequent scenes I mention) are distinctive to Chaucer's poem. They are not found in the *Filostrato*.

[33] The proverbial comment that closes this stanza is Chaucer's own, as are the two that follow in my discussion (5.97–98, 784).

And ner he com, and seyde, "How stant it now
This mury morwe? Nece, how kan ye fare?"
Criseyde answerde, "Nevere the bet for yow,
Fox that ye ben! God yeve youre herte kare!
God help me so, ye caused al this fare,
Trowe I," quod she, "for al youre wordes white.
O, whoso seeth yow knoweth yow ful lite." (3.1562–68)

Here, in the context of quick-witted dialogue, alert to the deceptive powers of speech, to Pandarus's dissembling, Criseyde translates the previous night's lyricism into "al this fare."

For Diomede, Chaucer creates a self-serving, deceitful speech that is without truth or content. Purely tactical and based on the psychology of the listener, speech is for Diomede a weapon that he can wield at will. He speaks, for example, of the winner of Criseyde as a "conquerour" (5.792–94) and indicates that the same *speche* that is for Pandarus valuable for its own sake is something of trivial worth:

"But whoso myghte wynnen swich a flour
From hym for whom she morneth nyght and day,
He myghte seyn he were a conquerour."
And right anon, as he that bold was ay,
Thoughte in his herte, "Happe how happe may,
Al sholde I dye, I wol hire herte seche!
I shal namore lesen but my speche."[34] (5.792–98)

More than any of the others, Diomede has simplified experience into a few formulations that make speech bluntly opportunistic and translate it directly into strategy. Proverbial wisdom is plucked (*ex post facto*) to validate his opportunism:

"I have herd seyd ek tymes twyes twelve,
'He is a fool that wol foryete hymselve.' " (5.97–98)

"For he that naught n'asaieth naught n'acheveth." (5.784)

---

[34] Although these particular instances of Diomede's taking stock without speaking are not found in the *Filostrato,* there is precedent for them there: see *Filostrato* 5.13 (Diomede sees the love of Troiolo and Criseida) and 6.10 (Diomede sees Criseida weeping).

He enters the action in Book 5 shrewdly reading the situation, observing Troilus's pale face and his silence. As he leads Criseyde's horse toward the Greek camp, he adapts his strategy of speech to the reality he observes. Words disguise his meaning—

> ". . . I shal fynde a meene
> That she naught wite as yet shal what I mene." (5.104–5)

And they buy him time. He draws Criseyde out, "in speche / Of this and that" (5.107–8) by asking questions, showing understanding for her new circumstance, and offering first friendship (127–33) and then a quasi-familial bond: "And that ye me wolde as youre brother trete" (5.134).

Near the place most symbolic of deceit—Calchas's tent[35]— Diomede then asserts that were it not for the fact that

> ". . . we ben so neigh the tente
> Of Calcas, which that sen us bothe may,
> I wolde of this yow telle al myn entente. . . ." (5.148–50)

Although Diomede's discourse may be reminiscent of the familiar chatter between Pandarus and Criseyde, it is employed—as Diomede's stated tactics more than once remind us—without reciprocal awareness and with a kind of lean self-interest that includes the pretense of being not only intimate but open. Diomede lacks Pandarus's love of talk, and he lacks his sense of the mutuality of speech. Like Jean's false lover, Diomede is expert at hiding in a speech that knowingly draws on the authority of the courtly without, in fact, subscribing to it.

Diomede's patent duplicity is an extreme instance of Chaucer's repeated turning in *Troilus and Criseyde* to the forces that prevent communication. The communicative transaction seems never to be simply assumed. Sometimes communication—especially for the courtly lover and as described in the commandments of Guillaume's God of Love—is thwarted simply because an utterance is not designed to communicate in the first place. Troilus's early and ample love "compleynte" in Book 1

---

[35] Though not in Boccaccio, this proximity to the tent is a detail that is found in Benoit de Sainte-Maure, *Le Roman de Troie*. See Windeatt, ed., *Troilus and Criseyde* 455.

achieves nothing: "Al was for nought: she herde nat his pleynte" (1.544). This is already ironic as well as factual.

More often, however, communication falters even when words have been heard. In Book 3, for example, after the massive flurry of activity—all the arranging by Pandarus for the meeting in Deiphebus's house—the two principals are together, and their discourse cannot achieve closure for the simple reason that Criseyde does not understand, or claims not to understand, Troilus's "entente." Since lack of communication is always possible in courtly discourse, it can be pretended and used tactically. Chaucer builds up to this anti-climax, juxtaposing the diverse *speche* (and, in Pandarus's case, gestures) to draw attention to the difficulty of the discursive transaction:

> "I, what?" quod she, "by God and by my trouthe,
> I not nat what ye wilne that I seye."
> "I, what?" quod he, "That ye han on hym routhe,
> For Goddes love, and doth hym nought to deye!"
> "Now than thus," quod she, "I wolde hym preye
> To telle me the fyn of his entente.
> Yet wist I nevere wel what that he mente." (3.120–26)

Criseyde states that she understands neither Pandarus's "poking" nor Troilus.

But communication in *Troilus and Criseyde,* as we have seen, can also be thwarted because "entente" is, in fact, often purposely hidden. As Criseyde remarks, the "goddes speken in amphibologies" (4.1406) and human discourse, too, is anything but straightforward. The poem provides an abundant supply of words for verbal deceit,[36] and not only Diomede but also Pandarus, Criseyde, and even Troilus practice (or provide comment on) the art of dissimulation.

The ambiguity, disparity of awareness, and uncertain "entente" that are common features of the characters' speech in *Troilus and Criseyde* are found, as well, in the narrator's. So, for example, in the midst of Pandarus's preparations for the dinner at Deiphebus's house, when he hurries on in the name of brevity, the narrator seems to partake in Pandarus's

---

[36] These include "feyne" and "feyned" (2.1528; 3.167; 4.1463; 5.846), "blende" (2.1496), "sleyghte" (2.1512), "wordes white" (3.901, 1567), "this paynted process" (2.424), Criseyde's statement that "It nedeth me ful sleighly for to pleie" (2.462), and Criseyde's calling Pandarus a "fox" (3.1565). And there are more.

verbal agility. We recall Pandarus's "What sholde I moore seye?" (2.321), followed by nine stanzas of his talk. Here, even his diction resembles Pandarus's:

> But fle we now prolixitee best is,
> For love of God, and lat us faste go
> Right to th'effect, withouten tales mo,
> Whi al this folk assembled in this place. . . . (2.1564–67)

We might legitimately wonder what makes it "best" to hurry at this particular moment. And we might also note that the apparently straight-forward promise to go "right to th' effect" will more likely yield further ambiguity.

The narrator is similarly dissembling in his comment on another central episode in Book 3. Here, the world may be blind to Pandarus's arrangements (3.526–30), but the poem's audience is more than once (and, indeed, unreliably) reminded that we are not blind:

> . . . it bifel right as I shal yow telle. . . . (3.511)

> Ye han wel herd the fyn of his entente. (3.553)

We seem to be privy to Pandarus's intentions and his assertion—notably punctuated by "he swor" (556, 566, 570, 589)—that Troilus is out of town (570), but we are, in fact, also victims of a deception. We watch Pandarus teasing Criseyde with the hypothesis that were Troilus in town, she need not fear, for Pandarus would rather die a thousand times than that men might see him there (568–74). The narrator draws further attention to Pandarus's lack of openness by teasing the audience just as Pandarus had teased Criseyde (3.554–74):

> Nought list myn auctour fully to declare
> What that she thoughte whan he seyde so,
> That Troilus was out of towne yfare,
> As if he seyde therof soth or no;
> But that, withowten await, with hym to go,
> She graunted hym, sith he hire that bisoughte,
> And, as his nece, obeyed as hire oughte. (3.575–81)

Although he will on another issue excuse himself by claiming that "I kan nat tellen al, / As kan myn auctour . . ." (3.1324–25), the narrator here suggests that it is his source which is incomplete. Then, having recounted Criseyde's concern for "goosissh poeples speche" (3.583) and Pandarus's extensive assurances (589–93), the narrator again draws attention to the incomplete nature of his account by commenting (almost off-handedly), "what sholde I more telle?" (593). Elsewhere, he promises the reader certainty when, in fact, he supplies none. His "for o fyn is al that evere I telle" (2.1596) is unconvincing, not unlike Pandarus's "Th'ende is every tales strengthe" (2.260) as he revels in process and Criseyde's emphasis on "conclusioun" (5.765, 1003) in the very midst of her uncertain status. In all these instances, Chaucer's focus seems to be rather on those aspects of speech that point us to the complexity of human communication and to the forces that make it so.

The subtlety and appreciation with which Chaucer himself has treated speech in *Troilus and Criseyde* must at least give us pause concerning the meaning of its endings.[37] The poem does not convincingly lead to the successive endings, nor do the endings resolve the complexity and conflict inherent in the poem, with speech or anything else. At its opening, *Troilus and Criseyde* introduces a treasonous figure who is honored for his speech: the Greeks

> Hym diden bothe worship and servyce,
> In trust that he hath konnynge hem to rede.
> In every peril which that is to drede. (1.82–84)

If the potentially complex political entanglements of knowledge and speech are thus indicated, the poem's ending, consonant with its treatment throughout, refuses to give convincing authority to any one kind of discourse. There is, first of all, the narrator's denial of responsibility:

> Bysechyng every lady bright of hewe,
> And every gentil womman, what she be,
> That al be that Criseyde was untrewe,
> That for that gilt she be nat wroth with me.

[37] There is also the odd detail that the endings are punctuated by references to speech: ". . . And this commeveth me / To speke . . ." (5.1783–84); "for ther is so gret diversite / In Englissh . . ." (5.1793–98); "But yet to purpos of my rather speche" (5.1799); and "Lo here, the forme of olde clerkis speche" (5.1854).

> Ye may hire gilt in other bokes se;
> And gladlier I wol write, yif yow leste,
> Penelopeës trouthe and good Alceste. (5.1772–78)[38]

Next, Chaucer's farewell to his book—"Go litel bok" (5.1786–99)— includes explicit acknowledgement of the difficulty of communication, whether due to miswriting, mismetering, or something even more basic in communication itself. In no way can understanding be assumed:

> And red wherso thow be, or elles songe,
> That thow be understonde, God I biseche! (5.1797–98)

The authoritative exhortation to young, fresh folks to repair home from worldly vanity and seek true love (1835–48), though moving and beautiful, is a purely conventional palinode, a pious sentiment that overleaps rather than resolves all that precedes. The rejection of "olde clerkis speche / In poetrie" (1854–55) hardly seems final in the context of the passage of veneration, the tribute to "Virgile, Ovide, Omer, Lucan, and Stace" (1789–92).

In his ending, as in the poem generally, Chaucer seems to be showing us that speech can show us numerous (and often necessarily conflicting) realities, that it provides us a way of looking at the world. Though we may look for a definitive statement that gives order to experience, the poem gives us, instead, a different and more difficult alternative.[39]

---

[38] This denial is followed by the narrator's rather surprising claim that

> N'y sey nat this al oonly for thise men,
> But moost for wommen that bitraised be
> Thorugh false folk—God yeve hem sorwe, amen!—
> That with hire grete wit and subtilte
> Bytraise yow. . . . (5.1779–83)

A similar move from one gender to another is found in the *Manciple's Tale* IX (H) 187–95, a passage discussed briefly in chap. 8, below. Here, as there, the effect of this shift in gender is to draw our attention to the poem's larger thematic concerns, especially as they relate to speech.

[39] Phillip Pulsiano's "Redeemed Language and the Ending of *Troilus and Criseyde*," in *Sign, Sentence, and Discourse: Language in Medieval Thought and Literature,* ed. Julian N. Wasserman and Lois Roney (Syracuse: Syracuse UP, 1989) 153–74, is an example of what I would call the simpler alternative. In a discussion of the last several stanzas of the poem, and quoting from *De doctrina Christiana* 1.4.4, Pulsiano summarizes as follows: "Like Dante, Chaucer has taken us on a journey from doubt to certitude, from ambiguity to truth. He becomes our guide through the world, so that 'by means of corporal and temporal things we may comprehend the eternal and spiritual' " (170).

The poem's treatment of speech suggests that in its concrete forms and manifestations, speech can provide a way of reading the complex and conflicting forces in human society, past and present, and thus a means of understanding them. By refusing finally to let discourse wrap up the experience of the poem conclusively, Chaucer points to that newly discovered potentiality of speech. Rhetorically directed towards its audience, *Troilus and Criseyde* may go some distance in remedying the credulousness that Boccaccio in *De casibus* diagnosed as constituting the greatest harm to the prince and the commonwealth.[40]

---

[40] See my discussion in chap. 1, esp., pp. 9–12 above.

4

The *Knight's Tale* and the Discourse of Authority

Chaucer's propensity for the dialogic is not only a dramatic matter, but an ethical and political one. For in Chaucer's conception, dialogue almost always confronts authority, exposing authoritative discourse to critical contradiction. The dialogic structure reveals culture as an interplay of multiple authorities, some agreeing and some disagreeing, some operating from the top down and some from the bottom up. Not limited to those who are nominally in authority or wield power directly, authoritative discourse belongs to any speaker who speaks within the embrace of authority, whether that authority be political, erotic, social, or religious. It can come from the mouths of victims, lovers, celebrants, suppliants, or anyone else, when they speak by the rules of an overarching authority—or an established frame of reference—that does not suffer questioning.

The kinds of speech to be found in the aura of authoritative discourse include political addresses, and philosophical lectures, but also invocations and apostrophes, lyric utterances[1] and prayers, sermons and

---

[1] The implications of lyric authority are persuasively argued in Thomas C. Stillinger, *The Song of Troilus: Lyric Authority in the Medieval Book* (Philadelphia: U of Pennsylvania P, 1992). Stillinger points out, for example, that in Guillaume's *Roman,* lines 2436ff., the "experience of love is . . . presented as a pre-existent discourse that is taken up and adopted as the individual lover's own inner life" (7). For an enumeration of the "lyric

complaints. Prescribing rather than describing, authoritative discourse tells us not how things are but how they should be.

The Clerk in the *General Prologue* is a model practitioner of authoritative discourse. He speaks "in forme and reverence." Though we are never told quite what form it is, nor to whom or to what the reverence is directed, whether it be a social, religious, or academic authority, it is clear that he speaks under the arch of its (here unspoken) commandments, and that he implicitly obeys them. The *General Prologue* has several other exemplars of authoritative speakers: the Knight's speech is in keeping with ideals of courtesy already discussed in relation to Troilus and Guillaume de Lorris's *Roman*. The Gospel is the source of the Parson's speech.[2] And there is at least one revealed anti-authoritarian in the *General Prologue*: the Monk, who openly carries on a dialogue with Augustine and the "text." But the literary plan promises to unfold a whole corpus of anti-authoritarian—and therefore subversive—discourse.

In the *Knight's Tale,* particularly in the speeches of Theseus, Chaucer does the fullest possible justice to the discourse of authority. Here, speech is the supreme political vehicle by which a ruler expresses his will, demonstrates his responsiveness to his people, and behaves judiciously or not:

> "And forthy I yow putte in this degree,
> That ech of yow shal have his destynee
> As hym is shape, and herkneth in what wyse;
> Lo, heere youre ende of that I shal devyse.
>> My wyl is this, for plat conclusioun,
> Withouten any repplicacioun—
> If that you liketh, take it for the beste. . . ." (I [A] 1841–47))

Imperative, unhurried, and assured, Theseus's speech stands on traditional associations and ancient wisdoms. It declares a coherent world in which logic and even syntax itself become weapons of authority. Au-

---

pieces" in *Troilus and Criseyde,* see James I. Wimsatt, *Chaucer and His French Contemporaries: Natural Music in the Fourteenth Century* (Toronto: U of Toronto P, 1991). Wimsatt counts fifty-six, or "about a fifth of the total lines" (142). See also in chap. 3, n5, above, Eugene Vance's comment concerning Troilus in "Marvelous Signals: Poetics, Sign Theory, and Politics in Chaucer's *Troilus,*" *New Literary History* 10 (1979): 293–337.

  [2] See the *General Prologue* I (A) 481, 498, and 527.

thoritative discourse seems to dwell *on* a given situation rather than move it in any practical way.[3] The discourse of authority makes decisions. Rather than opening an issue for discussion or seeking to generate response, it seeks closure: to resolve conflict and contain discussion.

Though the discourse may assume a listener, it does not require one. The listener to the authoritative discourse of the *Knight's Tale* is a silent presence, typically anticipating the speech with quiet respect. Even when delivered by proxy, as when the herald announces the restrictions on the weapons to be used in the tournament, the discourse emanating from authority has a majesty that demands stillness, not response. We witness opinion and dialogue being replaced by reverence and receptivity:

> Somme seyden thus, somme seyde "it shal be so";
> Somme helden with hym with the blake berd,
> Somme with the balled, somme with the thikke herd;
> Somme seyde he looked grymme, and he wolde fighte:
> "He hath a sparth of twenty pound of wighte."
> Thus was the halle ful of divynynge. . . . (I [A] 2516–21)

> Duc Theseus was at a wyndow set,
> Arrayed right as he were a god in trone.
> The peple preesseth thiderward ful soone
> Hym for to seen, and doon heigh reverence,
> And eek to herkne his heste and his sentence.
> An heraud on a scaffold made an "Oo!"
> Til al the noyse of peple was ydo,
> And whan he saugh the peple of noyse al stille,
> Tho shewed he the myghty dukes wille. . . . (I [A] 2528–36)

Self-contained and self-sufficient, authoritative discourse does not depend on reciprocity, though it may sometimes accept it.

The poem as a whole is full of this declaimed, unreciprocated speech. Speech is so important in the *Knight's Tale* that often the action of the tale is an occasion for, indeed, seems to exist for the sake of

---

[3] See the discussion of the style of the *Knight's Tale* in *Chaucer and the French Tradition* (Berkeley: U of California P, 1957), where Muscatine describes the pace of the *Knight's Tale* as "deliberately slow and majestic" and points out the frequency of the rhetorical devices *occupatio* and *descriptio* (177–78).

discourse, rather than vice versa. Thus, the imprisonment of Arcite and Palamon and their falling in love with Emily is the occasion for extensive philosophical speeches; their fighting in the woods is the occasion for Theseus's felt pity and speech on the power of love; Arcite's illness is the occasion for lyrical lament (I [A] 2765–97); Theseus's subsequent sorrow is the occasion for Egeus's wisdom on the world's transmutation (I [A] 2842–49)—to name only a few instances. In all these, while listeners are present, the discourse is complete without them.

The description of Theseus before his final speech of the tale is the crowning example of the power of his discourse. The respectful hush of the listener is only one reason why all the discursive transactions of the *Knight's Tale*—most of them touched, if not initiated by Theseus—are satisfactorily closed. His wisdom, his words, and his will are one:

> Whan they were set, and hust was al the place,
> And Theseus abiden hadde a space
> Er any word cam fram his wise brest,
> His eyen sette he ther as was his lest,
> And with a sad visage he siked stille,
> And after that right thus he seyde his wille. . . . (I [A] 2981–86)[4]

Theseus's discourse now stamps its rationale and its persuasive amplitude on the events of its world with unquestioned authority. His final speech on "the faire cheyne of love" (I [A] 2988) is the culmination of a tale in which the spoken word has unquestioned amplitude and stature.

The *Knight's Tale* allows us momentarily to experience a world in which discourse can convey a cosmology and a reasoned conclusion. Theseus's words at the tale's end move Palamon and Emelye to an action that makes "of sorwes two / O parfit joye" (I [A] 3071–72) in both the private and political realms. Like that in *The Consolation of Philosophy,* Theseus's consolation attends to the questions that have been raised by Palamon and Arcite[5] and by the events of the poem. His discourse asserts a wisdom based on law. Purposeful, cohesive, rational, Theseus's cosmology (with its rich heritage of classical and medieval thought) would seem to unify and give closure to human experience generally.

---

[4] Theseus's tribute to the god of love in part 2 is similarly introduced: "He gan to looken up with eyen lighte / And spak thise same wordes al on highte . . . " (I [A] 1783–84). In each case, godlike attributes accompany his speech.

[5] See esp. I (A) 1251–67 and 1303–22.

But it cannot. When viewed solely from the perspective of a given speaker, discourse appears to obey the rule of reason. The Knight thinks he has closed his tale; for the Miller, it is not closed at all.[6] The Miller cannot accept the Knight's discourse without accepting its values, so closely bound are discourse and the social order, language and ideology. In terms of speech, the Host's comment—after the general praise of the *Knight's Tale,* that "unbokeled is the male" (I [A] 3115)—is fully substantiated. The Miller, and with him humanity, is simply unable to keep still: "He nolde his wordes for no man forbere" (I [A] 3168). Speech—portrayed in the Knight's narrative as an authoritative and civilizing force—now establishes itself as the currency of conflict, a means by which to pay itself back. The group's sense of a "noble" story that is worthy of remembrance, especially by the gentry (I [A] 3111–13), becomes the Miller's

> . . . "By armes, and by blood and bones,
> I kan a noble tale for the nones,
> With which I wol now quite the Knyghtes tale." (I [A] 3125–27)[7]

As the Host hurries from pilgrim to pilgrim, urging thrift,[8] the frame of reference shifts audibly to the experiential world. The majestic pace of Theseus's speech is replaced by the rush of everyday life:

> "Abyd, and lat us werken thriftily. . . ." (I [A] 3131)

> "Sey forth thy tale, and tarie nat the tyme. . . ." (I [A] 3905)

---

[6] Paul A. Olson reads the *Miller's Tale* as an explicitly political statement; see *"The Canterbury Tales" and the Good Society* (Princeton: Princeton UP, 1986) 75–85. See also Lee Patterson, " 'No Man His Reson Herde': Peasant Consciousness, Chaucer's Miller and the Structure of *The Canterbury Tales,"* *South Atlantic Quarterly* 86 (1987): 457–95. Alfred David's characterization of the *Miller's Tale* as "a literary Peasants' Rebellion," in *The Strumpet Muse* (Bloomington: Indiana UP, 1976), is further developed by Paul Strohm in his *Social Chaucer* (Cambridge: Harvard UP, 1987) 151ff. On this general subject, see also John M. Ganim, "Chaucer and the Noise of the People," *Exemplaria* 2 (1990): 71–88.

[7] Alfred David, *The Strumpet Muse* 92; and Paul Strohm, *Social Chaucer* 153, note the "literary" nature of the Miller's rebellion: "the Miller's social revolt is transmuted into a matter of style (with his requital transferred from the Knight himself to the Knight's *tale)."* Strohm considers that, as such, "the Miller's rebellion is subject to a process of conciliation and integration far more rapid and less painful than that experienced by the rebellious peasants in 1381" (154).

[8] On "thrift" and its relation to Bakhtin, see Peggy Ann Knapp "Robyn the Miller's Thrifty Work," in *Sign, Sentence, Discourse: Language in Medieval Thought and Literature,* ed. Julian N. Wasserman and Lois Roney (Syracuse: Syracuse UP, 1989) 298–300.

"Now tell on, Roger. . . ." (I [A] 4345)

"Now telle on, gentil Roger by thy name." (I [A] 4353)

In the competitive, rushed, and pragmatic world of the *Miller's Tale,* speech is retribution. A fart is as effective as words (I [A] 3806–8), and reasoned argument is finally deposed altogether:

For what so that this carpenter answerde,
It was for noght; no man his reson herde. (I [A] 3843–44)

A justice may be operating in the *Miller's Tale,* but it is a comic justice that is not produced or supported by reasoned discourse, and its grammar is pragmatic rather than formal.

The Ciceronian sense of discourse as a binding element of society suffers further deterioration in the *Reeve's Prologue* and *Tale.*[9] Here, proverbial wisdom specifically denigrates discourse: "whan we may nat doon, than wol we speke" (I [A] 3881), and the tongue is "sely" (I [A] 3896). For the Reeve, as for the Miller, speech is revenge:

". . . I shal hym quite anoon;
Right in his cherles termes wol I speke." (I [A] 3916–17)

By his own report, he shares the Miller's kind of speech (his "cherles termes") and, by implication, its distrust of authority. But if the *Miller's Tale* suggests conflict with the political aspect of an authoritative discourse, the *Reeve's Tale* suggests conflict with its intellectual aspect. The *Reeve Tale*'s miller satirizes an "art" in which space itself is confected of nothing but discourse:

"Myn hous is streit, but ye han lerned art;
Ye konne by argumentes make a place
A myle brood of twenty foot of space.
Lat se now if this place may suffise,

---

[9] See Emily Jensen, "Male Competition as a Unifying Motif in Fragment A of *The Canterbury Tales,*" *Chaucer Review* 24 (1990): 320–28; the essay includes a discussion of what Jensen calls a "degenerative movement" in this fragment.

> Or make it rowm with speche, as is youre gise." (I [A] 4122–26)

The clerks' northern dialect (full of "mistakes") erroneously suggests stupidity to the miller, so he is reacting to both that and to their presumed intelligence as clerks. The miller satirically *imagines* intellectual discourse to equal making a universe out of nothing; but as the clerks rearrange the miller's bedroom and themselves to suit their purposes, their "magic" finally works. The *Reeve's Tale* vindicates the clerks' cleverness and in turn satirizes the miller's anti-intellectualism.

In this context of reciprocating perspectives, one of the key functions of the *Knight's Tale* is to provide a context for the related but different examples of authoritative discourse in the tales that follow. The *Clerk's Tale* is particularly illuminated by the *Knight's Tale* and vice versa. Both tales posit an all-encompassing philosophical and social order and the presence of an absolute ruler. While the discourse of authority, as embodied in Theseus, is neither naked nor arbitrary, in Walter it is arbitrary, subjugating, and oppressive. Walter, as we shall see momentarily, suppresses mercy and pity in his speech. Theseus, by incorporating these qualities, exhibits a discourse in which the private and the public blend into one another.

In the *Knight's Tale* Theseus seems to think aloud, and he navigates easily from inner to outer, from the private to the public. His speech is capable of exposing conflict and subjecting initial emotions to scrutiny and thoughtful modification. The *Knight's Tale* gives prominence to this quality by more than once describing the process by which Theseus's discourse translates an initial emotion into understanding and compassionate behavior. This attention to the civilizing power of discourse is notable given the almost overwhelming destructive forces also present in the *Knight's Tale*.[10]

Theseus's discourse in the *Knight's Tale* not only has unquestioned stature, but it is characteristically the tool by which the ruler tempers his judgement. His early question to the company of ladies—

> "What folk been ye, that at myn homcomynge
> Perturben so my feste with criynge?" (I [A] 905–6)—

---

[10] Muscatine remarks on the "constant awareness of a formidably antagonistic element" in the *Knight's Tale* (*Chaucer and the French Tradition* 181). On this topic, see also William Frost, "An Interpretation of Chaucer's *Knight's Tale,*" *Review of English Studies* 25 (1949): 289–304.

is but one instance of several in which Theseus first questions aggressively and then responds judiciously and sympathetically. His words and behavior are similarly modified when he comes upon Arcite and Palamon, who have broken the conditions of their liberty and set upon each other in the woods. Discourse tempers arbitrary judgements. Theseus's tribute to the god of love (I [A] 1785–90) is the outcome of a lengthy inner deliberation in which ire is replaced by reason:

> And though he first for ire quook and sterte,
> He hath considered shortly, in a clause,
> The trespas of hem bothe, and eek the cause,
> And although that his ire hir gilt accused,
> Yet in his resoun he hem both excused. . . . (I [A] 1762–66)

Nurtured and reflected upon, responsive to inner as well as outer impulses, Theseus's discourse is the vehicle by which human emotions can be understood and governed. It reflects on itself, noting both its limits and its power:

> And in his gentil herte he thoughte anon,
> And softe unto hymself he seyde, "Fy
> Upon a lord that wol have no mercy,
> But been a leon, both in word and dede. . . ." (I [A] 1772–75)

And noting these, it differentiates between "a proud despitous man" and one who has "repentaunce and drede" (I [A] 1776–77).[11] It is a measure of Chaucer's instinctive dialogism and openness in terms of discourse, that even Theseus, who is a most powerful speaker, still leaves room for dialogue. If only briefly and pointedly, phrases like "If that you liketh, take it for the beste," or "And if yow thynketh this is weel ysayd" (I [A] 1847, 1867), acknowledge the presence of a listener.

In the *Clerk's Tale*, the discourse of authority is less supple and more arbitrary. I have tried to show elsewhere that the particular questions raised by the Griselda story about the psychological and spiritual appropriateness of the testing of Griselda are central to the medieval contro-

---

[11] A similar movement in Theseus, from an initially harsher position to a gentler one, is found in the herald's announcement of Theseus's modification of the tournament rules and the destruction of life (I [A] 2537–60).

versy about political order, especially in fourteenth-century Italy.[12] As one historian has put it, the notion of absolute political order is not "compatible" with "the Christian notion of the absolute value of human personality."[13] The obedience and unity of will which lie at the very heart of political unity may, if pushed to the extreme in practice, conflict irrevocably with the value of the individual. When we look at the way in which discourse is used in the *Clerk's Tale,* it supports completely this thesis that at the axis of the tale is a tension between the needs of the state and the value of the individual: in her absolute obedience to Walter, Griselda tests the acceptability of absolute authority and therefore of absolute, arbitrary discourse.

The philosophical underpinnings and the judiciousness suggested by Theseus's speech give way in the *Clerk's Tale* to a diminished speech that is the agency of pure power. Though the ruler's discourse in both tales assumes a hierarchical, established order, Walter's, much more than Theseus's, draws attention to the distance between himself and others. Walter's speech is a means of maintaining hierarchy and the disparity of power. To this end, he asserts sharp—indeed, legal—distinctions between himself and the people, and between himself and Griselda. The first meeting with Janicula and Griselda is a "collacioun" (IV [E] 325). Terms like "charge," "assure," "swere," "assente," "requeste," and "grucche" describe and necessarily delimit the relationship among the speakers:[14]

> "Lat me allone in chesynge of my wyf—
> That *charge* upon my bak I wole endure.
> But I yow preye, and *charge* upon youre lyf,
> What wyf that I take, ye me *assure*
> To worshipe hire, while that hir lyf may dure,
> In word and werk, bothe heere and everywheere,
> As she an emperoures doghter weere.

---

[12] Michaela Paasche Grudin, "Chaucer's *Clerk's Tale* as Political Paradox," *Studies in the Age of Chaucer* 11 (1989): 63–92.

[13] A. P. d'Entrèves, *Dante as Political Thinker* (Oxford: Clarendon, 1952) 49.

[14] For the legal and political implications of the verb "grucchen" here (IV [E] 170, 354), see the *Middle English Dictionary*, ed. Hans Kurath and Sherman M. Kuhn (Ann Arbor, Mi.: U of Michigan P., 1954); and Alfred L. Kellogg, "The Evolutions of *The Clerk's Tale:* A Study in Connotation," in *Chaucer, Langland, Arthur: Essays in Middle English Literature* (New Brunswick: Rutgers UP, 1972) 276–329.

> "And forthermoore, this shal ye *swere*: that ye
> Agayn my choys shul neither *grucche* ne stryve;
> For sith I shal forgoon my libertee
> At youre *requeste,* as evere moot I thryve,
> Ther as myn herte is set, ther wol I wyve;
> And but ye wol *assente* in swich manere,
> I prey yow, speketh namoore of this matere." (IV [E] 162–75;
>   italics mine)

In the first meeting with Griselda, Walter is similarly legalistic, referring to his questions as "demandes" and asking whether Griselda will "assente, or elles yow avyse?" (IV [E] 348–50). His conditions for marriage specifically address Griselda's speech: the absolute obedience that Walter asks would efface what is most characteristic of the human being:

> "And eek whan I sey 'ye,' ne sey nat 'nay,'
> Neither by word ne frownyng contenance?
> Swere this, and heere I swere oure alliance." (IV [E] 355–57)

There is a sense in the *Clerk's Tale* that discourse, as characterized by Walter, is at once absolute and minimalist. In addition to a legal framework for speech that necessarily distances speaker and listener, Walter's speech curtails speech. So, for example, even as he asks his people's agreement to his conditions for marriage, he closes all other avenues of discourse:

> "And but ye wole assente in swich manere,
> I prey yow, speketh namoore of this matere." (IV [E] 174–75)

To Griselda's acceptance of the marriage contract (IV [E] 358–64), Walter responds: "This is ynogh, Grisilde myn" (IV [E] 365). He is similarly economical in his comments to the people gathered outside: the brief directive to honor and love his wife is followed simply by "ther is namoore to seye" (IV [E] 371). This phrase is echoed verbatim by the sergeant in the first encounter with Griselda, when he asks forgiveness and states the necessity of his mission (IV [E] 526–32).

In the *Knight's Tale,* the discourse of authority does its work openly. Theseus's speech reveals its reasonings and manifests the underlying structure of belief that gives it its authority. The underlying rationale of

Walter's speech, on the other hand, remains hidden, and its authority thus naked and arbitrary. Walter withholds explanations. To accomplish his ends, he orders his sergeant to misinform Griselda, misrepresents his people's views,[15] devises a false papal bull (IV [E] 736–49), sends secret letters, and uses "open audience" (IV [E] 790) to lie to Griselda. As though hidden even from himself, Walter's discourse does not, until the tale's end (IV [E] 1072–78), reveal its full intentions to anyone. Even his apparent openness with his sergeant—"He prively hath toold al his entente / Unto a man, and to his wyf hym sente" (IV [E] 517–18)—is also, in fact, another reminder of a discourse that conceals. The sergeant may be privy to Walter's intentions concerning the testing of Griselda, but here, too, the secretive aspect of communication is stressed. He reveals Walter's intentions to anyone "upon peyne his heed of for to swappe" (IV [E] 586).

Walter's speech not only does not navigate between the private and the public; it must negate the former for the latter, or vice versa. His speech excludes his own emotions and the acknowledgement of Griselda's. Walter notes Griselda's continued obedience, and hides his response:

> Glad was this markys of hire answeryng,
> But yet he feyned as he were nat so;
> Al drery was his cheere and his lookyng,
> Whan that he sholde out of the chambre go. (IV [E] 512–15)

> . . . And whan this markys say
> The constance of his wyf, he caste adoun
> His eyen two, and wondreth that she may
> In pacience suffre al this array;
> And forth he goth with drery contenance,
> But to his herte it was ful greet plesance. (IV [E] 667–72)

> "The smok," quod he, "that thou hast on thy bak,
> Lat it be stille, and bere it forth with thee."
> But wel unnethes thilke word he spak,

---

[15] See the *Clerk's Tale* IV (E) 481–90, 624–37, and 799–801. Walter's deceit and the roughness of his sergeant are, of course, complicated by the fact that Walter is shown to be gentle and caring behind the scenes.

But went his wey, for routhe and for pitee. (IV [E] 889–93)

The reference to Walter's eyes—"he caste adoun / His eyen two"—as he sees but cannot acknowledge Griselda's obedience, recalls, by contrast, the description of Theseus's eyes, "He gan to looken up with eyen lighte" as he addresses Palamon and Arcite and gives tribute to the god of love (I [A] 1783–1814), and later, "his eyen sette he ther as was his lest" (I [A] 2984). Theseus's speech is the supreme manifestation of his understanding and his governance. Walter's, on the other hand, is propelled by a hiddenness that impairs its capacity to represent the human condition.

When Chaucer's narrator, in the *Clerk Tale*'s extended ending, exhorts the "archewyves" (IV [E] 1195) among his listeners to use the arrows of their "crabbed eloquence" (IV [E] 1203), he exposes the discourse of authority to the same kind of dialogic treatment that immediately meets the *Knight's Tale* in the *Miller's Prologue*. But the dialogic in the *Clerk's Tale* is already in progress. For not only does Theseus's speech in the *Knight's Tale* provide a context for Walter's, but in the *Clerk's Tale* itself, Walter's speech is implicitly contrasted to Griselda's as a ruler. Here, even in the smaller confines of the *Clerk's Tale,* Chaucer would seem to be reminding his audience that the species of discourse that Walter embodies is severely limited in its scope.

In the *Clerk's Tale,* Griselda, as the event requires, is able to "redresse" the common profit and to "apese" discord, rancour, and sadness. Her words are so wise and ripe and her judgments of "so greet equitee" that she appears—"as men wende"—to be sent from heaven, "Peple to save and every wrong t'amende" (IV [E] 438–41). Often taken to be a reference to Christ,[16] the idea that Griselda was sent from heaven to amend every wrong is possibly also intended to evoke Cicero, and thus the eloquence for which the Italian humanists admired him. In Book 6 of Boccaccio's *De casibus,* the description of Cicero's virtues suggests Griselda's in the *Clerk's Tale,*[17] and the sense that he is sent from Heaven

---

[16] Cf. Matt. 1.21. See also Phillipa Hardman, "Chaucer's Tyrants of Lombardy," *Review of English Studies,* n.s., 31 (1980): 172–78, which cites the Apocryphal Gospel of the Infancy: "And when the multitude saw it, they were astonished, and said: 'This young child is from heaven' for he hath saved many souls from death, and hath power to save them all his life long." See *The Apocryphal New Testament: A Collection of Apocryphal Christian Literature in an English Translation,* ed. J. K. Elliott, trans. M. R. James (New York: Oxford UP, 1993) 54.

[17] See esp. the *Clerk's Tale* IV (E) 406–41.

is also the same: "Cicero, it seems to me was sent here from God;" though he already possessed "genius from Heaven," his skill in eloquence finally surpassed even Plato's.[18]

In Lydgate's translation of the *De casibus* (not directly from Boccaccio's Latin, but from Premierfait's French), we find some of the same language (and certainly the same concepts) found in Chaucer's description of Griselda: among these, that Cicero was "sent from aboue to been ther diffence" and that he could "appese bi his prudent langage / Folkis that stoode at discencioun" (6.3077, 3137–38).[19] Understood as an emblematic merging of Christian and Ciceronian eloquence, and, in fact, an eloquence like Theseus's, this rendition of Griselda's speech would seem to further substantiate our doubts regarding Walter's.

---

[18] Boccaccio, *The Fates of Illustrious Men*, trans. Louis Brewer Hall (New York: Ungar, 1965) 161–62. The Latin, from *De casibus*, VI.12, 10–12, reads: "Hic etenim ad hoc arbitror a Deo datus mortalibus, etsi celesti polleret ingenio, longo tamen et pervigili studio in tantam mirande eloquentie evasit facundiam . . . sed ipsam Platonis mellitam verborum dulcedinem. . . ."

[19] Below are the relevant passages from *Lydgate's Fall of Princes, Part III*, ed. Henry Bergen, Early English Text Society e.s. (London: Oxford UP, 1924; rpt. 1942) 123:

Thus koude he punshe tretours of the toun,
Outraie ther enmyes, of manhod & prudence;
Callid of ther cite gouernour & patroun,
Sent from aboue to been ther diffence,
Ther champioun, most digne of reuerence,
Chose of ther goddis ther cite for to guie
Bi too prerogatyues: knihthod & polycie. (6.3073–80)

He coude appese bi his prudent langage
Folkis that stoode at discencioun;
Bi crafft he hadde a special auauntage,
Fauour synguleer in pronunciacioun,
In hihs demenyng gret prudence and resoun:
For the pronouncyng of maters in substaunce,
His thank resceyveth bi cheer & contenaunce. (6.3137–43)

The name of Tulie was kouth in many place;
His elloquence in eueri lond was ryff;
His langage made hym stonde in grace
And be preferrid duryng al his lyff. (6.3151–54; italics mine)

5

Discourse and Freedom in the
Wife of Bath's Prologue

The association between women and uncontrollable speech was an active tradition in Chaucer's England. One community by common assent "ordained that all the women of the township control their tongues without any sort of defamation."[1] The "cucking-stool," a device for constraining disorderly women and "scolds" and exposing them to public ridicule, often by ducking, was a village institution; the court-rolls show that villages were "repeatedly fined, or threatened, for neglecting to provide them."[2] The contemporary records are not lacking in descriptions of the "common scold." There is, for example, the case of one Alice Stether, who was brought before the mayor of London on 4 September 1375

---

[1] G. G. Coulton, *Medieval Panorama: The English Scene from Conquest to Reformation* (New York: Meridian, 1955) 84, quotes from the Durham roll records: "From Agnes of Ingleby—for transgressions against William Sparrow and Gillian his wife, calling the said Gillian a harlot, to the damage of £2 whence they will take at their will 13s.4d; as was found by the jury—by way of penalty and fine 3s.4d; reduced in mercy to 6d. It is ordained by common assent that all the women of the township control their tongues without any sort of defamation."

[2] Coulton, *Medieval Panorama* 78. Although the cucking-stool (Latin: *cathedra stercoris*)—which was also referred to as "thewe"—was not exclusively for women, their disorderly talk was punished in this fashion. For their own such talk, men suffered the pillory and/or whetstone, or imprisonment. On the history of the cucking-stool, see

97

. . . for being a common scold; and for that all the neighbours, dwelling in that vicinity, by her malicious words and abuse were so greatly molested and annoyed; she sowing envy among them, discord, and ill-will, and repeatedly defaming, molesting, and backbiting many of them, sparing neither rich nor poor; to the great damage of the persons and neighbours there dwelling, and against the Ordinance of the City.[3]

Though Alice, on being questioned, denied the charges, claiming "she was in no way guilty of the things aforesaid," she suffered "the punishment of the pillory, called the *'thewe,'* for women ordained, there to stand for one hour." Official discourse proclaims the punishment for discourse: "And precept was given to the Sheriffs to have proclamation made of the nature of the offence."[4]

An entry in the Letter-Books on 27 June 1379, involving Ralph Strode as attorney to the aggrieved, and William Waleworthe (at various times alderman, sheriff, and, in 1380, mayor of London) describes the crime of yet another Alice—Alice Godrich—who ostensibly came to Waleworthe's house,

and there, and elsewhere within the City of London, did horribly raise the hue and cry upon the said William, as though against a thief, and without cause; calling him a false man, and imputing to him that he had unjustly disinherited her of 20 pounds' value of land yearly, and that he, by his mastery unjustly detained the aforesaid Robert, her husband, in prison, for that reason; to the great scandal of the offices which the said William had heretofore held in the city aforesaid, and to his own damage of 100£.

In response to this, Waleworthe "asked that the same Alice, for the cause before alleged, might be chastised, that so, such scold and she-liars [Latin: *mentitrices*] might dread in future to slander reputable men, without a cause." Though this Alice, too, was convicted, and "should have

---

T. N. Brushfield's *Obsolete Punishments, II: The Cucking Stool,* in *Journal of Architecture, Archaeology, and History,* Society of Chester, VI., 203 (1857–59).

[3] *Memorials of London and London Life in the XIIIth, XIVth and XVth Centuries,* A.D. 1276–1419, ed. and trans. Henry Thomas Riley (London: Longmans, 1868) 385.

[4] *Memorials of London* 385.

the punishment of the pillory, called the '*thewe*,' for such women provided, to stand upon the same for one hour in the day, with a whetstone in the meantime hung from her neck," William himself entreated for her to the mayor and aldermen, and she was released from prison.[5]

Extreme repressive measures, such as the cucking-stool, testify to the political frustration which women might have been expected to vent in language and to the male desire to keep these disruptive manifestations in check. With few outlets besides speech, women's authority was chiefly informal and domestic and, as such, was bound up with their moral substance and the power of speech. In the pages that follow, I will suggest that in the *Wife of Bath's Prologue,* Chaucer takes the traditional association between women and uncontrollable speech and turns it into an exploration of discursive freedom. The Wife's discourse and her sexuality are of a piece: excessive, redundant, and subversive, they both explode into improprieties and forbidden domains.

Nowhere else are the fullest implications of Chaucerian discourse more abundantly played out. Here, in the course of one performance, the qualities of mind and language that seek the problematic and resist closure proliferate before our eyes and ears. The dialogic landscape of the Wife's discourse abounds in open transactions, or what I have called "dynamic aperture"[6] in my discussion of the *Book of the Duchess*. She makes pronouncements and assertions not to close an issue but to provoke questions that generate more discussion. Her speech thrives on contradictions. Extremes necessarily suggest opposing extremes and bold assertions are accompanied by a palpable delight in the controversy that surrounds them.[7] Authorities are quoted against one another—the word

---

[5] *Memorials of London* 433–34.

[6] The first thirty-four lines of the *Wife of Bath's Prologue,* as speech generates more speech, provide a remarkable example of dynamic aperture. The Wife's assertions (e.g., "Housbondes at chirche dore I have had fyve") evoke provisos (e.g., "If I so ofte myghte have ywedded bee") which, in turn, provoke more assertions (e.g., "And alle were worthy men in hir degree"). The Wife's questions typically precipitate more questions; she at once raises and refines them: "If I so ofte myghte have ywedded bee / . . . But me was toold. . . ." She seeks out the problematic (e.g., "Herkne eek, lo, which a sharp word for the nones") and complicates the discourse with other authorities that suggest further doubt, refinement, and challenge (see the *Wife of Bath's Prologue* III [D] 1–34, and esp. 28–29, 30–34).

[7] Derek Pearsall remarks in his work *The Canterbury Tales* (London: Allen and Unwin, 1985) 76, that the Wife's monologue "demands to be looked *into,*" that it "puzzles and intrigues the observer, offers opportunities for contrary responses, creates, though itself a monologue, the effect of a dialogue, within the speaker and also within the reader."

is set against the word—and issues are raised, not to resolve them, but to generate further issues. Questions precipitate more questions:

> "Eek wel I woot, he seyde myn housbonde
> Sholde lete fader and mooder and take to me.
> But of no nombre mencion made he,
> Of bigamye, or of octogamye;
> Why sholde men thanne speke of it vileynye?" (III [D] 30–34)

> "Telle me also, to what conclusion
> Were membres maad of generacioun,
> And of so parfit wys a [wright] ywroght?" (III [D] 115–17)

In Chaucer's imagining of the Wife's mind, there is "nat a word that it nys quit" (III [D] 425). The ripping of the pages of Jankin's "book of wikked wyves" (III [D] 685) symbolizes what the Wife does with established discourse throughout the *Prologue*. Her many-sided attack on authority is particularly an attack on the discourse by which that authority is maintained. The *Prologue*'s sudden reversals and its dialectical quality embody the struggles inherent in discourse, particularly the struggle between the prevailing ideology and the forces that question it.[8]

The Wife is immediately controversial for delivering a prologue that threatens the etiquette of the tale-telling game established in the *Canterbury* frame. She is expected to tell a tale, and she knows it:

Pearsall argues that it is precisely this quality in her prologue that counsels against a strictly iconographic reading (76–86).

[8] Cf. Adrienne Rich's "Teaching Language in Open Admissions," in *On Lies, Secrets, and Silence: Selected Prose 1966–1978* (New York: Norton, 1979), which comments on the teaching of language at the City College of New York:

> At the bedrock level of my thinking about this is the sense that language is power, and that, as Simone Weil says, those who suffer from injustice most are the least able to articulate their suffering; and that the silent majority, if released into language, would not be content with a perpetuation of the conditions which have betrayed them. But this notion hangs on a special conception of what it means to be released into language: not simply learning the jargon of an elite, fitting unexceptionably into the status quo, but learning that language can be used as a means of changing reality. What interests me in teaching is less the emergence of the occasional genius than the overall finding of language by those who did not have it and by those who have been used and abused to the extent that they lacked it. (67)

"Abyde!" quod she, "my tale is nat bigonne." (III [D] 169)

"Now, sire, now wol I telle forth my tale." (III [D] 193)

"Now wol I seye my tale, if ye wol heere." (III [D] 828)

But as she delays and her prologue overflows, she reverses the hierarchical relationship between prologue and tale. Her *Prologue* unwraps dogma, spurs subversion, and invites unrest. If the primary object of a prologue is to make the listener *benevolus, attentus,* and *docilis,*[9] the Wife's does just the opposite. Simply by discoursing, the Wife threatens to topple an entire structure of assumptions, beginning with the rules of the game.[10] Established by males, the rules of the tale-telling game convey hierarchy, patriarchal authority, and closure. The Wife of Bath is profoundly in default of these rules. There is succinct disapproval in the Friar's interjection that

"This is a long preamble of a tale!" (III [D] 831)

Thus the Wife makes a sarcastic reference to the Friar's attempt to control her speech when she comments to the Host that she will now tell her tale,

". . . right as yow lest,
If I have licence of this worthy Frere." (III [D] 854–55)

The sarcastic comment on the Friar's potential control over the Wife's discourse will be enlarged in the tale that follows to suggest a similar control in society generally: especially notable is the thrice-re-

---

[9] Ernst Robert Curtius calls this "die bekannte Hauptregel der antiken Rhetorik für das Proemium," in his article "Mittelalter-Studien. XVIII," *Zeitschrift für romanische Philologie* 63 (1943): 246, cited in James A. Schultz, "Classical Rhetoric, Medieval Poetics, and the Medieval Vernacular Prologue," *Speculum* 59 (1984): 5.

[10] In his study of play "as a cultural phenomenon," Johan Huizinga observes that whereas the cheat "pretends to be playing the game and, on the face of it, still acknowledges the magic circle," the spoil-sport "trespasses against the rules or ignores them." Huizinga likens the cheat to the hypocrite and the spoil-sport to the revolutionary, pointing out that society prefers the cheat to the spoil-sport, that it can tolerate disorder as long as its values are observed. See Huizinga, *Homo Ludens: A Study of the Play Element in Culture* (Boston: Beacon, 1950) 11–12.

peated emphasis on *limiting* in "lymytours," "lymytour," and "lymytours and othere hooly freres" (III [D] 866, 874, 877). Where there were once (pagan) elves, there are now (Christian) "lymytours." And where there was once dancing "in many a grene mede"—

> The elf-queene, with hir joly compaignye,
> Daunced ful ofte in many a grene mede (III [D] 860–61)—

there are now

> . . . lymytours and othere hooly freres,
> That serchen every lond and every streem. . . . (III [D] 866–67)

The blessing and the saying of his matins and other holy things (III [D] 869, 876) only thinly obscures the more pronounced ubiquitousness of this loosely defined group of "lymytours and othere hooly freres" (III [D] 865). Even if we had not already been alerted to their power and control by the Wife's promise to tell her tale, "if I have licence of this worthy Frere" (III [D] 855), we would sense here a stifling presence:

> As thikke as motes in the sonne-beem,
> Blessynge halles, chambres, kichenes, boures,
> Citees, burghes, castels, hye toures,
> Thropes, bernes, shipnes, dayeryes—
> This maketh that ther been no fayeryes.
> For ther as wont to walken was an elf
> Ther walketh now the lymytour hymself
> In undermeles and in morwenynges,
> And seyth his matyns and his hooly thynges
> As he gooth in his lymytacioun.[11] (III [D] 868–77)

---

[11]It is tempting to read in this passage a guarded reference to the Fourth Lateran Council (November 1215), which "opened with a declaration of faith" and "laid down a machinery of persecution for Western Christendom, and especially a range of sanctions against those convicted, which was to prove adaptable to a much wider variety of victims than the heretics for whom it was designed." There is also evidence that in at least one instance (in Languedoc in 1233), papal authority was given to Dominican friars to act as inquisitors in the carrying out of the Council's decree. See R. I. Moore, *The Formation of a Persecuting Society: Power and Deviance in Western Europe, 950–1250* (Oxford: Blackwell, 1987) 7, 10, and 9, resp. The association between discourse and sexuality is rooted in the period, for, as Moore points out, "the metaphor of seduction was freely used in

One crowd has displaced another; it pervades every nook and cranny (of time as well as space) in town and country, on land and sea.[12]

The sense of challenge, even defiance, informs the Wife's discourse generally. It is found in the acknowledged preference, early in her prologue, for the Old Testament over the New. This preference is so notable that it has been remarked that the Wife's treatment of Old Testament figures forms "a kind of gloss on St. Paul, so that the Wife is, in effect, reversing the usual process and glossing the New Law in the 'light' of the Old."[13] The Old Testament, much more than the New, is a treasury of day-to-day things that happen to real people.[14] It is full of tales and "experience." Especially in their attitudes toward sensuality, the New Testament is characterized as harsh, the Old Testament as gentle:

> ". . . lo, which a sharp word for the nones,
> Biside a welle, Jhesus, God and man,
> Spak in repreeve of the Samaritan. . . ." (III [D] 14–16)

> "God bad us for to wexe and multiplye;
> That gentil text kan I wel understonde." (III [D] 28–29)

The Wife's prologue exploits the physicality and variety of the biblical text to precipitate debate:

> "Lo, heere the wise kyng, daun Salomon;
> I trowe he hadde wyves mo than oon.

---

association with heresy, and sexual libertinism ascribed as a matter of course to heretics and their followers." Moore cites the Le Mans chronicler's description of Henry of Lausanne: "Women and young boys—for he used both sexes in his lechery—became so excited by the lasciviousness of the man that they testified publicly to his extraordinary virility" (*The Formation of a Persecuting Society* 122).

[12] In England, canon law was generally administered by archbishops, bishops, and archdeacons in ecclesiastical courts. During Chaucer's time, there was "about one archdeacon to each county," and "this official was often called 'the bishop's eye' " (Coulton, *Medieval Panorama* 122).

[13] D. W. Robertson, *A Preface to Chaucer* (Princeton: Princeton UP, 1962) 326. See also Edmund Reiss, "Biblical Parody: Chaucer's 'Distortions' of Scripture," in *Chaucer and Scriptural Tradition,* ed. David Lyle Jeffrey (Ottawa: U of Ottawa P, 1984) 58.

[14] Edmund Reiss cites a 1968 dissertation which notes "approximately 700 biblical quotations and allusions" in Chaucer's work. Of these, "about three-fifths" come from the Old Testament; the Wife's preference for the Old Testament over the New would thus also seem to be Chaucer's own. See Reiss, "Biblical Parody: Chaucer's 'Distortions' of Scripture," in *Chaucer and Scriptural Tradition* 48.

As wolde God it leveful were unto me
To be refresshed half so ofte as he!
Which yifte of God hadde he for alle his wyvys!
No man hath swich that in this world alyve is." (III [D] 35–40)

The Old Testament provides such a richness of narrative material and example that some of it will necessarily survive glossing:

"What rekketh me, thogh folk seye vileynye
Of shrewed Lameth and his bigamye?
I woot wel Abraham was an hooly man,
And Jacob eek, as ferforth as I kan;
And ech of hem hadde wyves mo than two,
And many another holy man also." (III [D] 53–58)

The *Wife of Bath's Prologue* is openly critical of deductive readings that simply add gloss to gloss, denying empirical reality.[15] Whether from experience or from a text, evidence is repeatedly put forward to challenge established interpretations of the Biblical text.[16] To this

---

[15] On the Wife's readings of scripture, see Robertson, *Preface to Chaucer* 317ff. Graham Caie addresses the question of whether a fourteenth-century reader would recognize the Wife's misreadings, arguing that they would. See Caie, "The Significance of Marginal Glosses in the Earliest Manuscripts of *The Canterbury Tales*," in *Chaucer and Scriptural Tradition* 75–76. For a more skeptical view of Chaucer's sense of exegesis and glossing, see Lawrence Besserman, " 'Glossynge Is a Glorious Thyng': Chaucer's Biblical Exegesis," in *Chaucer and Scriptural Tradition,* 65–73. Besserman points out that "Chaucer was not a fourteenth-century exegete, and his allegiance to the orthodox view of biblical interpretation (in so far as there was a single view) needs to be proved, not merely assumed." He reminds us that, although "the fundamental premise of biblical exegesis was . . . that the letter kills and the spirit gives life (2 Cor. 3:6)," this, to Chaucer's Wycliffite contemporaries, "was no guarantee of true piety; it seems to have been the slogan of parties they regarded as corrupt" (66).

[16] Mikhail Bakhtin's comments on the complexity and ambiguity of "the relationship to another's word," particularly to "the authoritative and sanctified word of the Bible, the Gospel, the Apostles, the fathers and doctors of the church" seem particularly pertinent to the *Wife of Bath's Prologue*. He reminds us that this is "the primary instance of appropriating another's discourse and language" in the Middle Ages and that it suggests "a whole spectrum of possible relationships . . . beginning at one pole with the pious and inert quotation that is isolated and set off like an icon, and ending at the other pole with the most ambiguous, disrespectful, parodic-travestying use of a quotation." He notes the "transitions between various nuances on this spectrum," and that these are "to such an extent flexible, vacillating and ambiguous that it is often difficult to decide whether we are confronting a reverent use of a sacred word or a more familiar, even parodic playing with it. . . ." See "From the Prehistory of Novelistic Discourse," in *The*

end, the prologue urges a direct, or at least critical reading of the Bible:[17]

> "Wher can ye seye, in any manere age,
> That hye God defended mariage
> By expres word? I pray yow, telleth me.
> Or where comanded he virginitee?" (III [D] 59–62)

Even when embedded in satire, the Wife's prologue reminds us of distinctions that are freeing:

> "Men may conseille a womman to been oon,
> But conseillyng is no comandement.
> He putte it in oure owene juggement. . . ." (III [D] 66–68)

There is an insistence that empirical reality and the affections play a legitimate role in the process of understanding.

In the debate over the question of the Samaritan's allowed marriages, for example—"how manye myghte she have in mariage?" (III [D] 23)—the Wife asserts the role of experience and the natural affections. When she acknowledges God's command "to wexe and multiplye" as a gentle text that she can "wel understonde" (III [D] 29), "understonde" gains a richness in its association with the natural affections not unlike Boccaccio's treatment of sexuality throughout the *Decameron*.[18] Here, as there, humor acts as the vehicle for profound res-

---

Dialogic Imagination" Four Essays by M. M. Bakhtin, ed. Michael Holquist; trans. Caryl Emerson and Michael Holquist (Austin: U Texas P, 1981) 69.

[17] Besserman, " 'Glossynge Is a Glorious Thyng,' " in *Chaucer and Scriptural Tradition* 69–70. "In 1378 Wyclif in his *De veritate . . .* declared that it was the duty of all Christians to have firsthand knowledge of the Bible."

[18] In the Prologue to the Fourth Day, for example, Boccaccio tells a story in his own voice that illustrates the inevitability of natural desires. A father, turned widower, renounces the world. He attempts to isolate his son from the world's temptations, only to find that the son, on his first trip to Florence, is absolutely unable to keep his eyes off the young women—creatures with whom he is so profoundly inexperienced that he does not even know what to call them. The father, on being asked, tells his son that they are goslings and that they are evil. Like Chaucer's Wife, the son presses on, thereby reminding the audience of the power of experience and common sense. He tells his father that the goslings are more beautiful than the painted angels which have so often been pointed out to him and that even if they are evil, he must have one.

tiveness with the constraints of an established and limiting discourse.[19]
In the Wife's playful, almost taunting, "Sey ye no?" (III [D] 123) that
follows her discussion of God's purposes in making "membres . . . of
generacion" (III [D] 116), the transactive quality of the discourse first
mimics traditional argument, then immediately refutes its conclusions:

> "Glose whoso wole, and seye bothe up and doun
> That they were maked for purgacioun
> Of uryne, and oure bothe thynges smale
> Were eek to knowe a femele from a male,
> And for noon oother cause—sey ye no?
> The experience woot wel it is noght so." (III [D] 119–24)

To break out of the mental confines of establishment discourse, the
Wife's prologue takes contrasting and dialectical postures that precipitate
discussion and generate more moderate positions. The demand for virginity, for example, suggests a hypothetical (and correspondingly extreme) damning of marriage:

> "For hadde God comanded maydenhede,
> Thanne hadde he dampned wedding with the dede." (III [D]
>   69–70)

To bring this to consciousness is to appreciate the paradox that an extreme position against marriage is untenable, if only because it will en-
danger the existence of virginity itself:

> "And certes, if ther were no seed ysowe,
> Virginitee, thanne wherof sholde it growe?" (III [D] 71–72)

---

[19] Jill Mann has observed that Chaucer's treatment of the Wife and this "gentil text"
is distinctly unlike Gower's in the *Vox Clamantis*. She observes that Chaucer "has a more
flexible attitude to 'authority' than Gower": "even when Gower allows his sinners a
voice . . . their point of view is given only to be refuted." Mann remarks concerning
the Wife of Bath: "at such moments, as when she quotes the text bidding her 'increase
and multiply,' the reader's attitude to her may well take the form that it does towards
Gower's nuns—an awareness of another dimension, another point of view from which
her selection and manipulation of arguments looks unscrupulous and wilful." "But we
notice," Mann continues, "that the reader is not so securely supported in this point of
view as he is in Gower; only the Wife's voice is heard, while Chaucer himself is silent."
See "Chaucer and the Medieval Latin Poets," in *Geoffrey Chaucer*, ed. Derek Brewer
(London: Bell, 1974), esp. 176–78.

The inclusiveness of the Wife's discourse is rooted in the inclusiveness of her personality, ever embracing the various and the diverse.[20] Her marriages are a schooling—"Diverse scoles maken parfyt clerkes" (III [D] 44c)—and she remains an eager student. She will leave nothing uninvestigated:

"Of fyve husbondes scoleiyng am I.
Welcome the sixte, whan that evere he shal." (III [D] 44f–45)

Her activities, her astrological signs, and her tastes all attest to an encompassing temperament:

"Therfore I made my visitaciouns
To vigilies and to processiouns,
To prechyng eek, and to thise pilgrimages,
To pleyes of myracles, and to mariages. . . ." (III [D] 555–58)

"For certes, I am al Venerien
In feelynge, and myn herte is Marcien.
Venus me yaf my lust, my likerousnesse,
And Mars yaf me my sturdy hardynesse. . . ." (III [D] 609–12)

"I ne loved nevere by no discrecioun,
But evere folwede myn appetit,
Al were he short, or long, or blak, or whit. . . ." (III [D] 622–24)[21]

As does the mix of nostalgia and satisfaction with which she appreciates the entire experience of living:

"But—Lord Crist!—whan that it remembreth me
Upon my yowthe, and on my jolitee,
It tikleth me aboute myn herte roote.
Unto this day it dooth myn herte boote

<hr/>

[20] The Wife is inclusive regarding authority as well, first downplaying it—"Experience, though noon auctoritee / Were in this world, is right ynogh for me / To speke of wo that is in mariage" (III [D] 1–3)—and then turning to it (III [D] 180–83 and 323–25).

[21] The Wife's appreciation for diversity extends to her view of God; see esp. III (D) 102–4 and 142–46.

That I have had my world as in my tyme." (III [D] 469–73)

The Wife's inclusiveness, and the open transactions and contradictions on which her speech thrive, are features most emphatically not characteristic of the authoritative speech which she reports and against which she rebels: the proverbial wisdom of the good husbands and Jankin's "book of wikked wyves" (III [D] 669–772).[22] In the first place, the proverbial, oral wisdom of the first three husbands—the "goode men, and riche, and olde" (III [D] 197)—can be mouthed by anyone, even by the inebriated:

> "Thou comest hoom as dronken as a mous,
> And prechest on thy bench, with yvel preef!" (III [D] 246–47)

It is a rhetoric that moves unfailingly from conclusion to example, and its examples can be endless. If one proverb does not cover the subject, another, quite different one, will. Its formulas are all-embracing. Rich will follow poor; foul, fair:

> "Thou seist to me it is a greet meschief
> To wedde a povre womman, for costage;
> And if that she be riche, of heigh parage,
> Thanne seistow that it is a tormentrie
> To soffre hire pride and hire malencolie.
> And if that she be fair, thou verray knave,
> Thou seyst that every holour wol hire have . . ." (III [D] 248–54)

> "And if that she be foul, thou seist that she
> Coveiteth every man that she may se,
> For as a spanyel she wol on hym lepe,
> Til that she fynde som man hire to chepe." (III [D] 265–68)

In this all-encompassing view, woman is unchanging. She is always put down:

---

[22] It is noteworthy that Chaucer emphasizes the oral nature of the discourse of the good husbands with the repeated "thou seist," just as the written is emphasized in "tho redde he me" in the description of Jankin's book.

> "Been ther none othere maner resemblaunces
> That ye may likne youre parables to,
> But if a sely wyf be oon of tho?
>   "Thou liknest eek wommenes love to helle,
> To bareyne lond . . .
> . . . to wilde fyr. . . ." (III [D] 368–72)

Just as the fair woman is assailed from all sides (III [D] 253–56), so the recipient of this kind of wisdom is powerless to stop the proliferation of examples; and they all head in the same direction:

> "Thus goth al to the devel, by thy tale." (III [D] 262)

The Wife dismisses the entirety of this talk as "japes" (III [D] 242), as a fiend's chiding and preaching (III [D] 244–47), and finally, as deceit:

> "Thus seistow, olde barel-ful of lyes!" (III [D] 302)

Though oral, the husband's preaching has all the rigidities of authority ordinarily associated with the book. She responds to it with defiance, verbal wit, and her own deceit:

> "After thy text, ne after thy rubriche,
> I wol nat wirche as muchel as a gnat."[23] (III [D] 346–47)

> "A wys wyf, if that she kan hir good,
> Shal beren hym on honde the cow is wood,
> And take witnesse of hir owene mayde
> Of hir assent. . . ." (III [D] 231–34)

>   "Of wenches wolde I beren hem on honde,
> Whan that for syk unnethes myghte they stonde." (III [D] 393–94)

---

[23] Addressing issues of gender in the Wife of Bath's performance, Thomas Hahn cites these lines and points out that here "the Wife proclaims her resistance to the imposed boundaries, margins, rules that contain the text. In particular, 'rubriche'—the only occurrence of this word in Chaucer—evidently takes in the carefully pricked and ruled texts of St. Paul and other writers . . . of the ordered, formal, systematically organized discourse of masculine authority in general." See Hahn, "Teaching the Resistant Woman: The Wife of Bath and the Academy," *Exemplaria: A Journal of Theory in Medieval and Renaissance Studies* 4.2 (Fall 1992): 436.

"I swoor that al my walkynge out by nyghte
Was for t'espye wenches that he dighte;
Under that colour hadde I many a myrthe.
For al swich wit is yeven us in oure byrthe;
Deceite, wepyng, spynnyng God hath yive
To wommen kyndely, while that they may lyve."[24] (III [D]
  397–402)

In Jankin's book of wicked wives, proverbial wisdom is transformed into literary artifact and threatens to become the symbol of a whole culture. All sewn together and bound in one volume (III [D] 681), the book is clearly a typical medieval manuscript. It amounts to a personal collection of miscellaneous writings in which women are tried and condemned. Like that of its oral counterpart, its discourse is formulaic and predictable—

"Of Eva first, that for hir wikkednesse." (III [D] 715)

"Tho redde he me how Sampson loste his heres."
(III [D] 721)

"Tho redde he me . . .
Of Hercules and of his Dianyre" (III [D] 724–25)

"No thyng forgat he the care and the wo / That Socrates
hadde with his wyves two . . ." (III [D] 727–28)—

and so on.

The recitation of proverbs that follows—Jankin knows more proverbs than there are grass or herbs in this world (III [D] 772–74)—completes the stifling sense of closure.[25] Taken together, Jankin's proverbs and stories are as lacking in the full range of discourse, in question, contradiction, and surprise, as the Wife of Bath's own talk is rich

---

[24] For a discussion of verbal wit and deceit as described by Criseyde when she promises Troilus that she will return to Troy (4.1401–6), see chap. 3, pp. 66–68, above.

[25] Note the role of rime to emphasize the stifling of thought in Jankin's earliest proverb: "Whoso that buyldeth his hous al of *salwes,* / And priketh his blynde hors over the *falwes,* / And suffreth his wyf to go seken *halwes,* / Is worthy to been hanged on the *galwes!*" (III [D] 655–58; italics mine).

with them. So closely allied are discourse and power that the Wife's act of destroying Jankin's book is co-equal with the act of taking power away from him.[26]

The *Wife of Bath's Prologue* suggests a mind and an epistemology for which stasis and closure are anathema. Her prologue is itself riddled with open-endedness and surprise. The initial promise "to speke of wo that is in mariage" (III [D] 1–3) is radically modified when, 170 lines later, the Wife herself becomes "the whippe" (III [D] 175) rather than—more expectably—the subject of "tribulacion in mariage" (III [D] 173). Given the Wife's manifest physicality and the relish with which she describes at least two of her marriages,[27] the spirit of the discourse demonstrably contradicts its opening topic. And when the Wife claims of her experience with her fifth husband that "After that day we hadden never debaat" (III [D] 822), she claims it in a discourse that is itself fully committed to debate. The Wife is a *perpetuum mobile* of self-generating speech; if the Friar had not put the cap on her *Prologue,* she would still be going on today.

The *Wife of Bath's Prologue* is, indeed, the most radical example of Chaucer's dialogic in the *Canterbury Tales.* There is no closing off, except the critic's own. Citing scriptural contexts that Chaucer's Wife has overlooked and Christian doctrine she has misunderstood, the critic seeking closure tries to make the creative artist comply with an arbitrary measure. In this case it is, paradoxically, most frequently the very same arbitrary measure, the rigidity of established Church doctrine, that the poem is satirizing. The same applies when the Wife's prologue is read as a study of the Wife's character: "An interpretation of her 'Prologue' and therefore of her character," writes one critic, "depends on our ability to *recall* the text abused and so to appreciate the significance of the Wife's deafness to its fourteenth-century interpretation."[28] These critics see the Wife's performance as "carnal" and "myopic" and assert that it "reveals strikingly how overtly ironic Chaucer can be in his misapplications of

---

[26] The physical destruction of the book (or pages of the book) as a statement of non-compliance was for Chaucer an event close to home. For example, on 12 March 1387, the assembled mayor, aldermen, and sheriffs, along with other prominent citizens of London, agreed to the burning on that same day of "a certain quire, or book, called '*Jubile*' " because, they contended, its new oaths and ordinances were "repugnant to the old and approved customs" of London (*Memorials of London* 494).

[27] And these, the Wife's last two husbands, are notably first mentioned as "badde" (III [D] 196).

[28] Caie, "The Significance of Marginal Glosses," in *Chaucer and Scriptural Tradition* 75.

Scripture."[29] But surely the exaggerated or "grotesque" form this satire takes is a safety dodge, a protective irony, that has been used by others in the past (notably Boccaccio in the *Decameron*) and will be used again by Erasmus in *The Praise of Folly* and Swift in *Gulliver's Travels*. Given the circumstances, indirection and guile, even the "grotesque," would seem to be requirements of any art that is critical of an entrenched and powerful discourse.[30]

In its questioning not only of authority but of mental style in general—including freedom, self-awareness, response, and judgment—the Wife's prologue provides an anti-perspective to intellectual authority systems of Chaucer's time. With its reliance on common sense, emotion, and gusto, it challenges the exclusiveness and the closed nature of those systems. When the Wife points us to the psychological polarities inherent in the human condition—

> "The children of Mercurie and of Venus
> Been in hir wirkyng ful contrarius . . ." (III [D] 697–98)—

Chaucer may be implying that a discourse which would accurately cover these polarities cannot be shut tight or super rational, that it must be inclusive, providing for "wysdam and science" as well as "ryot and dispence" (III [D] 699–700). The Wife's proverbial

> "He is to greet a nygard that wolde werne
> A man to lighte a candle at his lanterne . . ." (III [D] 333–34)

---

[29] See Edmund Reiss, "Biblical Parody," in *Chaucer and Scriptural Tradition* 57–58.

[30] Per Nykrog makes a similar comment with reference to Jean de Meun's method in the *Roman de la Rose*:

> Et comme cela arrive souvent dans des situations de répression sociale sévère, il affuble son message audacieux, hétérodoxe et répréhensible, d'un vêtement désarmant de légèreté, de badinage, même de bouffonnerie. Son point de départ dans le texte de Guillaume de Lorris le place dans le genre badin. L'ambiguïté qu'il a donnée à son Génius, ce bouffon porte-parole de Dieu, peut servir à deux fins: par sa bonhomie joviale il prend démonstrativement le contre-pied des prédicateurs déchaux qui sèment la peur de la damnation éternelle—par sa bouffonnerie il met sa morale immorale (selon les idées courantes) à l'abri de la censure. Sa grande excommunication de tous les ennemis de la sexualité libre et naturelle est-elle une parodie de celle lancée par l'évêque de Paris contre les "naturalistes"?

See *L'Amour et La Rose: Le Grand Dessein de Jean de Meun*, Harvard Studies in Romance Languages, 14 (Lexington, Ky: French Forum Publishers, 1986) 87.

would apply to discourse as well as to sex. It is not diminished by use but enriched by it. Only one more connection (suggested by the prologue itself) allows us to see that just as one cannot have virgins unless sexuality is expressed—"And certes, if ther were no seed y-sowe, / Virginitee, thanne wherof sholde it growe?" (III [D] 71–72)—so a severely limited discourse will destroy the very conception and propagation of thought. Shimmering with energy, humor, and doubt, the *Wife of Bath's Prologue* reminds us of the limitless capacities of speech.

6

Words and Deeds in the *Squire's Tale* and the *Franklin's Tale*

The values of Cicero's rhetoric, especially the notion that the social order requires an eloquence allied with wisdom, surface repeatedly in the *Canterbury Tales*. These values, like others, are further defined—if not transformed—by the dialogics of the pilgrimage frame. Both the *Squire's Tale* and the *Franklin's Tale* at their outset turn our attention to the art of rhetoric or, as the Squire puts it, to the "colours longynge for that art" (V [F] 39). In a traditional modesty topos, both tellers deny their knowledge of that art, and both tales, of course, proceed in different ways to show substantial skill in it. Having established their stance toward rhetoric *per se,* the tales themselves each go on to explore more complex issues of discourse. As they do so, the knowledge of rhetorical colors—the Squire says it must be a "rethor excellent / That koude his colours," and the Franklin that "colours ne knowe I none" (V [F] 38–39, 723)—is shown to be a superficial aspect of an art which, at a deeper level, involves a complex and interdependent relationship between speech and truth, words and deeds, and finally, in the *Franklin's Tale,* an attitude toward human fallibility itself. The *Squire's* and *Franklin's Tales,* which appear together as a separate fragment of the *Canterbury Tales,* treat these deeper issues not only coherently, but in fact symmetrically, and may be seen on one level as a poetic essay on the uses and misuses of discourse.

This interpretation of the fragment reopens an issue of subject matter which has been accepted as settled by readers ever since G. L. Kittredge popularized the "marriage group," with the *Squire's Tale* interrupting, for purposes of variety, the discussion of an issue (among the pilgrims and the tales) which finds its best solution in the *Franklin's Tale*.[1] Both of these tales deal with seduction and love; and both are accepted generally as variations on the ever dependable, but sometimes over-ridden, medieval hobby-horse of courtly love.[2]

Our discovery of the true subject matter of these tales, and of the nature of their relationship in the F fragment, has been hindered by the critical assumptions of the "dramatic theory," in which the *Canterbury Tales,* as one adherent of the theory has put it, "cannot be properly understood if they are not apprehended as expressions of their tellers."[3] A dramatic reading would point to the overt competitiveness of the Franklin, as he (perhaps) interrupts, praises, and then betters the Squire in his own more adroit handling of the matter and manner of romance. Given the fact that both the Squire and the Franklin narrate versions of romance and that both comment extensively on themselves as narrators and on the art of rhetoric, the application of the dramatic theory seems particularly tempting here, if only, as one critic has pointed out, "to argue that the perceived faults in a specific pilgrim signal us to understand his tale as either severely flawed or deliberately 'bad.' "[4]

But in spite of all the apparent material for a dramatic reading of

---

[1] George Lyman Kittredge, "Chaucer's Discussion of Marriage," *Modern Philology* 9 (1912): 435–67. For a review of scholarship on the marriage debate in the *Canterbury Tales* and comment on the role of the *Squire's Tale* in this debate, see Marie Neville, "The Function of the *Squire's Tale* in the Canterbury Scheme," *Journal of English and Germanic Philology* 50 (1951): 167–79.

[2] That these thematic or "realistic" readings may, indeed, be inadequate to account for the tales is indicated in one critic's recent dismissal of the *Squire's Tale* as nothing more than "a meandering Oriental tale of fantasy, about talking birds, one of them a lady bird betrayed by a faithless lover." If the critic has mistaken its real subject matter, the *Squire's Tale* does not deserve short shrift. See Donald Howard, *Chaucer: His Life, His Works, His World* (New York: Dutton, 1987) 432–33.

[3] Harry Berger, Jr., "The F Fragment of the *Canterbury Tales*: Part I," *Chaucer Review* 1 (1966–67): 88. The dramatic theory of the *Canterbury Tales* is found more generally stated in Howard's *Chaucer: His Life, His Works, His World*: "The General Prologue is what makes *The Canterbury Tales* tick. It gives coherence to the whole, hovers over the arrangement of the tales and their assignment to appropriate tellers. The tales and tellers are uniquely a group in a complex dramatic relationship" (446).

[4] For a brief history of the dramatic theory and a cogent statement of its problems, see C. David Benson *Chaucer's Drama of Style: Poetic Variety and Contrast in "The Canterbury Tales"* (Chapel Hill: U of North Carolina P, 1986), particularly chap. 1, "Beyond

the fragment, including the Host's succinct putdown of the Franklin's pretensions, the dramatic readings do not and cannot account for the underlying themes in the tales themselves, themes that are only superficially those of romance. In fact, neither the *Squire's Tale* nor the *Franklin's Tale* places much narrative emphasis on the erotic event—the tercelet's seduction of the falcon or Aurelius's would-be seduction of Dorigen. Both events, rather, are presented in verbal contexts heavy with implications regarding the arts of discourse. In these contexts, the attempted seduction itself may be seen as a vehicle for exploration of the universal goal of sophistic rhetoric: winning the listener to one's will.[5]

Shortly after the opening of the *Squire's Tale,* a strange knight enters the court of King Cambyuskan and presents the monarch with four gifts. The first is a steed of brass that can carry its rider

". . . into every place
To which youre herte wilneth for to pace." (V [F] 119–20)

The second, a broad mirror of glass can confer powers of perception both in politics and in love. The ring of gold will enable its bearer to

the Dramatic Theory" (3–25). Benson points out that the uncritical acceptance of the dramatic theory will inevitably involve the critic in self-fulfilling prophecies.

[5] Sophistic rhetoric denies the Socratic emphasis on the necessary relationship between eloquence and wisdom, words and deeds, emphasizing not *what* is said but the *way* it is said. See James J. Murphy, *Rhetoric in the Middle Ages: A History of Rhetorical Theory from Saint Augustine to the Renaissance* (Berkeley: U of California P, 1974), particularly the discussion of the ancient traditions of rhetoric and their relation to the Middle Ages (3–132). The necessary relationship between words and deeds is central for Cicero, who opens the *De inventione* by observing that "wisdom without eloquence does too little for the good of states, but that eloquence without wisdom is generally highly disadvantageous and is never helpful." *De Inventione, De Optimo Genere, Oratorum Topica,* trans. H. M. Hubbell, Loeb Classical Library (Cambridge: Harvard UP, 1949) 3. See also my discussion in chap. 1, above.

Though modern scholarship has found essential affinities between the concerns of the Sophists (particularly Protagoras) and early humanism, the Italian humanists themselves—with less access to the relevant texts—considered the Sophists "diametrically opposed to Socrates and Plato and as the corrupt purveyors of a pseudo-knowledge or falsehood, or certainly no more than amoral orators." See Charles Trinkaus, "Humanism and Sophism," *The Scope of Renaissance Humanism* (Ann Arbor: U of Michigan, 1983) 169–91. The humanist attitude toward the Sophists is reflected in Chaucer's description of the tercelet in the *Squire's Tale*: "Ne koude man, by twenty thousand part, / Contrefete the *sophymes* of his art"; "Who kan sey bet than he, who kan do werse?" (V [F] 553–54, 600; italics mine).

understand the speech of every "fowel that fleeth under the hevene," "knowe his menyng openly and pleyn," and know the healing powers of "every gras that groweth upon roote" (V [F] 150–53). The fourth gift, the naked sword has the virtue of being able to strike through armor "as thikke as is a branched ook" (V [F] 159) and to heal the very wound it makes. These gifts, which carry heavy symbolic meaning and which promise to confer new power upon their possessor, are nonetheless misunderstood and misprized by members of Cambyuskan's court.

The meaning of the gifts has eluded modern criticism of the *Squire's Tale* about as thoroughly as it eludes the court into which the gifts are brought. Some say that the gifts are more or less ineffective instruments in a "romantic" structure; others, that they are elements in an "ironic" takeoff on the Squire. In general, the *Squire's Tale,* gifts and all, is written off as a failed contrivance, a "wreck" that cannot be salvaged by interpretation.[6] Before settling comfortably into that judgment, however, we might reconsider the tale's own observation that lack of understanding causes one to "demen gladly to the badder ende."

To begin with, the gifts invite interpretation in that they appear to be related to each other. They are all visual symbols whose meaning seems particularly connected with such powers as relate to human understanding and communication. The ring opens up lines of discourse between the human and the natural world. The mirror confers understanding of the honesty or dishonesty of its bearer's associates. The horse is a vehicle of fancy, compared immediately both to the expressive gifts of Pegasus and to the verbal dishonesty of Sinon. But it is the sword, the most problematic of the four gifts, that ultimately supplies them all with

---

[6] For generic treatments of the *Squire's Tale,* see particularly Gardiner Stillwell, "Chaucer in Tartary," *Review of English Studies* 24 (1948): 177–88; Stanley J. Kahrl, "Chaucer's *Squire's Tale* and the Decline of Chivalry," *Chaucer Review* 7 (1973): 194–209; and Robert M. Jordan, "The Question of Genre: Five Chaucerian Romances," in *Chaucer at Albany,* ed. Rossell Hope Robbins (New York: Burt Franklin, 1975) 77–103. For discussion of rhetoric in the tale and the idea that the tale is an ironic takeoff on the Squire, especially as its rhetoric is so self-conscious, see Derek A. Pearsall, "The Squire as Story-Teller," *University of Toronto Quarterly* 34 (1964): 82–92; Robert S. Haller, "Chaucer's *Squire's Tale* and the Uses of Rhetoric," *Modern Philology* 62 (1965): 285–95; John P. McCall, "The Squire in Wonderland," *Chaucer Review* 1 (1966): 103–9. See also Pearsall's more recent doubts about an ironic reading of the *Squire's Tale* in his *The Canterbury Tales* (Boston: Allen and Unwin, 1985) 138–44; it is here that Pearsall refers to the "temptation to salvage a wreck" and sensibly warns that this "must be recognized as a mere reaction to the dispersive tendency of Chaucer's style in tales that lack a commanding centre of attention" (141).

their thematic unity. With its paradoxical capacity both to wound and to heal, the sword can be symbolically interpreted as a reference to thought and speech.[7] The knight's bounty towards the Mongolian king thus appears to be more more than a romantic miscellany or a haphazard collection of useless and meaningless "paraphernalia."[8] It is a sequence whose harmonics imply the understanding and eloquence that will perfect Cambyuskan's rule.

Not having noticed the relationship of the gifts to one another, readers have also not seen the relationship of the gifts to the *Squire's Tale* as a whole. With the exception of Canace's ring, the gifts are almost universally regarded as having no point in the narrative that follows: "seldom has there been such a build-up for so little effect."[9] Yet seen as visual emblems of the power of discourse, the gifts and their prominence give the tale as we have it a remarkable coherence. They are framed on the one side by the eloquence of the strange knight and on the other by the falcon's description of the tercelet's duplicity, a duplicity accomplished entirely by his abuse of that same eloquence. Understood and applied, the gifts recall a Ciceronian view of speech and rhetoric as a powerful art of understanding as well as of communication. They provide a rationale for the eloquence of the strange knight; they also comprise an effective and powerful response to the "crouned malice" (V [F] 526) of the tercelet.

Before the strange knight can explain the virtues of the gifts to Cambyuskan's court, the narrative touches four times on the subject of rhetoric, once at great length. In all these instances, we are introduced to a use of speech and rhetoric that contrasts sharply with that of the tercelet

---

[7] The association between the sword and speech, as we shall see, occurs in Dante's *Inferno* 31, one of the recognized sources for Chaucer's reference to "Thelophus the kyng, / And of Achilles with his queynte spere" (V [F] 238–39) when the court later "wondred on the swerd" (V [F] 236).

[8] John P. McCall, "The Squire in Wonderland," *Chaucer Review* 1 (1966): 105.

[9] Stanley J. Kahrl, "Chaucer's *Squire's Tale* and the Decline of Chivalry," *Chaucer Review* 7 (1973): 197. Robert M. Jordan draws attention to the extent to which the *Squire's Tale* observes "the rhetorical imperative of *amplificatio*." While this emphasis on amplification, according to Jordan, is typical of Chaucer's romances, the *Squire's Tale* more than Chaucer's other tales in this genre—"lacks both plot and theme." See "The Question of Genre: Five Chaucerian Romances," *Chaucer at Albany* (83). Though I have no argument with calling these parts of the *Squire's Tale* amplifications, I would point out that our reading of medieval narrative (e.g., the digressions in *Beowulf*) has amply demonstrated that theme is almost never relegated entirely to plot, that, in fact, it finds most frequent presence in the so-called digressions and amplifications.

in the falcon's lament later in the poem. It is a rhetoric which emphasizes the relationship between eloquence and wisdom, words and deeds. Cambyuskan, "So excellent a lord in alle thyng" (V [F] 15), is "Sooth of his word" (V [F] 21); the Squire compares himself to "a rethor excellent" (V [F] 38). Later, having described the eloquence of the knight, the Squire claims that he cannot "sowne his stile" or "clymben over so heigh a style" (V [F] 105–6). And, finally, the narrative gives lengthy attention to the knight's eloquence. The knight is skilled in the mechanical aspects of speech and delivery—"Withouten vice of silable or of lettre"—but more important, his demeanor is appropriate to his words:

This strange knyght, that cam thus sodeynly,
Al armed, save his heed, ful richely,
Saleweth kyng and queene and lordes alle,
By ordre, as they seten in the halle,
With so heigh reverence and obeisaunce,
As wel in speche as in contenaunce,
That Gawayn, with his olde curteisye,
Though he were comen ayeyn out of Fairye,
Ne koude hym nat amende with a word.
And after this, biforn the heighe bord,
He with a manly voys seide his message,
After the forme used in his langage,
Withouten vice of silable or of lettre;
And for his tale sholde seme the bettre,
Accordant to his wordes was his cheere,
As techeth art of speche hem that it leere. (V [F] 89–104; italics mine)

Chaucer's gentle prodding, "As techeth art of speche *hem that it leere,*" draws attention to the teachings of Italian humanists, who were the first in early modern Europe to emphasize rhetorical education.[10] And in twice giving prominence to the consonance between the knight's words and deeds, the portrait asserts that he is true to the ancient tradition of the good man speaking well. This points back in time to "Gawain, with his olde curteisye," but it also points forward to the lover in this tale, the tercelet. As the falcon reports it, the tercelet's achievement, too, is

---

[10] See the discussion of Petrarch and Boccaccio in chapter 1, pp. 6–14, and n.23.

in the realm of speech. But what is portrayed as an ideal in the strange knight as well as in Cambyuskan and Gawain is precisely what the tercelet lacks: "Who kan sey bet than he, who kan do werse?" (V [F] 600).

Virtuous eloquence frames the gifts on the one side; its abuse, or what Cicero called the "depraved imitation of virtue,"[11] frames the other. The description of deceit in the falcon's lament is one of the most extended in Chaucer's poetry. Its vivid amplifications, colored with classical and biblical references and powerful emblems of duplicity (serpent, tomb, tiger),[12] convey the artfulness of hypocrisy. The tercelet, like the Pardoner, revels in his speech: "His manere was an hevene for to see" (V [F] 558; for the Pardoner, see VI [C] 398–99: "Myne handes and my tonge goon so yerne / That it is joye to se my bisynesse"). The tercelet's wickedness is so extreme as to reverse normal perceptions of good and evil: John the Baptist's prophesy, "There cometh one mightier than I after me, the latchet of whose shoes I am not worthy to stoop down and unloose," is powerfully turned about:

> Ne koude man, by twenty thousand part,
> Countrefete the sophymes of his art,
> Ne were worthy unbokelen his galoche,
> Ther doublenesse or feynyng sholde approche. . . . (V [F] 553–56)

The same "art" of rhetoric that provided the rationale for the exemplary manner of the strange knight is used by the tercelet to subvert the accepted purpose of speech itself. The tercelet communicates what he does not mean and serves his own "entente" so completely that "save the feend, noon wiste what he mente" (V [F] 522).

In the face of the tercelet's "crouned malice" (V [F] 526), the falcon's defeat seems inevitable:

---

[11] See the discussion of this in chapter 1, pp. 7–12, and n21.

[12] For the reference to a serpent in the *Squire's Tale*, see V (F) 512–13: "Right as a serpent hit hym under floures / Til he may seen his tyme for to byte." The reference to tomb, V (F) 518–19: "As in a toumbe is al the faire above, / And under is the corps" (cf. Matt. 23.27, "Woe unto you, scribes and pharisees, hypocrites! for ye are like unto whited sepulchres, which indeed appear beautiful outward, but are within full of dead men's bones, and of all uncleanness"). The reference to the tiger, V (F) 543: "Anon this tigre, ful of doublenesse." On the tiger image, see Melvin Storm's discussion of early medieval commentaries on Job 4.11 as source in his "The Tercelet as Tiger: Bestiary Hypocrisy in the Squire's Tale," *English Language Notes* 14 (March 1977): 172–74. In the *Squire's Tale*, the tercelet is also compared to Jason, Paris, and Lamech (V [F] 548–50).

"And shortly, so ferforth this thyng is went
That my wyl was his willes instrument." (V [F] 567–68)

And the tercelet's moral reversal to "repentant" (V [F] 655), as the plot
line of the *Squire's Tale* reports it, seems unlikely. To combat the skilled
hypocrite would necessitate not only learning the craft he practices, but
attaining the wisdom he lacks. It would involve a comprehensive understanding of the art of rhetoric as it is set forth and symbolized in the gifts.
The tercelet's successful use of discourse as deception vividly demonstrates the humanists' urgency concerning study in the arts of speech and
their sense that neglecting this imperils the commonwealth.

The centrality of the gifts is emphasized by the tale's frame, with its
attention to true eloquence on the one hand and the depraved imitation
of it on the other, and by the pervasive concern with the knowledge of
art or craft throughout the text. The tale's teller—in one of the first of
many modesty topoi—draws attention to his lack of "konnyng" in rhetoric and to the skill required in that "art" to "discryven every part"
(V [F] 35–41).[13]

Subsequently, the strange knight's eloquence is referred to as fulfilling the highest requirement of the "art of speche" (V [F] 103–4). The
members of the court which receives him are demonstrably learned in
contemporary science (including optics), magic, and poetry, but their
failure to understand the gifts is described as a deficient knowledge of
"craft." They are unable to move the horse of brass because "they kan
nat the craft" (V [F] 185). They wonder about Canace's ring, because
apart from knowing that Moses and Solomon had "konnyng in swich
art," they have not heard of the "craft of rynges" (V [F] 249–51). Finally, by contrast, there is the tercelet, who has so completely mastered
"the sophymes of his art," that no one could "countrefete" them "by
twenty thousand part" (V [F] 553–54).

By addressing the human virtues of understanding and communication, the gifts give context and meaning to the material of the tale's
frame as well as to the tale's general preoccupation with craft. All in all,
more than a third of the *Squire's Tale* is devoted to the subject of the
gifts. The gifts are treated so expansively that one critic concludes that

---

[13] Of the frequency of the modesty topos figure in the *Squire's Tale*, Pearsall remarks:
"there is a temptation in reading the Squire's Tale, and one which the present writer has
not resisted in the past, to see them, namely, as signs, ironically planted by Chaucer, of
real inadequacy on the Squire's part" (*Canterbury Tales* 140).

121

the poet, "far from making use of light, rather nervous *occupatio,*" says too much. Gardiner Stillwell finds that Chaucer lingers unnecessarily over the people and their speculations: "His lively interest in human nature keeps him from his story, just as in Part II. . . . The poet himself, it is possible, does not know precisely what he is trying to do: belittle the garrulous mob, obtain romantic effect by suggesting a whole tradition of magic gadgets, or dabble in scientific speculation."[14]

If we assume that Chaucer *does* know what he is doing, we notice that the rhetorical effect of all this attention to the gifts is to arouse our curiosity about their meaning. The knight describes in detail the virtue of each gift. We learn to whom each of the gifts is to be given, where it is to be kept, and how the court responds to it. Additionally, we have narrative comment on these responses, comment which suggests that while up-to-date and intellectual, the court's response to each of the gifts is severely limited. We learn what the gifts are *not,* and we sense the wrongheadedness of explanations that look primarily to science, magic, and historical analogues.[15] The narrative comments on the views expressed by members of Cambyuskan's court sharpen the issues of perception and understanding but do not resolve them. The further effect of all the speculation may well be to throw us back on the riddle-filled language of the knight himself.

The knight, whose most prominent feature, as we have seen, will be his eloquence, is at first visually defined by the gifts. They are what he rides, carries, and wears:

> In at the halle dore al sodeynly
> Ther cam a knyght upon a steede of bras,

---

[14] Stillwell, "Chaucer in Tartary," *Review of English Studies* 24 (1948): 187. The assumptions of this article, including the idea that Chaucer is primarily interested in human nature, are particularly relevant given the fact that Stillwell's essay is the "parent" of many subsequent essays on the *Squire's Tale,* and of commentary which, in John McCall's words, has "turned from viewing the story with sober enthusiasm as a promising fragment" to describing it "with realistic irony as a complete but rather silly performance." See McCall, "The Squire in Wonderland," *Chaucer Review* 1 (1966): 103.

[15] For the fullest treatment of the magical elements and their analogues, see W. A. Clouston, "On the Magical Elements in Chaucer's 'Squire's Tale,' with Analogues," *Chaucer's Squire's Tale,* London: Chaucer Society, 2nd ser. 23, 26, 1987–89. H. S. V. Jones prefaces the various oriental analogues with the comment that "we do not possess any unquestioned source of any portion of the tale or of any motif in it"; see Jones, in *Sources and Analogues of Chaucer's Canterbury Tales,* ed. W. F. Bryan and Germaine Dempster (Chicago: U of Chicago P, 1941) 357. Vincent D. DiMarco provides new findings,

And in his hand a brood mirour of glas.
Upon his thombe he hadde of gold a ryng,
And by his syde a naked swerd hangyng. (V [F] 80–84)

Here and in the descriptions that follow, the gifts are presented in an order that reinforces the sense of a group of contemplative and active virtues, with the ring and mirror framed in each instance by the steed and sword. Like Arthur's court in the presence of the Green Knight, Cambyuskan's court is silenced by the knight's uncommon entrance—"In al the halle ne was ther spoken a word/For merveille of this knyght" (V [F] 86–87)—and will be mystified by his descriptions of each of the gifts.[16] The contemplative ring and mirror will be given to Canace. Cambyuskan will receive the active aspects of power, the steed and the sword.

It is Canace's gifts, the ring and the mirror, that most directly address issues related to communication and understanding. Both are prominently described as enabling their bearer to see "openly" (V [F] 136, 141, 151). The mirror has the "myght" to reveal true intention in politics as well as in love. At the head of its listed virtues (V [F] 132–41) is its power to reveal "adversitee" to "youre regne or to yourself also." It is also able to identify the flatterer, that most subtle and dangerous threat to political well-being, for it shows you "openly who is your freend or

---

especially regarding Chaucer's "unrecognized debt in the Squire's Tale to the works of Roger Bacon, in "A Note on Canace's Magic Ring," *Anglia* 99 (1981): 399–405.

[16] The entrance of the "strange knight" into Cambyuskan's court in the *Squire's Tale* has more than once been compared to the Green Knight's entrance into Arthur's court in *Sir Gawain and the Green Knight*. For parallels, see particularly B. J. Whiting, "Gawain: His Reputation, His Courtesy and His Appearance in Chaucer's *Squire's Tale*," *Medieval Studies* 9 (1947): 234; C. O. Chapman, "Chaucer and the Gawain-Poet: A Conjecture," *Modern Language Notes* 68 (1953): 521–24; and Karl Heinz Göller, "Chaucer's Squire's Tale: 'The Knotte of the tale,' " in *Chaucer und Seine Zeit: Symposium für Walter F. Schirmer*, ed. Arno Esch, Buchreihe der Anglia, *Zeitschrift für Englische Philologie*, 14 (Tübingen: Max Niemeyer, 1968) 173–74. Given the accepted critical view of the gifts as useless magical "paraphernalia," it is understandable that the parallels between Chaucer's poem and *Sir Gawain and the Green Knight* would be seen as surface ones only. Göller, for example, writes that the suggestive festivities of Cambyuskan's court, in contrast to those of the Arthurian court, are "funktionslos" (without function), that expectations remain unfulfilled, and that the parallels to *Sir Gawain and the Green Knight* generally are superficial, tendentious, and partly misleading [Eine Fülle von Erwartungen bleibt unbefriedigt, die Parallelen zu Gawain and the Green Knight erweisen sich als oberflächlich und tendenzlos, teilweise sogar als irreführend] (174). A serious interpretation of the gifts significantly enlarges the parallel to the Gawain poem, for the gifts, like the Green Knight, challenge their respective courts to an entirely new understanding.

foo." In addition to giving knowledge of the healing powers of "every gras" and opening communication between the human and the natural world, the ring, too, enables its bearer to "knowe his menyng openly and pleyn" (V [F] 146–55).

This emphasis on "openly" and specifically on "openly that ther shal no thyng hyde" (V [F] 141) in the descriptions of mirror and ring contrasts with the hiddenness of the tercelet later in the poem—a hiddenness, moreover, achieved entirely with the skills and techniques of rhetoric:

> So peynted he and kembde at point-devys
> As wel his wordes as his contenaunce. (V [F] 560–61)

Images of duplicity—of hiding under, being wrapped in, and feigning all the appropriate "cerymonyes" and "obeisaunces"—abound in the falcon's early description of "this god of loves ypocryte" (V [F] 504–20). The infinite ingenuity of the deceiver is conveyed by the catalogue of subleties he masters, all of them stemming from the imitation of true eloquence: it is by dyeing his "coloures" and keeping "in semblaunt alle his observaunces / That sownen into gentillesse of love" (V [F] 511–17)[17] that the tercelet achieves a complete reversal of the accepted purpose of speech. He communicates that which is not true so successfully that no one except "the feend . . . wiste what he mente" (V [F] 522). In revealing intention "openly and pleyn," the mirror and ring provide a wisdom that penetrates false-seeming and hypocrisy and thus can effectively neutralize the subtlety of the deceiver.

The third gift, the "naked swerd," like the ring, has power to heal. The virtue of the sword is presented so paradoxically—both wounding and healing—as to suggest the work of speech rather than of metal:

> "This naked swerd, that hangeth by my syde,
> Swich vertu hath that what man so ye smyte
> Thurghout his armure it wole kerve and byte,
> Were it as thikke as is a branched ook;
> And what man that is wounded with the strook

---

[17] "That sownen into gentillesse of love" (V [F] 517) recalls Chaucer's use of "sownynge" in the adjacent descriptions of the Merchant and the Clerk in the *General Prologue* I (A) 275 and 307.

124

> Shal never be hool til that yow list, of grace,
> To stroke hym with the plat in thilke place
> Ther he is hurt; this is as muche to seyn,
> Ye moote with the platte swerd ageyn
> Stroke hym in the wounde, and it wol close." (V [F] 156–65)

When the court, wondering about the "swerd," "fille in speche of Thelophus the kyng, / And of Achilles with his queynte spere" (V [F] 238–39), they take us to canto 31 of Dante's *Inferno,* where Dante, just reprimanded by Virgil for looking on as Sinon and Adamo quarrel over whose hypocrisy is worse, reflects on the ability of one and the same *tongue* (Virgil's) both to wound and to heal. To elucidate the paradox this presents, Dante compares the apparently contradictory powers of speech to Achilles's spear or lance (traditionally, a sword):

> Una medesma lingua pria mi morse,
> sì che mi tinse l'una e l'altra guancia,
> e poi la medicina mi riporse;
> così od'io che solea far la lancia
> d'Achille e del suo padre esser cagione
> prima di trista e poi di buona mancia.

> [One and the same tongue first stung me, so that it tinged both my cheeks, and then it supplied the medicine to me; thus I have heard that the lance of Achilles and of his father was wont to be the cause, first of a sad and then of a good gift].[18]

Thus even the "swerd," the gift most explicitly symbolic of rule, is likely to be related to speech.[19] As the last of the four gifts described and

---

[18] In the *Inferno* Sinon is found (at the end of Canto XXX) in the eighth circle among the counterfeiters, who include counterfeiters of persons, of things, and of words. The description of the wounding and healing powers of Achilles's lance that opens Canto XXXI is thus textually adjacent to Sinon's verbal duplicity. Dante Alighieri, *Inferno,* vol. 1 of *The Divine Comedy,* trans. Charles S. Singleton, Bollingen Series 80 (Princeton: Princeton UP, 1970) 326–27.

[19] For another comparison between sword and speech in Chaucer, see the *Manciple's Tale* IX (H) 340–42:

> Right as a swerd forkutteth and forkerveth
> An arm a-two, my deare sone, right so
> A tonge kutteth freendshipe al a-two.

presented to the Mongolian king by the knight, and as an emblem of government, the sword directs our attention most fully to the role of speech in the political realm. The brief political allusions that accompany the horse, the mirror, and the ring are here given symbolic coherence.[20]

All the gifts and their virtues arouse wonder and diversity of opinion in the court, but none does so more than the brass steed. Indeed, its marvelous qualities distract one from solving the riddle it presents. Like the court, we so focus on its mechanical aspect that we may ignore the plainer indications of its meaning in the knight's description of its virtues. The critical effect of this is evident in one critic's description of the brass horse as "nothing more than a curious mechanical contrivance, a flying machine, round which the townsfolk congregate and speculate in an excitement of credulous curiosity."[21]

To look at the plainer suggestions of the horse's meaning in the knight's description of its virtues (V [F] 115–27) is to see that like speech (and poetry) itself, the steed of brass can transport us, free of the normal constraints of space and time. Providing a mental or spiritual journey, the steed allows the body to remain unaffected by its flight, even when it soars as high as an eagle:[22]

> "This steede of bras, that esily and weel
> Kan in the space of o day natureel—
> This is to seyn, in foure and twenty houres—
> Wher-so yow lyst, in droghte or elles shoures,
> Beren youre body into every place
> To which youre herte wilneth for to pace,
> Withouten wem of yow, thurgh foul or fair;
> Or, if yow lyst to fleen as hye in the air
> As dooth an egle whan hym list to soore,
> This same steede shal bere yow evere moore,
> Withouten harm, til ye be ther yow leste,
> Though that ye slepen on his bak or reste,

---

[20] The court's response to the horse includes reference to Sinon and the destruction of Troy (V [F] 209–10). The mirror has powers that enable its bearer to see "adversitee" to the reign and to oneself, and to neutralize the flatterer (V [F] 132–36). The ring opens a whole sphere of communication to its possessor (V [F] 146–55).

[21] John Speirs, *Chaucer the Maker* (London: Faber and Faber, 1964) 163.

[22] For the eagle as suggestive of contemplation and inspiration, see the *House of Fame,* lines 499–508, and Dante's *Purgatorio* 4.19–20, 28–30.

And turne ayeyn with writhyng of a pyn.
He that it wroghte koude ful many a gyn.
He wayted many a constellacion
Er he had doon this operacion,
And knew ful many a seel and many a bond." (V [F] 115–31)

When the court shortly afterward is unable to move the brass horse, the narrative highlights their inability by pausing to ask, "And cause why?" The blunt response (delivered in the same line), "For they kan nat the craft" (V [F] 185), serves to remind us of the multiple layers of this narrative. At one level the court's lack of knowing is simply mechanical. At that level it will quickly be resolved, at least for Cambyuskan himself, by the strange knight's operating directions:

". . . Sire, ther is namoore to seyne,
But, whan yow list to ryden anywhere,
Ye mooten trille a pyn, stant in his ere. . . ." (V [F] 314–16)

At another level, however, the court's lack of knowledge is more thorough and complex. They are witnessing something whose imitation of nature both fascinates and disturbs. The horse's perfection—"Nature ne art ne koude hym nat amende" (V [F] 197)—lies in its giving the illusion of a real and living horse, "so horsly, and so quyk of ye (V [F] 196)."[23]

---

[23] Just how pertinent is Chaucer's description of the horse's "realism" ("so horsly and so quyk of ye") to fourteenth-century developments in art, especially in Italy, can be seen by comparing it to a passage in Boccaccio's *Decameron* 6.5 (ca. 1350) describing the same phenomenon. Boccaccio pauses in his narrative to give extended praise to Giotto's (d. 1337) realistic portrayal of nature:

> e l'altro, il cui nome fu Giotto, ebbe uno ingegno di tanta eccellenzia, che niuna cosa dà la natura, madre di tutte le cose e operatrice col continuo girar de' cieli, che egli con lo stile e con la penna o col pennello non dipignesse sì simile a quella, che non simile, anzi più tosto dessa paresse, in tanto che molte volte nelle cose da lui fatte si truova che il visivo senso degli uomini vi prese errore, quello credendo esser vero che era dipinto. *Decameron*, vol. 4 of *Tutte le Opere di Giovanni Boccaccio* (Milano: Arnoldo Mondadori, 1983) 550.

> [The other, whose name was Giotto, was a man of such genius that there was nothing in Nature—the mother and moving force behind all created things with her constant revolution of the heavens— that he could not paint with his stylus, pen, or brush, making it so much like its original in Nature that it seemed more like the original than a reproduction. Many times, in fact, while looking at paintings by this man, the observer's visual

The court expresses diverse opinions as they marvel at the horse's presence among them. While fascinated, they do not understand. And not understanding, they respond with distrust. They "demen" "it was a fairye" and come up with as many opinions as there are heads—"As many heddes, as manye wittes ther been" (V [F] 203). Two, however, are given prominence: the references to Pegasus and Sinon point us to the entire range of poetry and rhetoric. At one extreme is Pegasus, the winged horse whose hoof caused the fountain of the Muses to spring from Mount Helicon; at the other, Sinon, the hypocrite, abusing, indeed, the medium of the poet and bringing political ruin to Troy:

> They murmureden as dooth a swarm of been,
> And maden skiles after hir fantasies,
> Rehersynge of thise olde poetries,
> And seyden it was lyk the Pegasee,
> The hors that hadde wynges for to flee;
> Or elles it was the Grekes hors Synon,
> That broghte Troie to destruccion,
> As men in thise olde geestes rede. (V [F] 204–11)

Has the court unwittingly identified the relationship of hypocrisy to poetry and inspiration? The character of the horse, the things it can do for the rider, and the court's reference to Pegasus and Sinon suggest that Chaucer is reminding his audience that poetry and rhetoric share the same medium and, with it, the potential for the highest inspiration as well as for the lowest deceit. Just as the sword, whose description completes the group of four gifts, sharpens the political aspect of the gifts that precede it, so the horse's virtues provide a thematic framework for the mirror, ring, and sword that follow it.

The comprehensively political idea of discourse suggested by the *Squire's Tale* hearkens less to the medieval rhetorical manuals[24] than to

---

sense was known to err, taking what was painted to be the very thing itself]. *The Decameron,* trans. Mark Musa and Peter Bondanella (New York: Norton, 1982) 392.

[24] James J. Murphy lists six "preceptive" works about verse-writing from between about 1175 and 1280: Matthew of Vendome's *Ars versificatoria;* Geoffrey of Vinsauf's *Poetria Nova* and *Documentum de modo et arte dictandi et versificandi;* Gervase of Melkley's *Ars versificaria;* John of Garland's *De arte prosayca, metrica, et rithmica;* and Eberhard the German's *Laborintus* (see *Rhetoric in the Middle Ages* 135).

the heroic model of rhetoric expressed by Cicero and inherited by the Italian humanists, including Petrarch and Boccaccio. Taken together, the four gifts of the *Squire's Tale* suggest a view of eloquence deeper and more far-reaching than the emphasis on style and technique found in medieval rhetorical manuals and accepted as the poet's own in recent studies of Chaucer's "rhetorical poetic."[25] The gifts suggest that true eloquence is based on much more than style, delivery, and a knowledge of the "colours longynge for that art" (V [F] 39). They imply that it is accompanied by wisdom and, as such, is a powerful political tool. This obtains because eloquence, the art of effective expression, necessarily carries with it understanding, the art of effective analysis. As both Cicero and the Italian humanists urged in their concern with credulousness and the "depraved imitation of virtue," we cannot understand what we say without understanding what we hear. The eloquent politician is thus in control at once of communicative and interpretative interaction.

The curious circumstance that the theme of eloquence is given to the self-conscious and sometimes clumsy Squire directs our attention not only to the importance of eloquence, but to the manifold difficulties in gaining it.[26] Like the strange knight, the Squire is presenting a gift. If

---

[25] In *The Key of Remembrance: A Study of Chaucer's Poetics* (New Haven: Yale UP, 1963), Robert O. Payne describes Chaucer's view of poetry as "a way of managing language" (85) and summarizes as follows: "Chaucer started from (and never grew away from) the primary definitions of purpose and method in art as laid down by the orthodox tradition in medieval aesthetics: poetry is a process of manipulating language so that the wisdom evolved in the past will become available, applicable, and operative in the present. Its most distinctive characteristic as poetry is its ability to stir emotion—to move knowledge into operation" (89).

In a similar vein, Robert M. Jordan, in *Chaucer's Poetics and the Modern Reader* (Berkeley: U of California P, 1987), draws our attention to a distinction between *homo rhetoricus* and *homo seriosus* and argues that Chaucer, like rhetorical man, "centers his vital awareness on the word. He develops an overpowering self-consciousness about language. His orientation to life is social and pragmatic, committed to no single construction of the world, no single set of values" (8).

[26] One instance of the Squire's clumsiness with, even misuse of, rhetorical conventions might be the astrological allusions (V [F] 48–51, 263–65, 671–72). Such allusions are traditionally used to introduce and frame action, but here they seem to point away from, rather than toward, the main significance of the tale. They are in every case rhetorical flourishes that indicate a plot only thinly developed. In the last of these ("Appollo whirleth up his chaar so hye / Til that the god Mercurius hous, the sly—") the plot is palpably absent: the poem stops. The fact that the astrological allusions follow the natural course of the sun, and thus suggest Vinsauf's "natural order" (opposed to the "artistic order" he favors), makes the element of fun greater and, indeed, may tempt us to consider whether Chaucer is not here drawing on the well-founded reputation of Mercury, the god of eloquence. Traditionally believed to have been born at dawn, Mer-

he does not himself understand its full significance, he is in the best Chaucerian tradition of narrators whose limitations help to illuminate the world they create.

In the *Squire's Tale,* the tercelet deceives purposely. In the *Franklin's Tale,* the early *sententia* reminds us that there are circumstances in which human beings speak amiss without intending to do so:

> For in this world, certein, ther no wight is
> That he ne *dooth or seith* somtyme amys.
> Ire, siknesse, or constellacioun,
> Wyn, wo, or chaungynge of complexioun
> Causeth ful ofte to *doon amys or speken.* (V [F] 779–83; italics mine)

Later, as though to emphasize the degree to which tolerance is in order given the human propensity to do or speak amiss, the narrative that precedes Dorigen's rash promise to Aurelius gives extended attention to her loneliness for Averagus and her fear for his safe return. These emotions find their most serious expression in a complaint (to God) in which Dorigen concentrates obsessively on the "grisly feendly rokkes blake" (V [F] 868). Subsequently, and most appropriately, it is then the removal of the same grisly rocks "stoon by stoon" which becomes the condition of her promise to love Aurelius "best of any man" (V [F] 989–98). Dorigen speaks "amys" and she does so, not (as the tercelet or the hypocrite) from duplicity, but from the heart of her psychological condition.

Just as it is the tercelet's misuse of speech which dominates the lament of the falcon in the *Squire's Tale* (V [F] 409–620)—and thus the second part of the tale—so it is now Aurelius's deliberate misinterpretation of Dorigen's "biheste" which dominates the *Franklin's Tale.* Before Dorigen speaks amiss, her response to Aurelius's expression of love includes a string of terms germane to the subject of speech, particularly to its interpretation by the listener: "Is this your wyl," "and sey ye thus?" She focuses on Aurelius's intention and her perception of that intention, claiming that she did not, until now, understand his "entente." Having now understood it, her response is unconditional:

---

cury shares with Apollo the power of eloquence, but for him it is coupled with ingenuity and slyness. To be attuned to these qualities in a speaker whose "wyl is good" (V [F] 8) may, in a sense, train us in the rhetorical skills of perception that will elsewhere identify the deceiver.

"By thilke God that yaf me soule and lyf,
Ne shal I nevere been untrewe wyf
In word ne werk, as fer as I have wit." (V [F] 983–85)

If our attention has been drawn to the act of interpreting, so has Aurelius's. Even after Dorigen suddenly and "in pley" (V [F] 988) promises a condition—that she will love Aurelius "best of any man" if he removes all the rocks, stone by stone—Aurelius's immediate response is a complete and correct realization of the spirit of her words: "Is ther noon oother grace in yow?" (V [F] 999). In his subsequent despair, however, Aurelius ignores the spirit of Dorigen's words and attends solely to their letter. For help in his distress, Aurelius turns first to the gods, in particular to Apollo—here described as a kind of male Natura figure who is

". . . god and governour
Of every plaunte, herbe, tree, and flour." (V [F] 1031–32)

Nature, as it is portrayed in this poem, will not perform miracles on request. Apollo is silent. The narrative simply moves on to a description of Aurelius's brother, who caught him up and brought him to bed (V [F] 1083). When Dorigen later responds to the rock's apparent removal as being against the process of nature (V [F] 1345), she corroborates what Aurelius's bootless plea to Apollo has already implied.

If nature's process is reliable, however, Aurelius's is not. Given elaborate build-up in the narrative, the solution to which Aurelius now turns is a branch of science that specializes in appearance and seeming (V [F] 1139–51) and is full of terminology understood only by the initiated. In the *Squire's Tale,* the tercelet was associated with such emblems of hypocrisy as the serpent, the tiger, and the "feend" (V [F] 512, 543, 522). In the pagan context of the *Franklin's Tale,* Aurelius is twice associated with the furies.[27] His torment is so extreme as to arouse his brother's pity and with that the memory of a book of natural magic. In turning to magic and in creating "illusioun" (V [F] 1123–36) to set up an appearance of reality, Aurelius will, like the tercelet—whose description is also dominated by references to "seeming" (see V [F] 504–61)—pervert

---

[27] Aurelius "langwissheth as a furye dooth in helle" (V [F] 950), and "In langour and in torment furyus / Two yeer and moore lay wrecche Aurelyus" (V [F] 1101–2).

communicative symbols. Having ignored the spirit of Dorigen's words for their letter, he will now use magic to set up a false construct that temporarily substitutes for reality.

Though in some ways so like the artist, the magician is rather a "subtil clerk" (V [F] 1261), practicing a science of "apparence" (V [F] 1157) with the help of esoteric books, subtle calculations, ingenious advertising, and the ability to drive a bargain so elusively, but persistently, that Aurelius himself is caught in a rash promise:

> . . . "Fy on a thousand pound!
> This wyde world, which that men seye is round,
> I wolde it yeve, if I were lord of it." (V [F] 1227–29)

While artistic process enlightens and enhances, the magician's craft confuses and diminishes.

When Aurelius later conveys to Dorigen the result of the magician's labor, his speech imitates on a rhetorical level the self-serving craft of the magician. Masterful in its use of circumlocution and evasion, Aurelius's speech works subtly on Dorigen's sense of "trouthe" and "honor." It reserves the one (and only) important detail—"the rokkes been awaye"—for its very end:

> "But of my deeth thogh that ye have no routhe,
> Avyseth yow *er that ye breke youre trouthe.*
> Repenteth yow, for thilke God above,
> Er ye me sleen by cause that I yow love.
> For, madame, *wel ye woot what ye han hight—*
> *Nat that I chalange any thyng of right*
> *Of yow, my sovereyn lady, but youre grace—*
> But in a gardyn yond, at swich a place,
> *Ye woot right wel what ye bihighten me;*
> *And in myn hand youre trouthe plighten ye;*
> To love me best—*God woot, ye seyde so,*
> Al be that I unworthy am therto.
> Madame, *I speke it for the honour of yow*
> Moore than to save myn hertes lyf right now—
> *I have do so as ye comanded me;*
> And if ye vouche sauf, ye may go see.
> Dooth as yow list; *have youre biheste in mynde,*

> For, quyk or deed, right there ye shal me fynde.
> In yow lith al to do me lyve or deye—
> But wel I woot the rokkes been aweye." (V [F] 1320–38, italics
>   mine)

In his emphasis on Dorigen's words rather than her intention, Aurelius willfully misinterprets the spirit of her original "biheste." He turns speech into a self-serving vehicle with little or no relation to truth and communication. To deny the spirit of words and to reify them instead is to destroy not only the relationship of words and deeds, but the very power of speech to communicate.

In the narrative that follows Dorigen's recognition of what has happened (V [F] 1342–45), the central issues of words and deeds, discourse and reality, are treated simply and briefly. Arveragus returns, and his question "why that she weep so soore" (V [F] 1461) looks for clarification and gets it. Dorigen's "Thus have I seyd . . . thus have I sworn" (V [F] 1464) prompts Arveragus, as though to be assured that words and *not* deeds are at issue here, to ask "Is ther oght elles, Dorigen, but this?" (V [F] 1468).

When Aurelius later meets Dorigen in the garden, he too sees the distinction between speech and reality. He sees not only Arveragus's "gentillesse" but also Dorigen's sadness (V [F] 1527–28). In releasing Dorigen of "every serement and every bond" (V [F] 1534), he recognizes that to pursue the letter of the agreement would be to deny the reality of the unwilling woman before him. In this recognition, the intention and the spirit of Dorigen's words about the rocks have been restored. Finally, reality and discourse are also restored to their appropriate spheres in the clerk's response to Aurelius.

Like Arveragus, the clerk asks questions which bring about clarification, "Hastow nat had thy lady as thee liketh?" (V [F] 1589) and "What was the cause? Tel me if thou kan" (V [F] 1591). Discovering that nothing came of the verbal agreement between them, the clerk, too, makes a distinction between words and deeds and releases Aurelius of his word. The freedom of "Which was the mooste fre, as thynketh yow?" (V [F] 1622) is thus in every case defined at one level by perception and questioning that reasserts the distinction between words and deeds, discourse and reality, and recognizes the fitting relationship between them. In a world in which "ther no wight is / That he ne dooth or seith somtyme amys" (V [F] 779–80), gentility must also be concerned with the interpretation of speech and the ability to redress misinterpretation when it occurs.

Having at their outset directed our attention to the art of rhetoric, particularly that more superficial aspect of rhetoric that involves a mastery of the "colours longynge for that art," the tales of the F fragment direct our attention finally to the entire gamut of the use and interpretation of speech. When explored in these terms, the seduction scenes of the tales not only gain meaning, but exhibit a remarkable symmetry. The fragment suggests an echoing system based on the relationship of words to deeds, but while one tale concentrates its attention on the use of speech, the other concentrates on its interpretation. The tercelet *uses* words falsely and against their spirit to get what he wants; to get what he wants, Aurelius *interprets* words falsely. The symmetry is further carried out in that both victims, the falcon and Dorigen, are females. While the falcon is deceived by words, Dorigen is misunderstood. In both tales of the fragment, too, there is finally a return to the "proper" relationship between words and deeds. Writ large, the "gentility" referred to so frequently at the end of both tales might be seen as an image of enlightened poetic sensibility and concern with the nature of action and discourse generally.

7

The *Monk's Tale* and Chaucer's Idea
of the Listener

In the links of the *Canterbury Tales,* by introducing listeners and
interjecting the dynamics of dialogue, Chaucer suggests that it is precisely the listener that makes discourse such an unsettling experience.[1]
Chaucer's listeners remind us, among other things, that it is characteristic
of a listener to hear subjectively. Just as the Miller senses his exclusion
from the world of the *Knight's Tale,* so the Reeve, imagining himself the
subject of the Miller's discourse, "gan to grucche" (I [A] 3863).[2] For the
Cook, listening is itself a passionate act:

---

[1] See Brenda Deen Schildgen, "Jerome's *Prefatory Epistles* to the Bible and *The Canterbury Tales,*" *Studies in the Age of Chaucer* 15 (1993): 111–30. Schildgen describes Jerome's
expressed uneasiness about the difficulty of controlling responses to the vernacular translations of the Bible and sees parallels with Chaucer's sense of interpretation in the *Canterbury Tales*: The "divergent commentaries" within the *Tales,* she writes, "attest to
Chaucer's awareness, like Jerome's, of the interpreter's or reader's ability to perceive
various possibilities in spoken or written discourse and to create competing interpretations; they point, in contrast to Jerome's efforts to make readers' interpretive choices
informed by some self-reflexive method, to Chaucer's own abdication of power or
authority over the interpretations assumed by the participants in the literary
drama" (125).
[2] On the uses of "grucchen," and especially its political overtones, see John S. P.
Tatlock and Arthur G. Kennedy, *A Concordance to the Complete Works of Geoffrey Chaucer
and to "The Romaunt of the Rose"* (Washington, DC: Carnegie Institution, 1927), and

> The Cook of Loundoun, while the Reeve spak,
> For joye him thoughte he clawed him on the bak. (I [A] 4325–26)

In the *Cook's Prologue,* the Host's response to Roger's promise to tell "a litel jape that fil in oure citee" is to remind him of his professional practices, of little shortcuts and risks to his customers' health (I [A] 4342–48) that make him equally vulnerable to retribution as a speaker.

Elsewhere in the *Canterbury Tales,* Chaucer's interest in the listener spills over into the tales themselves, as a teller is interrupted or a narrator suddenly changes tactics. Here the frame narrative gains a fluidity which asserts that the listener is not outside the frame but palpably within it. So, for example, the Wife of Bath is more than once interrupted by the Pardoner (III [D] 163–68, 184–87). The inescapable presence of the listener is asserted, as well, in the final stanzas of the *Clerk's Tale* when the narrator asks for "o word, lordynges" (IV [E] 1163) and then subjects Walter's authoritative discourse (and Griselda's submission to it) to a proliferation of voices.[3]

Chaucer's interest in the listener receives sustained attention, as well, in the *Prologue of the Nun's Priest's Tale* where the Knight and the Host make contradictory comments on the nature of tragedy. While the Knight interrupts the Monk's tragedies because the Knight considers that a "litel hevynesse" goes a long way, the Host is less tolerant. He debunks the performance wholesale, and reveals, as he does so, that he has heard little and understood less. The contradictory nature of these responses throws light not only on Chaucer's methods in the *Monk's Tale* but also on his idea of the listener throughout the *Canterbury Tales.*

It has long been assumed that Chaucer had the material of the *Monk's Tale* in a desk drawer unfinished and that he included this particular "link" as a dramatic justification for its unfinished condition. Derek Pearsall describes this assumption, or "hypothesis": "A pleasing hypothesis would run thus: Chaucer composed a series of poetic exercises in the

---

the *Middle English Dictionary,* ed. Hans Kurath and Sherman M. Kuhn (Ann Arbor, MI: U of Michigan P, 1954).

 [3] The narrator's "I crie in open audience" (IV [E] 1179) here echoes its earlier use in the description of Walter's third test (IV [E] 790), where Walter, in fact, lies to Griselda. The narrator's reference to "crabbed eloquence" (IV [E] 1203) is only one of many such allusions to discursive disruption in the "Lenvoy": "Lat noon humylitee youre tonge naille" (IV [E] 1184); "Folweth Ekko, that holdeth no silence, / But evere answereth at the countretaille" (IV [E] 1189–90); "Ay clappeth as a mille, I yow consaille" (IV [E] 1200).

'fall of princes' tradition . . . he subsequently added a group of 'Modern Instances' (Peter of Spain, Peter of Cyprus, Barnabo and Ugolino) in order to give the theme a contemporary relevance . . . at the same time or subsequently, allocated the series to the Monk. . . ." While rejecting the dramatic principle as an explanation for the *Monk's Tale* and claiming that "the tale is not told 'badly,' " Pearsall makes only the briefest allusion to its "variety in the rhetoric of narration," "vivid touches," and hints of "swift, pregnant narrative technique."[4] Modern criticism of the *Monk's Tale* has shown a tendency to agree with the Knight's and Host's responses, which confirm the modern disinclination toward *exempla*:[5]

"Hoo!" quod the Knyght, "good sire, namoore of this!
That ye han seyd is right ynough, ywis,
And muchel moore; for litel hyvynesse
Is right ynough to muche folk, I gesse.
I seye for me, it is a greet disese,
Whereas men han been in greet welthe and ese,
To heeren of hire sodeyn fal, allas!
And the contrarie is joye and greet solas,
As whan a man hath been in povre estaat,
And clymbeth up and wexeth fortunat,
And there abideth in prosperitee.
Swich thyng is gladsom, as it thynketh me,
And of swich thyng were goodly for to telle."

"Ye," quod oure Hooste, "by Seint Poules belle!
Ye seye right sooth; this Monk he clappeth lowde.

---

[4] Derek A. Pearsall, *The Canterbury Tales* (London: Allen and Unwin, 1985) 280. See also R. E. Kaske, "The Knight's Interruption of *The Monk's Tale*," *English Literary History* 24 (1957): 249–68.

[5] Donald R. Howard reads the *Prologue of the Nun's Priest's Tale* as a semi-legitimate criticism of the *Monk's Tale* and attributes to Chaucer the fact that the other travelers seem to find the Monk's narratives boring: "the Monk's stories, perfectly well told, are interrupted and denounced because they're cheerless and tedious. Chaucer didn't write them with this in mind, as he wrote the singsong verses of *Sir Thopas*, but capitalized on the fact that they *would* be boring if told one after another in this relentless way." See *Chaucer: His Life, his Works, His World* (New York: E.P. Dutton, 1987) 446. Though Trevor Whittock, like others, makes an exception of the Hugelino episode, Whittock's judgment of the tale is severe: "The Monk produces a series of mechanical 'tragedies' in which human interest surrenders to the inevitable 'fall' of the plot." See Whittock, *A Reading of the "Canterbury Tales"* (Cambridge: Cambridge UP, 1968) 218. See also Paul G. Ruggiers, *The Art of "The Canterbury Tales"* (Madison: U of Wisconsin P, 1965).

He spak how Fortune covered with a clowde
I noot nevere what; and als of a tragedie
Right now ye herde, and pardee, no remedie
It is for to biwaille ne compleyne
That that is doon, and als it is a peyne,
As ye han seyd, to heere of hevynesse.
"Sire Monk, namoore of this, so God yow blesse!
Youre tale anoyeth al this compaignye.
Swich talkyng is nat worth a boterflye,
For therinne is ther no desport ne game. . . ." (VII 2767–91)

Often seen as a semi-legitimate criticism of the *Monk's Tale,* this "link," as we shall see momentarily, may more usefully serve to illuminate Chaucer's fascination with the complexity of language as it is heard. The *Prologue of the Nun's Priest's Tale,* with its so-called "roadside comedy," raises questions concerning the nature of audience and it raises them, quite appropriately, around a genre that more than any other carries assumptions of moral efficacy.[6]

The *Monk's Tale* does not, in fact, fulfill the quality of immoderate "hevynesse" (VII 2769) accorded it by the Knight, nor the boredom suggested by the comments of the Host. Nor does it show the obvious signs of deliberate dullness: mishandled tropes, repetition, needless digression, self-contradiction, chopped logic, and clichés. Quite the contrary, it is more variegated, rhetorically and otherwise, than most anything else in the *Canterbury Tales.* John Gardner's discussion of the *Monk's Tale* is notable for its awareness that the tale is "a subtler and more entertaining work than critics have generally noticed." Gardner reconstructs the positive contemporary response to the poem and attributes it in large measure to its listeners being "startled . . . with something new to most of them, in all probability, humanism's at once

---

[6] Richard Firth Green, *Poets and Princepleasers: Literature and the English Court in the Late Middle Ages* (Toronto: U of Toronto P, 1980) includes reference to the *Monk's Tale* and its histories in his chapter on the court poet's role as "An Advisor to Princes" (135–67). On the role of exempla, Green comments that "it is easy to dismiss the use of exempla as merely a form of stylistic ornamentation (which is how they appear to be treated by Geoffrey of Vinsauf, for instance), and to forget how seriously they were intended to be received; yet in a work such as the *Monk's Tale,* this 'ornamentation' usurps the very matter of the story, and we can be fairly sure that it is the 'lessons of history' that are there in question 'be war by thise ensamples trewe and olde' (line 1998)" (137).

intellectual and gossipy love of things current." Gardner rightly differentiates between the kind of "moralistic rhymes" written in the Anglo-
Saxon period on Lucifer, Adam, and Cain that "would continue to be
written, mainly for schoolboys, down into the eighteenth century" and
the Italian humanist influence on Chaucer in the *exempla* of the *Monk's
Tale*. "To English aristocratic ears," he writes, "the poem was in some
respects a new kind of work, an original and fascinating creation." It is
Gardner's view that Chaucer's contact with Italian humanism not only
provided him with new stories, but prompted him with new ways of
treating the older poetic traditions.[7] More recently, Renate Haas has
demonstrated quite compellingly the early humanists' interest in Sene-
can tragedy and reads the *Monk's Tale* in this context. The *Monk's Tale,*
in Haas's estimation, "no longer appears to be a mere experiment in
form, which is extremely boring to the modern reader, but an ingenious
response to the most advanced contemporary literary and philosophical
discussion."[8]

---

[7] John Gardner, *The Life and Times of Chaucer* (New York: Knopf, 1977) 221–23. See
also Green, *Poets and Princepleasers*. Green points out that it is not until Premierfait's
translations early in the fifteenth century that Boccaccio is generally known in northern
Europe; with his *Monk's Tale,* which is "undoubtedly indebted" to Boccaccio's *De casibus,* "Chaucer was in fact anticipating a later fashion" (160).

[8] See Renate Haas, "Chaucer's *Monk's Tale*: An Ingenious Criticism of Early Humanist Conceptions of Tragedy," *Humanistica Lovaniensia* 36 (1987): 44–70. Haas's assessment of the *Monk's Tale* as an "ingenious" response to the early humanist discussion
of tragedy is more convincing than her discussion of the tale itself, which relies heavily
on a dramatic reading of the *Canterbury Tales* (see 57–62). Haas argues that Chaucer plays
off the Monk's character, his shortcomings and misunderstandings, to draw attention to
"the inadequacies of the current definitions of tragedy" (57); the Monk is a "would-be
humanist completely entangled in the snares of the contemporary concepts of tragedy"
(62). The poetry never comes under discussion. But more generally, her reading of the
tale also provokes one to ask whether Chaucer would not be demanding too much of
his audience by at once introducing new material and then qualifying it with dialogic
irony.

Paul Strohm, too, casts doubt on traditional critical perceptions of the *Monk's Tale*
when he comments that "the Monk's *tragedies* are not at all the kind of thing that a
monk would be expected to have lying around his cell, but were in the 1380s the
province of an international and Latinate literary elite of the highest order of humanistic
pretension. . . ." See Strohm, *Social Chaucer* (Cambridge: Harvard UP, 1989) 70–71.
Strohm sees the "assignment of tragedies to the Monk," however, as a "subtle literary
joke" (71) and avers that "Chaucer must be suspected of some irony in turning a currently fashionable international form over to the relentlessly monologic
Monk . . ." (170).

See also the essay by Peter Godman, "Chaucer and Boccaccio's Latin Works," in
Chaucer and the Italian Trecento, ed. Piero Boitani (Cambridge: Cambridge UP, 1983)
269–95. Godman, too, believes that the *Monk's Tale* "has received a bad press" and cites

What, then, could Chaucer's motives in the Nun's Priest's prologue have been? Like Boccaccio in *De casibus virorum illustrium,* one of the acknowledged sources of the *Monk's Tale,* Chaucer seems concerned with the manifest tension between discourse and its receivers. Boccaccio addresses this issue directly in *De casibus* when he opens with general remarks that reflect the Italian humanists' concern with the relationship between poetry and knowledge (art and behavior); he refers specifically to his own efforts to effect the good of the state and to his collection of stories—or histories, as he calls them—and voices a realistic skepticism regarding the potential of art to accomplish reform. He often wondered, he writes in the introduction, how the labor of his studies could be of utility to the state, and as he did so, he remembered the scandalous behavior of famous princes: their debauchery, lack of restraint, and mis-use of power. Others have tried, and he will try also, to "penetrate their guard" and to "shatter an illusion that may cause their death." For his part, he knows how difficult it is to influence people "who make a habit of sensuality." Because these people are difficult to sway by the "eloquence of history," he will, instead, relate

> examples of what God or (speaking their own language) For-
> tune can teach them about those she raises up. And so that
> there can be no accusation against any specific time or sex,
> my idea has been to present succinctly, yet still with useful
> detail—those rulers and other famous persons, women as well
> as men, who have been overthrown from the beginning of
> the world until now.

By showing them what Fortune does to people she raises up, he may cause them to recognize their fragility and take counsel for their own good. Finally, in the tradition of the early humanists, Boccaccio closes his opening remarks by promising that he will introduce variety into what might otherwise be a tiring sameness of histories by flavoring them with direct encouragements to virtue and away from vice: "In order that an unbroken succession of stories be not tiresome to the reader, I think it will be both more pleasant and useful from time to time to add induce-

---

R. K. Root, who, in Godman's words, "regarded the work as so boring that he could not believe that Chaucer had intended it seriously" (278). See Root, *The Poetry of Chaucer,* 2nd ed. (Boston: Houghton, 1906) 206–7.

ments to virtue and dissuasions from vice." In the introduction to the second book, Boccaccio also considers the issues of length and repetition as they affect a listener: "As a constant flow of water will penetrate the hardest stone, so an adamantine heart is softened by a long narration."[9]

Boccaccio's comments regarding the style of his narrative and its effect on the listener should give us some perspective on similar concerns in the *Monk's Tale*. As Chaucer's Monk begins his tale, he, too, makes an implicit connection between the tragic genre, its *sentence,* and the response of the listener:

> I wol biwaille in manere of tragedie
> The harm of hem that stoode in heigh degree,
> And fillen so that ther nas no remedie
> To brynge hem out of hir adversitee.
> For certein, whan that Fortune list to flee,
> Ther may no man the cours of hire withholde.

---

[9] Giovanni Boccaccio, *De casibus virorum illustrium*, Proemio, 1; 6; 9; and Incipit secundus, 3, *Tutte Le Opere di Giovanni Boccaccio*, 12 vols (Milano: Arnoldo Mondadori, 1983) vol. 9.

> Exquirenti michi quid ex labore studiorum meorum possem forsan rei publice utilitatis addere, occurrere preter creditum multa; maiori tamen conatu in mentem sese ingessere principum atque presidentium quorumcunque obscene libidines, violentie truces, perdita ocia, avaritie inexplebiles, cruenta odia, ultiones armate precipitesque et longe plura scelesta facinora. . . . Sane cum tales, obscenis sueti voluptatibus, difficiles animos demonstrationibus prestare consueverint, et lepiditate hystoriarum capi non nunquam, exemplis agendum ratus sum eis describere quid Deus omnipotens, seu—ut eorum loquar more—Fortuna, in elatos possit et fecerit. . . . Porro, ne continua hystoriarum series legenti possit fastidium aliquod inferre, morsus in vitia et ad virtutem suasiones inseruisse quandoque tam delectabile quam utile arbitratus adnectam. . . .
>
> . . . ut, uti assiduo aque casu durissimus perforatur lapis, sic et adamantinum cor talium longa narratione molliatur. . . .

The translation is found in Boccaccio, *The Fates of Illustrious Men*, trans. Louis Brewer Hall (New York: Ungar, 1965) 1–2, 48. Boccaccio's concern with the relationship between style and persuasion is a feature of Italian humanism. Just how new and unusual this is in the fourteenth century is borne out by Robert O. Payne's observation in *The Key of Remembrance: A Study of Chaucer's Poetics* (New Haven: Yale UP, 1963) that the medieval rhetorical manuals concentrate on style and that they have little or nothing to say about how poetry moves its reader: "The analysis made in the rhetorical treatises is an analysis of causes in the structure of poetry, rather than of effects in the reader. Its ultimate aim was, of course, to instruct in the art of producing a poetry which *would* move its readers, and it is no doubt a limitation in the instruction that it has so little to say about how those effects follow from the causes listed, or what effects may follow" (50).

> Lat no man truste on blynd prosperitee;
> Be war by thise ensamples trewe and olde. (VII 1991–98)

In their subsequent encouragements to virtue and away from vice
Chaucer's tragedies, like Boccaccio's, are remarkably diverse. His material is drawn from biblical, classical, and contemporary sources.[10] His
characters, both male and female, are wicked *and* good. He introduces a
causality so various that we are continually surprised by a new source of
mutability. Now the cause of a fall is "synne" (Lucifer), now "mysgover-
nauce" (Adam), lack of discretion (Sampson), lack of self knowledge
(Hercules), pride, envy (Petro Rege de Cipre and others), treachery
(Hugelino), self-delusion (Nero). These do not exhaust the possibilities.
And the figure of Fortune herself, as Peter Braeger has noted, is by turns
philosophical, sly, strong, playful, frightening, laughing, or lecherous.

Contrary to the opinion of the Host, the poetry, too, is full of "so-
laas," showing artful and bountiful variation throughout, as much, or
more, as anything else in the *Canterbury Tales*.[11] It ranges from the biblical cadences of the tragedies of Nabugodonosor and Balthasar, to the
highly descriptive, compact style of the tragedy of Sampson, to moments
of heart-rending dialogue and pathos in the Hugelino episode.[12]

The vivid description and specificity that distinguish Chaucer's pathos support manifestations of the macabre in the *Monk's Tale* as well.

---

[10] In addition to Boccaccio's reasoning (already mentioned) on the mixing of old and
new examples when attempting to persuade, see Jean de Meun's Raison in the *Roman
de la Rose,* who, when she moves from ancient examples to more recent ones, prefaces
them with the pointed observation that: "Et se les prueves riens ne prises / d'anciennes
estoires prises, / tu les as de ton tens noveles . . ." (6601–3). [if you give no value to
these proofs taken from old stories, you have others from your own recent times . . .].
See Guillaume de Lorris and Jean de Meun, *Le Roman de la Rose,* ed. Felix Lecoy, 3 vols.
(Paris: Champion, 1965–70) 1:203.

[11] This view of the *Monk's Tale* as a tour de force of rhetorical variation is not one
generally taken by modern criticism, which has mainly accepted the tenor of the comments of the Knight and Host. It does, however, comport with John M. Manly's assessment of the percentages of rhetorical devices in several *Canterbury Tales,* ranging from
nearly 100% in the *Monk's Tale* to almost none in the *Friar's* and *Summoner's Tales.*" The
modern disapproval of the *Monk's Tale* may well reflect a persistence of Manly's view
that Chaucer, in his mature poetry, relied less on rhetoric and more on the direct observation of life. For a contrary view, see Muscatine, *Chaucer and the French Tradition,* 173–
75. See Manly, *Chaucer and the Rhetoricians, Proceedings of the British Academy,* 12 (London,
1926) 95–113. Manly's view is dismissed by Payne (see *The Key of Remembrance* 10).

[12] On the Hugelino episode, see Charles Muscatine, *Chaucer and the French Tradition*
(Berkeley: U of California P, 1957) 193.

The description of Antiocho, injured in his fall from a litter, is splendidly gruesome:

> For he so soore fil out of his char
> That it his limes and his skyn totar,
> So that he neyther myghte go ne ryde,
> But in a chayer men aboute hym bar,
> Al forbrused, bothe bak and syde.
>
> The wreche of God hym smoot so cruelly
> That thurgh his body wikked wormes crepte,
> And therwithal he stank so horribly
> That noon of al his meynee that hym kepte,
> Wheither so he wook or ellis slepte,
> Ne myghte noght the stynk of hym endure.
> In this meschief he wayled and eek wepte,
> And knew God lord of every creature.
>
> To al his hoost and to hymself also
> Ful wlatsom was the stynk of his careyne;
> No man ne myghte hym bere to ne fro.
> And in this stynk and this horrible peyne,
> He starf ful wrecchedly in a monteyne.
> Thus hath this robbour and this homycide,
> That many a man made to wepe and pleyne,
> Swich gerdoun as bilongeth unto pryde. (VII 2610–30)

As the concluding lines here demonstrate, Chaucer's direct encouragements to virtue are also well and variously embedded in the narrative. Only occasionally are they given a special prominence, as in the tragedy of Balthasar when the narrator seems to address the court directly, "Lordynges, ensample heerby may ye take" (VII 2239).

A concern for variety is found as well in the arrangement of the tragedies. The Monk draws attention to their ordering when he excuses himself, "I by ordre telle nat thise thynges. . . . / But tellen hem som bifore and som bihynde, / As it now comth unto my remembraunce" (VII 1985–90). In spite of the puzzle posed by manuscript discrepancies concerning the placement of the modern figures—sometimes placed centrally in the *Monk's Tale,* sometimes at the conclusion—there is a sense that there is something more than randomness at work in the ordering we have.[13] The tale begins—not like Boccaccio's *De casibus,* with Adam—but with Lucifer, who, though himself immune to fortune ("For though Fortune may noon angel dere") "yet fel he for his synne" (VII 2001–2). In the tragedies that follow, figures of enormous physical strength (Samson and Hercules) who nonetheless lack self-knowledge are juxtaposed with idolaters (Nabugodonosor and Balthasar), and the cruelest leaders (Nero, Oloferno, Antiocho) with the most virtuous and successful (Alexandro and Julio Cesare). There is also a tragedy (that of Pompeus, "this noble governour") within a tragedy:

> But now a litel while I wol biwaille
> This Pompeus, this noble governour
> Of Rome, which that fleigh at this bataille.
> I seye, oon of his men, a fals traitour,
> His heed of smoot, to wynnen hym favour
> Of Julius, and hym the heed he broghte.
> Allas, Pompeye, of th'orient conquerour,
> That fortune unto swich a fyn thee broghte! (VII 2687–94)

The fifth tragedy, that of Nabugodonosor, does not quite fit the stated definition of the genre. It takes us beyond the fall, to the "remedie." Nabugodonosor suffers a sudden loss of "his dignytee" and experiences the condition and attributes of a beast:

> This kyng of kynges proud was and elaat;
> He wende that God, that sit in magestee,
> Ne myghte hym nat bireve of his estaat.
> But sodeynly he loste his dignytee,
> And lyk a beest hym semed for to bee,
> And eet hey as an oxe, and lay theroute
> In reyn; with wilde beestes walked hee
> Til certein tyme was ycome aboute.
>
> And lik an egles fetheres wax his heres;
> His nayles lyk a briddes clawes weere;

---

[13] For a brief discussion of the manuscript disparities and a bibliography on the issue of the placement of the "Modern Instances" in the *Monk's Tale,* see *The Riverside Chaucer,* ed. Larry D. Benson et al. (Boston: Houghton, 1987) 930.

Til God relessed hym a certeyn yeres,
And yaf hym wit, and thanne with many a teere
He thanked God, and evere his lyf in feere
Was he to doon amys or moore trespace;
And til that tyme he leyd was on his beere
He knew that God was ful of myght and grace. (VII 2167–82)

The passage prolongs the experience of Nabugodonosor's being "lyk a beest," and makes the subsequent reinstatement of his humanity emotionally powerful. Its poetry is sudden and specific—"Til God relessed hym a certeyn yeres, / And yaf hym wit" (VII 2177–78)—and ironically seems to throw into relief the innumerable and futile ways in which humans use wit to outwit Fortune. Momentarily "wit" not only distinguishes man from beast but may also suggest the human component that, properly used, can free the human being from Fortune. God's power is made graphic, and so, too, is the appropriate use of human reason.

By now juxtaposing Nabugodonosor and Balthasar—tragedies of father and son—Chaucer gives specificity and further variety to the exhortation to virtue, here from the negative example. Nabugodonosor's story does not touch someone even as close as his own son: Balthasar "by his fader koude noght be war, / For proud he was of herte and of array" (VII 2185–86). Here, as elsewhere in the *Monk's Tale,* Chaucer's rhetorical variety fulfills the aims of Boccaccio's sense that "inducements to virtue and dissuasions from vice" contribute to the listener's persuasion.

The material of the *Monk's Tale,* then, is hardly defective. This tale and the contradictory remarks of the Knight and Host that follow it suggest Chaucer's interest in issues similar to those raised by Boccaccio in *De casibus* and demonstrate the difficulty, in practice, of the generic and explicit command, "Be war by these ensamples trewe and olde." Is it possible, even in a genre so overtly aimed at moral improvement, to penetrate the guard of the listener? How does human nature express itself in the act of listening and responding? What social and psychological factors help determine how we listen? The *Prologue of the Nun's Priest's Tale* is a comment on the listener's response rather than on the character of the piece itself.

In the *Prologue of the Nun's Priest's Tale,* Chaucer neglects his prior characterizations of the Knight in the *General Prologue* and in the *Knight's Tale* to use him, instead, as a representative of the class of the well-to-do. Let us look at what the Knight is really saying. As he interrupts the

145

Monk—and perhaps only the Knight among the *Canterbury* pilgrims has the social stature to do so—he narrows the Monk's earlier definition of tragedy. What the Monk had more broadly defined as a fall from great prosperity and high degree (VII 1975–77), becomes, for the Knight, a more specifically material fall from great wealth and ease. There is a subtle sense both in his criticism of tragedy and in his enthusiasm for its opposite (the Knight's interruption is divided almost equally between these) that the Knight is seeing tragedy and its "contrarie" through a grid of material loss and material gain. After his initial and sudden interruption of the Monk, the Knight uses deferential and moderate language (with the enveloping and limiting, "I seye for me" at its beginning and "as it thynketh me" at its conclusion) to explain his taste and preference. His language does not, however, entirely cloak his position. It is not the Monk's performance or style that the Knight finds lacking. It is emphatically the subject matter itself. He is visibly uncomfortable with a subject matter that warns against trusting in "blynd prosperitee" and that reminds him of the precariousness of his own material well-being. He says it is a "greet disese," and there is no reason not to believe him. We can see, then, that the response of the Knight in the Nun's Priest's prologue is really a comment on the inhibitions to understanding of certain kinds of discourse by virtue of the interests dictated by class and economic position.

The Knight yearns for a genre that records the rise to "prosperitee." The cluster of phrases, "clymbeth up," "wexeth fortunat," "abideth in prosperitee," all give the sense of a satisfaction with—and celebration of—material well-being. To experience these is "gladsom," and to tell of them "were goodly." Just as the tragedies of the *Monk's Tale* are a "greet disese," so their "contrarie," he asserts, would be "joye and greet solas." Such a genre, presumably, would mirror and validate his own situation and suggest its continuance. If there is any genre that by definition cannot do this it is tragedy.

The Host, who now expectably jumps in to support (and impress?) the Knight, is less moderate than he and less rational. Obviously part of the Host's agreement with and echoing of the Knight is class-based deference too. His language is assertive and punctuated by expletives ("by Seint Poules belle! / Ye seye right sooth," and "As ye han seyd"). The import of the Knight's words has mainly escaped the Host. Suddenly mobilized, he grasps for key words from the Monk's performance to back up his agreement with the Knight. As he picks up the Monk's *last* image first—"he spak how Fortune covered with a clowde / I noot never what" (VII 2782–83)—he gives the distinct impression, an impression he will soon verify, of having slept through most of the tale. In his later reference to the Monk's first words—"I wol biwaille in manere of tragedie" (VII 1991)—he misses the generic sense of "biwaille" completely and concentrates, instead, on the more literal bewailing of, or complaining, about something that can no longer be helped, "and pardee, no remedie / It is to biwaille ne compleyne / That that is doon" (VII 2784–86). He summarizes his so-called agreement with the Knight and asserts that it is not only useless to bewail what is already done, but "als it is a peyne, / As ye han seyd, to heere of hevynesse" (VII 2786–87).

Seeming to partake of the Knight's ethos, the Host now moves into hyperbole and wholesale debunking of the Monk's performance. His "namoore of this" repeats the Knight verbatim, but what follows claims universal agreement among "al this compaignye." For the Knight's "I seye for me" and "as it thynketh me," we now have:

> "Sire Monk, namoore of this, so God yow blesse!
> Youre tale anoyeth al this compaignye.
> Swich talkyng is nat worth a boterflye." (VII 2788–90)

The Host claims that were it not for the "clynkyng of youre belles," "I sholde er this han fallen doun for sleep" (VII 2794–97) and attempts to summarize with the proverbial wisdom: "Whereas a man may have noon audience, / Noght helpeth it to tellen his sentence" (VII 2801–2).[14] Well observed, but how does it apply in the present instance?

The Host's reference to the Monk's bridle's clinking bells suggests that Chaucer's mind is on the *General Prologue*. This makes all the more curious the fact that Chaucer does not, in the *Prologue of the Nun's Priest's Tale,* invoke the moral authority of the gentle Knight of the *General Prologue* and the *Knight's Tale*. Indeed, the Knight of the Nun's Priest's prologue is surprisingly unlike the Knight of the *General Prologue,* who is not notably wealthy, to judge by his armor; and he seems to be totally allergic to tragedy, which is the essential structure of the *Knight's Tale*.

---

[14] Pandarus's "Yet were it bet my tonge for to stille / Than seye a soth that were ayeyns youre wille" in *Troilus and Criseyde* (2.230–31) is spoken under similarly dubious circumstances. See my discussion above.

Like the Knight, the Host, too, is a new character. The Host, who is elsewhere variously most responsive to the storytellers—polite to the Prioress, medical to the Physician—is here neither deferential nor sympathetic. In the *Prologue of the Nun's Priest's Tale,* the Host's response underlines the class orientation of the Knight's response through its servile agreement, and both responses demonstrate the incompetence of segments of society to comprehend certain material. Chaucer is not saying that the *Monk's Tale* is dull, but that the Host, for all his protean sensibilities, is incapable of appreciating a certain level of discourse and, furthermore, that he attributes this lack of appreciation to the rest of the company. For the Knight's class, self-interest turns a deaf ear to morality. In a sense, this is one of the few places in Chaucer's poetry where we see Chaucer's acute, if good humored, awareness of the possible deficiencies of the literary artist's audience.

8

The *Manciple's Tale* and the Poetics of Guile

Since the publication of Donald Howard's *The Idea of the Canterbury Tales* in 1976, the *Manciple's Tale* has become the cornerstone of an interpretation of the *Canterbury Tales* in which the last tales "collapse the structure that has gone before." Along with the *Canon's Yeoman's Tale* and the *Second Nun's Tale*, the *Manciple's Tale*, in Howard's reading, creates a major and qualitative change in our attitude toward the tales that precede them:

> The three tales have the effect of an ironical *De contemptu mundi*—they let us see the vanity of earthly pursuits, the mutability of human deeds, the disappointing uselessness of human striving, the corruptness of human nature. They make us change our point of view—we look back on all that has gone before and it looks different. The Knight's vision of the noble life, the Wife's *joie de vivre,* the story-telling game itself, the wit, the intellect, the ironic games, and the fabulous masquerade—what does it all amount to? And this pessimistic effect prepares us perfectly for the Parson, who begins "Thou getest fable noon ytold for me."[1]

---

[1] Donald R. Howard, *The Idea of "The Canterbury Tales"* (Berkeley: U of California P, 1976) 304. For an early instance of a discussion of the *Manciple's Tale* in the design of

149

Similarly, Lee Patterson sees the Manciple preparing us "for the Parson not just by rehearsing one of the fables the Parson is going to reject but by casting doubt upon the whole poetic enterprise." Like Howard, Patterson argues that the Manciple's prologue and tale "provide a bitter parody of the tale-telling game" and that the "festivity in which it began . . . is now reduced to the querulous cynicism of the Manciple." All that goes before is qualified not only by the "sacramental language of penance" and the "terms defined by the Parson," but by a view of discourse found in the *Manciple's Tale*.[2]

These are captivating arguments. In spite of the poetic complexity of the *Manciple's Tale,* recent readings of the tale have not challenged them. In general, it is agreed not only that "the subject of the tale is language"[3] but also that the tale suggests a view of discourse and the poet which "finally leaves the poet no function at all."[4] Most simply put, we are to believe that Chaucer concludes the *Canterbury Tales* by negating the assumptions about discourse and poetry that shaped it.

This reading suggests that Chaucer, in this penultimate tale, bitterly attacks the great received tradition of speech as an enhancement given to man by God.[5] According to this tradition, as we recall, "it is speech that distinguishes men from animals, and it is speech that has the power to unite men in a single place, to extract them from their bestial and

---

the *Canterbury Tales,* see Wayne Shumaker's "Chaucer's *Manciple's Tale* as Part of a Canterbury Group," *University of Toronto Quarterly* 22 (1953): 147–56. For a survey of criticism of this tale, see the *Manciple's Tale,* ed. Donald C. Baker (Norman: U of Oklahoma P, 1984) 19–38, vol. 2 of *A Variorum Edition of the Works of Geoffrey Chaucer.*

[2] Lee W. Patterson, "*The Parson's Tale* and the Quitting of the *Canterbury Tales,*" *Traditio* 34 (1978): 377–79.

[3] Britton J. Harwood, "Language and the Real: Chaucer's Manciple," *Chaucer Review* 6 (1972): 268.

[4] Helen Cooper, *The Structure of the Canterbury Tales* (Athens: U of Georgia P, 1984) 199. See also Richard Hazelton, "The *Manciple's Tale*: Parody and Critique," *Journal of English and Germanic Philology* 62 (1963): 1–31; Stephen Knight, *Ryming Craftily: Meaning in Chaucer's Poetry* (London: Angus and Robertson, 1973) 161–83; V. J. Scattergood, "The Manciple's Manner of Speaking," *Essays in Criticism* 24 (1974): 124–46; Richard M. Trask, "The Manciple's Problem," *Studies in Short Fiction* 14 (1977): 109–16; R. D. Fulk, "Reinterpreting the *Manciple's Tale,*" *Journal of English and Germanic Philology* 78 (1979): 485–93; James Dean, "The Ending of the *Canterbury Tales,*" *Texas Studies in Language and Literature* 21 (1979): 17–33; F. N. M. Diekstra, "Chaucer's Digressive Mode and the Moral of the Manciple's Tale," *Neophilologus* 67 (1983): 131–48; Louise Fradenburg, "The Manciple's Servant's Tongue: Politics and Poetry in the *Canterbury Tales,*" *English Literary History* 52 (1985): 85–118; Robert M. Jordan, *Chaucer's Poetics and the Modern Reader* (Berkeley: U of California P, 1987) 149–62.

[5] See my discussion of the humanist estimation of speech in chap. 1, above.

savage condition, to bring them to civility, and to sustain laws and justice."[6] Civilized society, according to the classical tradition voiced by
Boccaccio and the other early humanists, could not exist without
speech. As it is currently read, Chaucer's *Manciple's Tale* questions the
validity of this tradition.

The discussion that follows will challenge these conclusions, on the
premise that there are networks of meaning in the tale and its prologue
that have not been adequately exposed.[7] While disturbing in tone, the
Manciple's prologue and tale, rather than negating the poetic principles
of the *Canterbury Tales,* explains and reinforces those principles. The dark
strains of the fragment—its return again and again to the troubled and
the imperfect in human nature, in the individual, in love, in politics, and
in the relationship of discourse to truth—are, in fact, the foundation
upon which Chaucer's poetics are built. That foundation is present not
only in the plot but also in the rhetorical amplifications of the tale.

There is much in the prologue and tale to point us to the general
area of speech, poetry, and song. The Manciple is the teller of the tale.
The crow can "countrefete the speche of every man / . . . whan he
sholde telle a tale" (IX [H] 134—35). Phebus, the protagonist, identified
as god of light, healing, music, and poetry, is compared to "the king of
Thebes, Amphioun / That with his syngyng walled that citee" (IX [H]
116–17). Sorrow for having killed his wife causes Phebus to "brak his
mynstralcie / Both harpe, and lute, and gyterne, and sautrie" (IX [H]
267–68). The crow's punishment is not only, as in Ovid, to be forever

---

[6] Cicero's *De oratore* 1.8.33, as paraphrased by Eugene Vance in "Marvelous Signals: Poetics, Sign Theory, and Politics in Chaucer's *Troilus,*" *New Literary History* 10 (1979): 294.

[7] One reason for this situation may be that criticism of the tale so frequently reverts, in the words of Robert M. Jordan, "to an extratextual teller—be he the Manciple or not—as the source of meaning. In other words, rhetoric is finally subordinated to drama as critical interpretation shifts from the text to its speaker" (*Chaucer's Poetics and the Modern Reader* 160).

Modern critical theory, with its greater emphasis on literature *as communication* (whether open or hidden), may encourage a change of emphasis which will allow us to attend more fully to the satire itself and the interaction between Chaucer and his audience. In the case of the *Manciple's Tale,* given its complexity and its tone, it seems truly ironic that discussions of truth-telling and discourse have so repeatedly focused on the Manciple rather than on the poet and the political conditions in Chaucer's England vis-à-vis truth-telling. Even Paul A. Olson, in a work which recognizes the political context of the tales, refers to it as "an Ovidian fable misglossed to spite a fellow pilgrim." See *"The Canterbury Tales" and the Good Society* (Princeton: Princeton UP, 1986) 279. (This is something like reading Swift's Brobdingnags as a satire of the Lilliputians.)

black but also to be forever bereft of song and speech.[8] And finally, the concluding moral warns, "My sone, be war, and be noon auctour newe / Of tidynges" (IX [H] 359–60).

The tale's tone is disturbing.[9] If Amphioun and Phoebus Apollo (and even the snow-white crow) suggest a golden age of speech and song, the moral, the fable itself, and the tale's amplifications suggest a world in which discourse is fallen. Verbal echoes reinforce the sense of something drastically metamorphosed. The tale is framed on the one side with a reference to an ideal, legendary monarch "that with his syngyng *walled* that citee" and on the other with a warning and reminder that "God of his endelees goodnesse / *Walled* a tonge with teeth and lippes eke" (IX [H] 117, 322–23; italics mine). With its advice of quietude, in which the best response is to hold one's "tonge . . . / At alle tymes, but whan thou doost thy peyne / To speke of God, in honour and preyere" (IX [H] 329–31), the overt moral of the tale is distinctly anti-speech. The advice to hold one's tongue would seem to follow from the crow's experience with truth-telling as well as from the tone of the tale's amplifications.[10] The crow's bluntness brings only suffering. The amplifications are leveling in their assessment of human nature and

---

[8] Chaucer's use of his sources in the *Manciple's Tale* is taken up by Burke Severs in "Is the *Manciple's Tale* a Success?" *Journal of English and Germanic Philology* 51 (1952): 1–16, and is studied by Britton Harwood in "Language and the Real," *Chaucer Review* 6 (1972): 268–79. Though Harwood does not say so, several of his findings are particularly significant to a reading like the present one in that they result in an emphasis on the poet and poetry. These include the following: (1) "apparently only in Chaucer's version is Phebus responsible for having taught the bird to speak"; (2) "the color change is altogether subordinated in the *Manciple's Tale* to the vengeance taken by Phebus upon the bird's voice, a punishment not even mentioned in the *Metamorphose,* the *Ovide moralisé,* or the *Confessio Amantis*"; and (3) the "wyf's" lack of a name in Chaucer's version and the lack of detail regarding her pregnancy (characterization found abundantly elsewhere) also serve to sharpen Chaucer's focus on the dilemma of Phebus himself [IX [H] 269–70). Significant, too, is Severs's finding that "though the analogues give virtually no characterization of him, the first 25 lines of the *Manciple's Tale* extravagantly celebrate his virtues and accomplishments" (4). Phebus, in Chaucer's version, most fully *represents* all that is civilized.

[9] That the tale is disturbing is now a commonplace among those who see its subject as language—so commonplace that references can be as brief as A. J. Minnis's "The Manciple is an unsympathetic character, and his tale is a sordid one." See *Chaucer and Pagan Antiquity* (Cambridge, Eng.: Brewer, 1982) 19.

[10] Cf. Jean de Meun, *Roman de la Rose,* 7007: "The tongue should be reined in." In the *Roman,* the context of this saying of Ptolemy, cited by Raison, is extremely complex. It is spoken in the midst of a philosophical defense of speech that includes Raison's, quoting from the *Timaeus* of Plato, to the effect that speech was "given us to make our wishes understood, to teach and to learn" (7065–72). Cf. above pp. 62–64.

crude in their assertion of the predominance of appetite. In the world of guile and appetite which the fable and the amplifications describe, keeping quiet would seem to be the best course.

But the manifest paradoxes of the *Manciple's Tale* continue to invite speculation. If this is a tale about silence, it is, as Robert Jordan has observed, "proclaimed in a torrent of language."[11] Furthermore, the fable of an apparently ideal Phebus is riddled with amplifications describing a fallen world. In addition to these paradoxes, there are signs of a structural method in the prologue and the tale in which Chaucer sets up networks of meaning and runs them against each other. One of these is the relationship, noticed in recent years, between prologue and tale.[12] To read any one part of the tale, especially its moral counseling silence, as Chaucer's final statement on human discourse is to miss his artfulness. Chaucer is doubling, or looping, around discourse to give us a philosophical understanding of words themselves.

The *Manciple's Prologue* provides a narrative which parallels—up to a point—the plot of the tale. One function of this parallelism, and its bifurcation as the action develops, is to focus our attention on the issue of truth-telling. In his prologue, the Manciple, like the crow whose story he will soon tell, observes reality and reports it truthfully. The Cook is drunk, and the Manciple minces no words in telling him so: "thy visage is ful pale, / Thyn eyen daswen"; "thy breeth ful soure stynketh"; "see how he ganeth, lo, this dronken wight"; "fy, stynkyng swyn!" (IX [H] 30–31, 32, 35, 40). His description is vivid enough for the Cook to "wax wrooth and wraw" (IX [H] 46), be reduced to silence, and, finally, fall off his horse. Realizing the dangers of such open truth-telling, the Host is quick to remind the Manciple that the Cook may in the future have occasion to take revenge precisely where it will hurt most:

---

[11] Jordan, *Chaucer's Poetics* 162. Cf. Chaucer, *Troilus and Criseyde* 3.1635, where the loquacious Pandarus advises Troilus: "Bridle alwey wel thi speche and thi desir."

[12] Though S. S. Hussey refers to the tale's "lack of an obvious relation to its narrator or even to its own prologue," the prologue and tale are now generally viewed as related; see Hussey, *Chaucer: An Introduction* (London: Methuen, 1971) 141. Scattergood, for example, points out that "there is a coherence of subject matter, for both the Prologue and Tale are concerned with the necessity for self-control, particularly self-control in speech"; see "The Manciple's Manner of Speaking," *Essays in Criticism* 24 (1974): 124. Derek Pearsall comments that while "The parallels are certainly there, and intended to be observed," what they contribute to the tale is "nothing indispensable"; see Pearsall, *The Canterbury Tales* (London: Allen and Unwin, 1985) 243.

"I meene, he speke wole of smale thynges,
As for to pynchen at thy rekenynges,
That were nat honest, if it cam to preef." (IX [H] 73–75)

The Host's reminder of society's in-built powers of retaliation for open-ness brings immediate results. Not only does the Manciple cease insult-ing the Cook, but he claims he said it "in my bourde" (IX [H] 81) and proceeds to give the Cook more wine (IX [H] 82–86).

As though to draw our attention to the Manciple's action, the narra-tor remarks, "What nedeth hym? He drank ynough biforn" (IX [H] 89). The Manciple's earlier assertion, "Of me, certeyn, thou shalt nat been yglosed," is thus turned on its head: having begun by speaking the truth, the Manciple now not only takes advisement but denies his own criti-cism and becomes a collaborator in the evil he began by criticizing.

The Manciple's own tale concerns a crow who, like the Manciple himself in his prologue, tells the truth, but who, unlike the Manciple, suffers the consequences of his truthfulness. The crow has been taught to imitate human speech and, like Phebus himself, is peerless in song (IX [H] 131–38). He uses both skills to convey truthfully what he wit-nesses in Phebus's house, first with a song—"Cokkow! Cokkow! Cok-kow!" (IX [H] 243)—that puns on the wife's infidelity, and then, "by sadde tokenes and by wordes bolde" (IX [H] 258).

In both the Manciple's prologue and his tale, the protagonists know the truth and both speak it. Like the Manciple of the prologue, the crow reports the reality he sees. What follows, however, is not capitulation, but a punishment for truth-telling complete with the crow's banish-ment. Phebus's first response to the crow's words is to kill his wife, an action which brings a sorrow so intense it causes him to break "his mynstralcie" and "his arwes and his bowe" (IX [H] 267–69). He then turns on the crow and accuses him of treachery and flattery, or "tonge of scorpioun" (IX [H] 271), precisely the vice the crow was guiltless of.[13] Phebus, having destroyed his own power to make music, now de-stroys that power in the crow, both song and speech. Unlike the Manci-ple, who maintains his position in society by denying the truth and perpetuating the evil he began by criticizing, the crow speaks with dig-

---

[13] The scorpion as an image of treachery, particularly flattery, occurs also in the *Book of the Duchess* (636–41); the *Man of Law's Tale* (II [B¹] 404–6); and the *Merchant's Tale* (IV [E] 2057–60).

nity and suffers for it. His punishment is emphasized in the plot's con-
centration on Phebus's anger; we never return to the crow. The crow is
literally silenced; in social terms, he is disenfranchised.

Though both the Manciple's prologue and tale suggest that society
is not at ease with total truth, neither of the alternatives posed seems a
satisfactory solution to the dilemma of truth-telling. The crow's alternative has dignity, but ends in total failure. The Manciple's seems like a
dangerous capitulation. The third alternative, quietism, suggested by the
Manciple's mother in the moral, is not much better. While it brings
neither capitulation nor punishment, it denies free expression of what is
most human. But the solutions posed in the fables do not exhaust the
possibilities for confronting the problem. The alternatives suggested
within a work do not constitute a closed world. They exist in the structure of a coherent poem. The Manciple's prologue and tale imply yet
another alternative, that exercised by the poet himself. Chaucer everywhere in the tale draws our attention to creative expression. Both the
Manciple and the crow are explicitly tellers of tales; Phebus is defined
by his "mynstralcie" and singing. The fable closes with references to
"tale," "auctour," and "tidynges."[14]

This attention to artistic expression in the poem and its coincidence
with the poet's own craft concentrate our attention on the example of
Chaucer himself, a poet writing in the court of Richard II and conveying the truth in the most effective way possible. As we know, this task
was not always an easy one, especially in the late 1380s and '90s.[15] That
the *Manciple's Tale* reflects Chaucer's preoccupation with corruption in
the court and the reality that it "can be dangerous to lecture a king" is
suggested by Nevill Coghill, who senses the poem's political dimension
and describes it as a "little masterpiece" which ventures "on the criticism
of his hearers." Coghill concentrates on the poem's explicit advice, even
though offered "obliquely" through the "carefully constructed dummy"
of the Manciple:

> "The advice he gives has its cynical side, in that it concludes
> with a heavy warning against exposing oneself to the 'lo-
> sengeours' and 'totelere accusours,' who, as we know from

---

[14] The use of "tydynges" in reference to the poet and poetry is also found in the
House of Fame; see, for example, 641–60 and 1025–29.
[15] See my discussion in chap. 1, above.

the BF version of the *Prologue to The Legend of Good Women*
(D352–4) infested the Court."[16]

The poem's pertinence to fourteenth-century London is sensed, as well,
by Carl Lindahl, who comments that here "a manciple channels dangerous thoughts into a socially commendable tale which simultaneously
describes and deplores the limitations of speech that his creator knew
first hand."[17]

It is in the amplifications of the *Manciple's Tale* that we find the
most compelling evidence of Chaucer's concern with that contemporary
world. Superficially awkward, even backtracking, the amplifications
seem not to fit the Ovidian fable in which they are found. While it is
now generally recognized that they are not rhetorical "padding," their
purpose in the tale is still debated.[18] I suggest that the amplifications
describe a reality both within the poem and within the audience to
whom the tale is addressed, the society of the poet. If the amplifications
accurately describe Chaucer's world, it is noteworthy that the reality
they portray is precisely the reality not recognized by Phebus, the singer
or poet of the fable. So sharp is this disparity that the amplifications may
well constitute Chaucer's attempt to demonstrate the necessity of a poetic that combines elements of prologue and tale and thus eludes the

---

[16] See Nevill Coghill, "Chaucer's Narrative Art in the *Canterbury Tales*," in *Chaucer and Chaucerians: Critical Essays in Middle English Literature,* ed. Derek Brewer (University: U of Alabama P, 1966) 136–39.

[17] Carl Lindahl, *Earnest Games: Folkloric Patterns in the "Canterbury Tales"* (Blooming-ton: Indiana UP, 1987) 13. Chaucer's references to flattery are so frequent as to be a *topos* of his poetry: in addition to the F version of the *Prologue* to the *Legend of Good Women* (352–54), mentioned by Coghill, see the lament of the falcon in the *Squire's Tale* V (F) 499–628; the *Nun's Priest's Tale* VII (3325–30); the *Summoner's Tale* III (D) 2074–75—"Beth war, therfore, with lordes how ye pleye. / Syngeth *Placebo* and 'I shal, if I kan . . .' "—and Placebo in the *Merchant's Tale,* who has been "a court-man" all his life, has never contradicted "lordes of ful heigh estaat," and thinks "any conseillour" who presumes to do so is a "ful greet fool" (IV [E] 1492–1504).

[18] Hussey refers to the tale's "slight story, its evident rhetorical padding and its lack of any obvious relation to its narrator or even its own prologue" (*Chaucer: An Introduction* 141). Recent criticism of the tale has given more attention to its amplifications, agreeing on their tone, but usually considering them in relation to the character of the Manciple. One exception to this latter tendency is F. N. M. Diekstra in "Chaucer's Digressive Mode and the Moral of the Manciple's Tale," *Neophilologus* 67 (1983): 131–48. See also Alan M. F. Gunn's excellent discussion of amplification in *The Mirror of Love: A Reinterpretation of "The Romance of the Rose"* (Lubbock: Texas Tech P, 1952).

unpleasant alternatives presented in the poem to the dilemma of truth-telling.

Tonally of a piece, the amplifications describe a world of appetite and prejudice, where to lack caution and guile is not to survive. The amplifications throw us off track and fail to fulfill the promises they make. Narrative intrusions more than once demand that the reader refocus attention from the specific material of the fable to broader and more troublesome human issues. In the first amplification in the *Manciple's Tale*—on the futility of keeping a "shrewe, for it wol nat bee" (IX [H] 151)—the narrator announces, "But now to purpos as I first bigan" (IX [H] 155), implying that he will move back to plot. Instead, there follows the lengthiest amplification in the tale (IX [H] 160–95), drawing on the examples of "bryd," "cat," and "she-wolf," in their ascending order of wildness and "appetit" (IX [H] 182), to illustrate the desire for "libertee" (IX [H] 174) and the "dominacioun" of "lust" (IX [H] 181, 186). Though Phebus's wife has clearly provided the impetus for the lengthy amplification on the impossibility of restraining nature, the narrator issues a puzzling denial, asserting that these examples apply to men, "that been untrewe, and nothyng by women" (IX [H] 188). Such backtracking is pointedly reminiscent of the Manciple's with the Cook (IX [H] 81–85). But in a context which now alludes to the human propensity for "newfangelnesse" (IX [H] 193–95), this apparent backtracking directs us beyond the figures of the fable to a broader definition of "untrewe" and the troubling condition of society.[19] Men are unfaithful in their way much more than women are—"we ne konne in nothyng han plesaunce / That sowneth into vertu any while" (IX [H] 194–95).[20]

The examples of bird, cat, and she-wolf vividly demonstrate the dominance of nature and lust in society. In the lengthy amplification on "lemman" (IX [H] 205–37), language itself points us to the darker unevennesses of human nature and society. Though some see the Man-

---

[19] For another instance of this shift in gender, see *Troilus and Criseyde* 5.1779–83, a passage discussed briefly on p. 82, n.38 above.

[20] For a discussion of Chaucer's use of words like "sad" and "trewe," both found in the *Manciple's Tale,* see Derek Brewer, "Some Metonymic Relationships in Chaucer's Poetry," *Poetica* 1 (1974): 1–20; rpt. in *Chaucer: The Poet as Storyteller* (London: Macmillan, 1984) 37–53. See also J. D. Burnley, *Chaucer's Language and the Philosophers' Tradition* (Cambridge, Eng.: D. S. Brewer, 1979) 72–73 and 78–79; and Jill Mann, "Satisfaction and Payment in Middle English Literature," *Studies in the Age of Chaucer* 5 (1983): 17–48, esp. 38–41.

ciple's character reflected in this passage, its idea of discourse is consonant with that found elsewhere in the *Canterbury Tales*.[21] The narrator defends his use of the word "lemman" by reminding the reader of Plato's injunction that "the word moot nede accorde with the dede," or "the word moot cosyn be to the werkyng," and concludes by asserting that being a "boystous man, right thus seye I" (IX [H] 205–11).[22]

What begins as an explanation of "knavyssh," or crude, speech, metamorphoses into an extended statement on the relationship of speech to reality. Not only do words reflect on social circumstance, which determines whether one is a "lemman" or a "lady" (and here there is a sudden change in the gender of "lemman"), but they validate alternate versions of reality: we apply words of opposite meaning—"capitayn" or "outlawe"—to men who have done similar things, though on a different scale.[23] The world, impressed by the one's greater potential to destroy— "By force of meynee for to sleen dounright, / And brennen hous and hoom, and make al playn" (IX [H] 228–29)—calls him "capitayn" instead of "theef."[24]

Though Phebus represents all that is most civilized, he is out of

---

[21] See particularly the *General Prologue* I (A) 725–42, and the *Miller's Prologue* I (A) 3176–80. For a brief discussion of critical comment on the Manciple's use of "lemman," see Baker, ed., *The Manciple's Tale* 109–10.

[22] The use of "boystous" to defend plain-speaking and consonance between words and deeds has a contemporary parallel in the prologue of Thomas Usk's *Testament of Love,* where Usk refers to his "rude wordes and boistous," arguing that they, more than "semelyche colours," can "drawe togider to make the calthers therof ben the more redy to hent sentence." See *Chaucerian and Other Pieces,* ed. Walter W. Skeat, Supplement to *The Complete Works of Geoffrey Chaucer* (London, 1897), 7:1.

Editors' punctuation of Chaucer has helped to confuse the interpretation of the passage discussed here (IX [H] 203–11). F. N. Robinson, in *The Works of Geoffrey Chaucer,* 2nd ed. (Boston: Houghton, 1957), for example, puts a comma at the end of line 211; thus, "I am a boystous man, right thus seye I," introduces the discussion of "lady" and "lemman" that follows. *The Riverside Chaucer* has a colon after line 211, thereby also suggesting its connection to what follows. Context alone makes this punctuation questionable, for line 211 brings to a close the problem raised in line 205 and defended by reference to Plato in lines 207–10.

[23] Cf. the related instance of this diversity in the meaning of words in *Troilus and Criseyde* 3.395–406, particularly regarding "gentillesse" and "bauderye."

[24] In "Lak of Stedfastnesse" (with its "Lenvoy to King Richard"), the focus is similarly on society's perception of worth: ". . . among us now a man is holde unable, / But if he can by som collusioun / Don his neighbour wrong or oppressioun" (10–12). The shift to the plural—as in "for among *us* now"— occurs in the *Manciple's Tale* only once, and that is when what is really the theme of all the amplifications is explicitly equated

158

touch with the darker reality of nature and society described in the amplifications. He does not share society's skewed perception. He is described as embodying both active and contemplative virtue—he slew "Phitoun, the serpent" (IX [H] 109), and he can play on "every mynstralcie" (IX [H] 113) and surpass even the "kyng of Thebes, Amphioun" (IX [H] 116) in his singing. He is "the semelieste man / that is or was sith that the world bigan" (IX [H] 119–20) "fulfild of gentillesse, / Of honour, and of parfit worthynesse" (IX [H] 123–24). But he knows "no gile" and therefore suspects none (IX [H] 196–97). Especially as Phoebus's gullibility is portrayed as having consequences reaching far beyond his own fate, Boccaccio's comments in *De casibus* on the dangers of credulousness to the prince and the commonwealth are here most pertinent:

> Credulousness is the mother of errors, the stepmother of artifice, the cause of hatred, a precipice to fall over, and always the neighbor of repentance. If we are human, if we examine ourselves, if we are careful, we will follow the authority of ancient laws which abhorred ready credulousness.[25]

Phebus has not done what Boccaccio and others describe as most essential for the prince to do: that he master the arts of rhetoric, if only to enable him to read others, to recognize deception when it occurs.

Twice the narration makes Phebus's guilelessness specific and connects it with his fate and with the fate of "mynstralcie." The extended amplification on the power of appetite to drive out discretion—"Lo, heere hath lust his dominacioun, / And appetit fleemeth discrecioun" (IX [H] 181–82) is juxtaposed with Phebus's "jolitee," or civility. What juxtaposition alone would suggest, that such a world requires awareness and caution, the poetry then makes explicit. In spite of "al his jolitee," guilelessness invites deception:

with the society of the poet and the audience to whom the poem is addressed:

> Flessh is so newefangel, with meschaunce,
> That we ne konne in nothyng han plesaunce
> That sowneth into vertu any while. (193–95)

[25] Boccaccio, *De casibus,* trans. Louis Brewer Hall (New York: Ungar, 1965) 26. See my discussion in chapter 1, pp. 9–12.

> This Phebus, which that thoghte upon no gile,
> Deceyved was, for al his jolitee. (IX [H] 196–97)

Later, the crow yet more specifically connects Phebus's blindness with his civilized virtues, implying that without caution (or guile), none of them are worth a whit. The poetry is emphatic in its assertion that no amount of civility alone can prevent one's being deceived:

> "Phebus," quod he, "*for al* thy worthynesse,
> *For al* thy beautee and thy gentilesse,
> *For al* thy song *and al* thy mynstralcye,
> *For al* thy waityng, *blered in thyn ye*. . . ."[26] (IX [H] 249–52; italics mine)

Phebus's lack of guile has tragic consequences. Being deceived, this figure of "mynstralcye" will destroy not only his own creativity, by breaking his musical instruments (IX [H] 267–68), but also the crow's, a creativity he had painstakingly "fostred" (IX obH] 131):

> "Thou songe whilom lyk a nyghtyngale;
> Now shaltow, false theef, thy song forgon,
> And eek thy white fetheres everichon
> Ne nevere in al thy lif ne shaltou speke." (IX [H] 294–97)

In punishing the crow, in depriving the world of song and speech, Phebus even more fully punishes himself.

Beginning without perception of guile, Phebus ends in a total breakdown of perception. He describes his dead wife as "so *sad* and eek so *trewe*" (IX [H] 275; italics mine), using words that carry a certain moral weight elsewhere in Chaucer's poetry.[27] The one figure who has, in fact, been "trewe" and who has also been associated with the word "sadde"—"By sadde tokenes and by wordes bolde" (IX [H] 258)—is

---

[26] A similar emphasis on credulousness (with the image of blindness) is found in Books 2 and 3 of *Troilus and Criseyde*. Pandarus advises Criseyde, "While folk is blent, lo, al the tyme is wonne" (2.1743); and later, in the midst of Pandarus's great deliberations and preparations for the lovers's first meeting, the narrator remarks:

> "Now al is wel, for al the world is blynd
> In this matere, bothe fremde and tame." (3.528–29)

[27] See note 20, above.

repeatedly designated as "traitour" (IX [H] 271, 298), as "false" (IX [H] 292, 295), and as having told a "false tale" (IX [H] 293). The moral order has literally been reversed; black has become white, white black. The terrible consequences of Phebus's lack of guile suggest that not even the singer, nor especially the poet, can afford to be guileless. Given the darker side of human nature, the poet's lack leads to the loss of moral perception and the destruction of poetry itself.

The symmetry of plot in the Manciple's prologue and tale and the contrast between the dark world of the amplifications and the nature of Phebus's civility (which has everything but guile and the suspicion of it) directs us to the occupation and thus to the dilemma of the poet. Given human nature, truth-telling is highly problematic. Both the prologue and the tale demonstrate that society takes measures to protect itself from truth, continuously threatening retaliation small and large. The instinctive response of the crow to speak the truth openly and plainly, though it may maintain his dignity, is ultimately destructive to poetry itself. How, then, is the poet to speak the truth?

If the poet's craft provides the hypothetical and alternative fable, what is the difference between truth-telling in the *Canterbury Tales* and the Manciple's in his prologue or the crow's in the *Manciple's Tale*? Does the *Canterbury Tales* express truth, and if so, how does it manage this? Or, more generally, can poetic discourse be permitted to express truth, and if so, how? An answer may be found not only in the suggestion that Phebus would have been much better off having guile but also in an otherwise rather puzzling comment at the end of the Manciple's prologue.

Though we have just seen the dire effects of "the beste galon wyn in Chepe" (IX [H] 23) and have heard the narrator say, "What neded hym? He drank ynough biforn" (IX [H] 89), the Host now praises "good drynke" as something that can "turne rancour and disese / T'a-cord and love, and many a wrong apese" (IX [H] 96–97). He blesses Bacchus for turning "ernest into game" (IX [H] 99–100)[28] and thus suggests that truth is possible when tempered with delight. The poet's

---

[28] The words "ernest" and "game" are, of course, found together elsewhere in Chaucer's poetry; see the *House of Fame* 822 and the *Miller's Prologue* I (A) 3186. Bacchus is discussed by James Dean, who seems to read literally the critical lines "For that wol turne rancour and disese / T'acord and love, and many a wrong apese." See Dean, "The Ending of *The Canterbury Tales*," *Texas Studies in Literature and Language* 21 (1979): 17–33.

creations are metaphoric and guileful, like Bacchus they change truth into forms that can be conveyed excitingly but without threat. The hypothetical third fable, the fable of the poet, thus evades the conclusions reached in either of the explicit alternatives to the dilemma of truth-telling in the prologue and the tale. What makes Chaucer's poetic in the Manciple's prologue and tale different from its expression elsewhere in the *Canterbury Tales* is its attempt to demonstrate its own necessity.

Society—situated somewhere between the ideal world of Amphion, who walled Thebes with his singing (IX [H] 116–17), and a world in which God's "endelees goodnesse" is reduced to having "*walled* a tonge with teeth and lippes" (IX [H] 322–23)—requires a discourse and poetry roughly attuned to its nature. From the very beginning of the *Canterbury Tales,* Chaucer has drawn our attention to the fact that poetic discourse mirrors a reality imperfect or fallen. In the *General Prologue,* the narrator defends his discourse both by the example of Christ's "ful brode" speech in "hooly writ" (I [A] 739) and Plato's injunction that "the wordes moote be cosyn to the dede" (I [A] 742). If the poet's discourse is sometimes "rudeliche and large" (or, like the Manciple's, "boystous"), it is because it is true to the reality—"hir wordes and hir cheere"—which it reports (I [A] 725–38). We recall that in the *Miller's Prologue,* the narrator similarly insists on the poetic necessity to be inclusive, both in its discursive style and in its subject matter. Not to be would be to "falsen som of my mateere" (I [A] 3171–75). From the beginning, too, Chaucer's juxtaposition of styles and tales has suggested that the fabliau can describe human nature as well (if not better, according to the Miller) as the courtly romance. In all these instances (and by example), Chaucer would seem to be telling us that if the poet's words are sometimes "knavyssh," they nonetheless describe a truth in the best way possible.[29] Thus in the apparently awkward defense of "knavyssh speche," and particularly the defense of the word "lemman," we can sense the basis for a defense of the *Canterbury Tales* as a whole. By its very nature, Chaucer seems to be saying, poetry must use gross images to describe true things.[30]

Rather than abandoning human discourse and poetry in this penulti-mate *Canterbury* tale, Chaucer may be demonstrating how, even under

---

[29] On this subject, see also my discussion of the *Wife of Bath's Prologue,* esp. pp. 111–13, above.

[30] Scattergood points out that the frequent use of the word "lemman" elsewhere in the *Canterbury Tales* would suggest that if the word "was felt to be a coarse expression then it must have been only mildly so"; see "The Manciple's Manner of Speaking," *Essays in Criticism* 24 (1974): 139.

the most difficult of conditions, the poet can survive. The symmetry of prologue and tale raises the issue of truth-telling, but does not resolve it. The Manciple's warning against speaking at all, except in prayer, is spoken in a fiction that has all the guile that Phebus, the singer of his fable, lacks. By pointing us not only to the world within the poem but also, inevitably, to the world of the audience outside it, the amplifications demonstrate the necessity of guile. The *Manciple's Prologue and Tale* would seem to suggest that if the poet is to speak and to survive in a world in which "Flessh is so newefangel, with meschaunce" (IX [H] 193)—the world not perceived by Phebus, whose eye is "blered" for all his "worthynesse" (IX [H] 249–52)—the poet's creations necessarily require artfulness, if not guile. If Chaucer's *Manciple's Tale* exemplifies the guile it prescribes, it does so because there are conditions under which, as the tale itself tells us, it would be foolish not to.

9

Discourse and Closure in the
Canterbury Tales

Again and again over recent years, critics have expressed dissatisfaction with Chaucer's "unfinished" narrative endings. The assumption that his sense of closure should conform to medieval rhetorical tradition, with its heavy emphasis on structural beginnings and conclusions, would certainly account for such dissatisfaction. Why should a poet who is variously alert to this tradition violate one of its most basic and simple requirements? Why, too, would he culminate a career already strewn with "unfinished" poems with a work whose very narrative frame (and the storytelling game it proposes) requires inordinate attention to the problem of beginnings and endings, even of prologues and epilogues? Perhaps Chaucer is not so much uncomfortable with structural endings as impelled to explore the expectations they arouse and the power of their absence. The critical restiveness with his handling of endings may, indeed, reflect a sense of one of his most profound strategies. Conventional closure implies that discourse can settle some vivid issues of human experience—the result dreamed of in philosophy and politics generally. By refusing to supply such a closure, Chaucer focuses our interest instead on the processes of communication, on the dynamics of discourse as social interaction itself.

Critics who assume Chaucer's sense of closure to be conventional and formal find his endings consummately unsatisfying. Thus, for example, Elizabeth Salter contends that his "endings and reconciliations are often made in a spirit of stoicism or weariness, with rarely the sense that they are the ineluctable consequence of what has gone before, and often coming with surprising suddenness."[1] Piero Boitani complains that the *Parliament of Fowls, Troilus,* the *Legend of Good Women,* and the *Canterbury Tales* have "disturbing, unsatisfactory, ambiguous, problematic, incomplete conclusions."[2] Donald Rowe notes "the frequency with which Chaucer disappoints our expectations, especially when it comes to endings."[3] And Barry Windeatt quite explicitly points to structural considerations when he refers to "the strain and challenge that Chaucer found in inventing an appropriate close to the structures that he had created in his poems."[4]

The relation between closure and poetic structure that is presupposed in these comments has ample basis in modern critical theory as well as in medieval rhetoric. Since the publication in 1967 of Frank Kermode's *The Sense of an Ending,* closure has been discussed both as an organizing phenomenon of narrative and as an essential aspect of human experience. In *Poetic Closure: A Study of How Poems End* (1968), Barbara Herrnstein Smith argues that our "sense of closure is a function of the perception of structure, defining structure as "the product of all the principles, both formal and thematic, by which a poem is generated." She describes the conditions under which closure occurs and the role of closure in defining our experience of the poem: "closure occurs when the concluding portion of a poem creates in the reader a sense of appropriate cessation"; it "gives ultimate unity and coherence to the reader's experience of the poem by providing a point from which all the preceding elements may be viewed comprehensively and their relations grasped

---

[1] Elizabeth Salter, *Fourteenth-Century English Poetry: Contexts and Readings* (Oxford: Oxford UP, 1983) 116.

[2] Piero Boitani, *Chaucer and the Imaginary World of Fame* (Cambridge: Cambridge UP, 1984) 208.

[3] Donald Rowe, *Through Nature to Eternity: Chaucer's "Legend of Good Women"* (Lincoln: U of Nebraska P, 1988) 109.

[4] Barry A. Windeatt, "Literary Structures in Chaucer," in *The Cambridge Chaucer Companion,* ed. Piero Boitani and Jill Mann (Cambridge: Cambridge UP, 1986) 195. See also Jerold C. Frakes, " 'Ther is na moore to seye': Closure in the *Knight's Tale,*" *Chaucer Review* 22 (1987): 1–7.

as part of a significant design." And closure "reinforces the feeling of finality, completion, and composure which we value in all works of art."[5]

Subsequent studies of closure query such all-embracing assumptions as what "we value in all works of art" and the explicit valuation that Smith and others place on concepts like "completion," "composure," "unity," and "coherence." In discussing "the set of assumptions common to both Western ideas of history and Western ideas of fiction"— including "notions of narrative, of character, and of formal unity" and "the sense of an ending"—J. Hillis Miller implicitly exposes the degree to which our sense of closure is culturally and historically contingent.[6] There is also growing skepticism about the "totalizing powers of organization" that critics claim for closure.[7] Even the "metaphoric thrust" of the term has come under fire. Is closure, or even our sense of it, necessarily formal or structural? Is it not, as one critic contends, simply one of a number of "traditional spatial and temporal coordinates" (like "Inside/ Outside," "Before/During/After," "Beginning/End"), and is not our interest in it a response to "a modern intellectual climate characterized by decenteredness, isolation and absence of meaning . . ."?[8]

Most pertinent to what ultimately characterizes Chaucer's endings (and to the critical readings of these endings) are some observations that originate in feminist theory. Susan Winnett comments on "the gender bias in contemporary narratology" and finds that "the meanings generated through the dynamic relations of beginnings, middles, and ends in traditional narrative . . . never seem to accrue directly to the account of the woman" and that they point, at best, "toward a rereading that evaluates the ideology of narrative dynamics according to whose desire they serve." She suggests a serious questioning of "the determinants that

---

[5] Barbara Herrnstein Smith, *Poetic Closure: A Study of How Poems End* (Chicago: U of Chicago P, 1968) 4–6, 36.

[6] J. Hillis Miller, "Narrative and History," *English Literary History* 41 (1974): 455–73.

[7] D. A. Miller, *Narrative and Its Discontents: Problems of Closure in the Traditional Novel* (Princeton: Princeton UP, 1981) xiii–xiv. Though he is wary of the "totalizing powers of organization" that critics (including the Russian formalists, Jean-Paul Sartre, Frank Kermode, Roland Barthes, Gerard Genette, Julia Kristeva, and Charles Grivel) claim for closure, the phenomenon of closure nonetheless remains central in Miller's own analyses, especially when he speaks of a modern novelist's "evasion" of "traditional formal requirements of plot and ending" (195). For a brief summary of contemporary discussions of closure, see Wallace Martin, *Recent Theories of Narrative* (Ithaca: Cornell UP, 1986) 85–89.

[8] David F. Hult, preface to *Concepts of Closure, Yale French Studies* 67 (1984): iii–vi.

govern the mechanics of our narratives, the notion of history as a sense-making operation, and the enormous investment the patriarchy has in maintaining them."[9] Discerning a similar gender bias, Carolyn Dinshaw specifically relates closure to a "masculine reading" of *Troilus and Criseyde* and suggests that the structure imposed on the poem when one reads " 'like a man' . . . resolves or occludes contradictions and disorder, fulfills the need for wholeness." "Such rest and closure," she continues, "are what every ideology provides; but the problem with 'soothing and harmonious ideologies' is that they achieve their vision of wholeness by unacknowledged exclusion, elimination, constraint."[10]

As one would expect, however, the closure Smith describes as creating "appropriate cessation" and "ultimate unity" is profoundly traditional in medieval poetic theory, which inherits from the *Poetics*—along with classical rhetoric—the tradition of a beginning, a middle, and an end. Geoffrey of Vinsauf opens his *Poetria Nova* (ca. 1210) with an analogy between the planning and building of a house and the planning and structuring of poetry; subsequently he compares the greeting, entertaining, and leave-taking of guests to a poem's beginning, middle, and end:

> Let the beginning of your poem, as if it were a courteous servant, welcome in the subject matter. Let the middle, as if it were a conscientious host, graciously provide it hospitality. Let the ending, as if it were a herald announcing the conclusion of a race, dismiss it with due respect. In each section, let everything in its own way do honor to the poem; neither let anything in any section sink or in any way suffer eclipse.[11]

Dante also assumes a relation between closure and poetic structure: "that upon which the speaker doth purpose to lay chiefest stress," he asserts, "should ever be reserved for the last; because that which is last said doth most abide in the mind of the hearer."[12] Petrarch betrays a

---

[9] Susan Winnett, "Coming Unstrung: Women, Men, Narrative, and Principles of Pleasure," *PMLA* 105 (1990): 505–18; see esp. 506 and 516.

[10] Carolyn Dinshaw, *Chaucer's Sexual Poetics* (Madison: U of Wisconsin P, 1989) 51. Dinshaw acknowledges that she is "indebted to Burlin's view of the end of the poem," which takes "soothing and harmonious ideologies" from Erich Fromm's *Man for Himself* (New York: Rinehart, 1947). See Robert B. Burlin, *Chaucerian Fiction* (Princeton: Princeton UP, 1977) 133.

[11] Geoffrey of Vinsauf, *The New Poetics,* trans. Jane Baltzell Kopp, in *Three Medieval Rhetorical Arts,* ed. James J. Murphy (Berkeley: U of California P, 1971) 35.

[12] Dante, *Il convivio* 2.9, trans. Philip H. Wicksteed (London: Dent, 1931).

similar sentiment when, in a letter to Boccaccio, he confesses that he read "more carefully at the beginning and at the end" of the *Decameron.*[13] And Boccaccio himself announces, in the Prologue to the Fourth Day, that the incompleteness of his own "novella" in that section distinguishes it from others in the *Decameron.* By the time Chaucer, in *Troilus and Criseyde,* has Pandarus say to Criseyde, "Th'ende is every tales strengthe" (2.260), the relation between structure and closure is surely a cliché. After all, do not readers, like lovers, hope for a satisfying consummation?

Yet reality often frustrates such desires, and Chaucer, who was intensely aware of human aspiration and fallibility in other areas, may well have projected that sense of incompleteness into his perspective on conclusion as well. His apparent inability to close may be, instead, an artful and conscientious imitation of reality. In the hands of an innovative artist, closure—like other poetic conventions, as Smith has rightly pointed out—will reveal more than "the operation of its own laws."[14]

Chaucer's sense of closure, which indeed seems different from and more powerful than the traditional one, is intimately bound up with the idea of a *response* to the structural narrative itself. Though the conventional structural closure is everywhere signaled in the *Canterbury Tales,* Chaucer seems remarkably little content with it. The well-plotted *Knight's Tale* and *Miller's Tale* both signal conventional endings. The *Knight's Tale* receives a formal summary and the customary, if brief, prayer: "Thus endeth Palamon and Emelye; / And God save al this faire compaignye! Amen" (I [A] 3107–08). A similar signal is found in the *Miller's Tale*: "This tale is doon, and God save al the rowte!" (I [A] 3814). The lived-happily-ever-after "conclusions" of the *Wife of Bath's Tale* and the *Clerk's Tale* are hardly less formal signals. There is no question that Chaucer is fully aware of the convention of structural closure.

Of course, some of the ambiguity in Chaucer's closure—especially that which is caused by his delaying the ending past the purely structural close—comes from the medieval habit of moralizing. The rhetorical manuals, including Geoffrey of Vinsauf's *Poetria Nova,* all mention the use of *sententiae* at the beginning and end of a poem.[15] But though the

---

[13] Petrarch, *Epistolae rerum senilium* 17.3, in *Chaucer: Sources and Backgrounds,* ed. Robert P. Miller (New York: Oxford UP, 1977) 137–38.

[14] Smith, *Poetic Closure: A Study of How Poems End* 30.

[15] For a brief discussion of the treatment of beginnings and endings in Jean de Garlande (*Exempla vitae honestae*) and Matthieu de Vendôme (*Ars versificatoria*), as well as in

aim of a concluding *sententia* is to encapsulate the meaning of what has preceded, to intensify structural closure that is already present, Chaucer's *sententiae* more often do not. In the *Nun's Priest's Tale,* for example, the *sententia* concerning Paul and the interpretation of literature—along with the advice to "Taketh the fruyt, and lat the chaf be stille" (see VII 3436–37, 3443)—is belied by the experience of that tale. Indeed, every image and turn of this poem work against the closure of the *sententia,* as the poem dishes out, instead, delectable subtleties of "chaf" to eye and ear. The literary sophistication required by the poem's delightful mock-heroics suggest, at the least, a skeptical response to the denial of such pleasure.

In the *Physician's Tale,* the narrative comment on the punishment suffered by the offenders—"Heere may men seen how synne hath his merite" (VI [C] 277ff.)—seems awkward and trivial in the context of the events and the pathos just witnessed. The Manciple moralizes on his tale for fifty-one verses (IX [H] 311–62) by quoting his "dame" on the wisdom of "lasse spekyng" (IX [H] 336). The warning is remarkably ample, even repetitive, given its explicit thesis of verbal restraint: "My sone, thenk on the crowe, a Goddes name! / My sone, keep wel thy tonge, and keep thy freend" (IX [H] 318–19). In the context of the fable the Manciple has just rehearsed (and the tale-telling game it figures in), the admonition to restrain one's tongue "at alle tymes" (IX [H] 330) seems curious indeed. In the last chapter, I argued that this irony is illuminated by the implied presence of the author, who uses veils of fiction to combine the force of speech with the safety of silence. The Manciple's overt advice, while it may close the fiction, raises issues that cry for a hearing.

The *Clerk's Tale* is another striking example of a tale that "goes on" in other terms—in this instance, for some twelve stanzas, after its principals live happily ever after (see IV [E] 112–29). What follows the tale's structural "end" may seem simply to partake of the medieval habit of moralization, but it actually does much more. The narrative is closed in the process of generating responses to its own argument. This closing is in effect anti-closural. In rapid succession, the narrator imagines into his narrative a variety of listeners whose contrasting responses demonstrate the impossibility of closure. He reminds them how difficult it is to find

---

Vinsauf, see Edmond Faral, *Les Arts poétiques du XIIe et du XIIIe siècle* (Paris: E. Champion, 1924) 58–60.

"now-a-dayes / In al a toun Grisildis thre or two" (IV [E] 1164–65).
Whereas Griselda was "noght ameved / Neither in word or chiere, or
contenaunce" (IV [E] 498–99) by her husband's cruelty, the "Lenvoy"
exhorts the archwives, by contrast, to "Be ay of chiere as light as leef on
lynde, / And lat hym care, and wepe, and wrynge, and waille!" (IV [E]
1211–12).[16] Finally, there is in "the murye words of the Hoost" a pilgrim
listener's specific response to the tale, including his enigmatic, "As to
my purpos, wiste ye my wille; / But thyng that wol nat be, lat it be
stille" (IV [E] 1211f–12g).

In these responses, the narrative of Griselda's extreme "stedefasten-
esse" is placed in a social and psychological context that alerts us to its
limitations. Not a further commendation of Griselda's patience but,
rather, the reverse, the advice to the archwives would imply that any
absolute stance inevitably suggests its opposite. The successive "frames"
of this ending have recently been described as allowing "an exhilarating
effect of release."[17] I would suggest that they are exhilarating, not because they act as release, but because they irrevocably engage us in the
dialogical processes of discourse itself.

The tales as a whole show a surprising array of additional ways in
which Chaucer ignores, skirts, transcends, and even anticipates structural
closure in favor of an engagement between the narrative and its responding audience that fundamentally works against closure. Most easily recognized is a straight comment after a structurally closed piece (a
"closure" found most notably, before Chaucer's *Canterbury Tales,* in
Boccaccio's *Decameron*).[18] Even when such closure appears to intensify

---

[16] The "Lenvoy de Chaucer" (IV [E] 1177–1212) is, of course, Chaucer's addition
to his sources. There have been many theories as to the function of these final stanzas,
most influential among them being G. L. Kittredge's dramatic interpretation in his *Chaucer and His Poetry* (Cambridge: Harvard UP, 1951) 194–200.

[17] Windeatt, "Literary Structures in Chaucer," in *The Cambridge Chaucer
Companion* 202.

[18] Variously extensive and detailed, this kind of comment after a structurally closed
piece is a salient feature of the the *Decameron*. So, for example, before Neifile begins her
story (1.2), the comment on the Cepparello story (1.1): "Panfilo's story was praised in
its entirety by the ladies, and parts of it moved them to laughter; after all had listened
carefully and it had come to an end, the Queen ordered Neifile. . . ." And before
Fiammetta begins in 6.6: "The ladies were still laughing over the well-phrased and quick
reply made by Giotto when the Queen ordered Fiammetta to go on with the next
story. . . ." Of the relationship of the *Canterbury Tales* to Boccaccio's *Decameron,* Burlin
observes that we find in Chaucer "the increasing fascination of a new game, inspired
by Boccaccio and perhaps Sercambi, but carried to unprecedented dramatic length by

the structural closure already present, anti-closural forces often prevail. Thus the straight comment after the *Knight's Tale,* "In al the route nas ther yong ne oold / That he ne seyde it was a noble storie / . . . And namely the gentils everichon" (I [A] 3110–13), voices the social exclusion that will account for the Miller's subsequent, "I kan a noble tale for the nones, / With which I wol now quite the Knyghtes tale" (I [A] 3126–27).

More extended and particularized instances of this kind of closure would include the Merchant's comparison of his own "wyf the passyng crueltee" to "Grisildis grete pacience" after the structural close of the *Clerk's Tale,* and the Host's similar response after the structural close of the *Merchant's Tale*: "Now swich a wyf I pray God kepe me fro!" (IV [E] 2420). The issue of marriage raised by both these closures recurs, of course, throughout the *Canterbury Tales,* especially in the so-called "marriage group," first described in detail by George Lyman Kittredge.[19] The prayer that accompanies the signal of structural close in the *Wife of Bath's Tale*—"And thus they lyve unto hir lyves ende / In parfit joye" (III [D] 1257–58)—goes on to decenter the discourse it presumably closes. If the late events of the Wife's tale suggest an equilibrium between the sexes, the prayer, a benediction turned malediction, declares woman's ascendancy and rebellion: "And olde and angry nygardes of dispence, / God sende hem soone verray pestilence!" (see III [D] 1258—64). Closure here consists of the narrator's own commentary on her tale and a reopening of the issues of the Wife's prologue and tale. A variation on this closure occurs in the *Summoner's Prologue,* where the vivid anecdote about Satan's tail at least temporarily closes the foregoing *Friar's Tale,* which so angers the Summoner "that lyk an aspen leef he quook for ire" (III [D] 1667).

Rarely is Chaucer done with a tale at its structural close, nor are his readers. In the *Franklin's Tale,* the conventional *demande* or *jugement* offered to the audience, "Lordynges, this question, thanne, wol I aske now / Which was the mooste fre, as thynketh yow?" (V [F] 1621–22), is an obvious example of the structural closure's merging with, or giving way to, a transaction with the listeners and envisioning a comment from

---

Chaucer" (*Chaucerian Fiction* 151). A brief but comprehensive discussion titled "The Genre of the Story-Collection" can be found in Helen Cooper, *The Structure of The Canterbury Tales* (Athens: U of Georgia P, 1984) 8–55.

[19] See Kittredge, *Chaucer and His Poetry* 185–211.

them.[20] The perfect "gentillesse" (see V [F] 1595–1612) of each character would suggest that the debate over "which was the *mooste* fre"—even with the question's implication of hierarchy and resolution—cannot be resolved and that Chaucer's interest lies, rather, in precipitating the discussion and mental ferment implied by "as thyketh yow?"

The same sort of transaction with the audience marks the endings of three of Chaucer's tales that do not in fact come to structural closure at all. The *Squire's Tale* is followed by "the wordes of the Frankeleyn to the Squier." What the Franklin calls "a word or two" (V [F] 701) is actually twenty-one lines that remark on the Squire's eloquence—"In feith, Squier, thow hast thee wel yquit / And gentilly" (V [F] 674–75)—and express the Franklin's concern for his own son. The tale of *Sir Thopas* is interrupted by the Host's "Namoore of this, for Goddes dignitee" (see VII 919ff.), and the *Monk's Tale* by the Knight's "Hoo! . . . good sire, namoore of this!"—which the Host soon seconds (VII 2767, 2780).[21] Although the attractive dramatics of these interruptions may make them seem to be extraneous incidents on the pilgrimage, they are actually, like the Franklin's comment on the *Squire's Tale,* quite specific responses by the audience to the style or content of the narratives themselves. The illusion of realism—the narrative appearing to be unfinished because it is interrupted—underscores Chaucer's innovative sense of closure. If his artful and various uses of narrative in the tales—and the listeners' responses in the links—are seen as continuous, the *Sir Thopas* ends, not with the Host's interruption but with the end of the audience engagement that follows it. Similarly, the *Monk's Tale* is less an unfinished tale than a fiction whose stance shifts abruptly to consider the problem of the listener.

Closure in the *Canterbury Tales* can also be delayed: a tale is sometimes completed, after its structural closure, with the comment supplied by the tale immediately following. Within the eight *Canterbury* fragments that each comprise two or more tales, one narrative seems to close its predecessor—in some cases more clearly and pointedly than in others. Often invited and made explicit by the text itself—e.g., "I kan a noble tale for the nones, / With which I wol now quite the Knyghtes tale"

---

[20] For another instance of the *demande* or *jugement* offered to the audience, see the end of the first part of the *Knight's Tale* (I [A] 1347–54): "Yow loveres axe I now this questioun: / Who hath the worse, Arcite or Palamoun?"

[21] See my discussion of these lines and the *Prologue of the Nun's Priest's Tale* in chapter 7 above.

(I [A] 3126–27)—this kind of delayed closure, often discussed in terms of Chaucer's dramatics, is a commonplace of Chaucer criticism. Thus, to note only a few examples, we may recall that the *Miller's Tale* (further) closes the *Knight's Tale*, the *Reeve's Tale* the *Miller's*, and the *Summoner's* the *Friar's*. On the juxtaposition of the *Canon's Yeoman's Tale* and the *Second Nun's Tale*, Charles Muscatine points out that "there is something more than coincidence in the contrast between St. Cecilia, unharmed in her bath of flames, conquering fire through faith, and the blackened, sweating believers in earth, whose fire blows up in their faces."[22] In general, this contiguity of tales and points of view undermines closure and suggests, as Paul Strohm observes, "that the truth about a subject is not unitary or closed, but is open and additive and can best be approached by entertaining a variety of points of view."[23]

Chaucer's play with closure adds complexity to individual tales and appreciably deepens one's sense of his irony and meaning in the *Canterbury Tales* as a whole. In the *Summoner's Tale,* closure proceeds in a complicated sequence that makes it all but impossible to define the location of the structural close. The story of the friar's gift of Thomas's fart (III [D] 2139ff.) is retold and commented on at least three times before the definitive structural "end" of the tale. In each instance, an audience within the *Summoner's Tale* comments on the events of the narrative and gives the tale a provisional closure. First the friar tells his "odious meschief" (III [D] 2190) to a "worthy man was lord of that village" (III [D] 2165). The response to the tale broadens to include that of the suddenly present "lady of the hous" who "ay stille sat / Til she had herd what the frere sayde" (III [D] 2200–1). Her observation that "a cherl hath doon a cherles dede" (III [D] 2206) is then expanded by her husband's. When the friar reveals the charge put on him—"To parte that wol nat departed be / To every man yliche" (III [D] 2214–15)—the lord launches into

---

[22] Charles Muscatine, *Chaucer and the French Tradition* (Berkeley: U of California P, 1957) 216.

[23] Paul Strohm, "Form and Social Statement in *Confessio amantis* and the *Canterbury Tales*," *Studies in the Age of Chaucer* 1 (1979): 35–36. The juxtaposition of the *Canon's Yeoman's Tale* and the *Second Nun's Tale* is further developed by Bruce A. Rosenberg in "The Contrary Tales of the Second Nun and the Canon's Yeoman," *Chaucer Review* 2 (1968): 278–91. The most frequently discussed juxtaposition is surely that of the *Knight's* and *Miller's Tales*; for a brief summary of the ways in which the former comments on the latter, see Constance B. Hieatt, ed., the *Miller's Tale* (New York: U of Western Ontario P, 1970) 4–5 and (bibliography) 55–60. For juxtaposition in the fragments of the *Canterbury Tales*, see Larry Sklute, *The Virtue of Necessity: Inconclusiveness and Narrative Form in Chaucer's Poetry* (Columbus: Ohio State UP, 1984), particularly chap. 6.

an extended tour de force of amplification on the amazing wit, if not mystery, of both the source and the expression of the problem the friar describes (III [D] 2216–42). This response, and the direction in which it takes the humor and the satire, is in turn developed further when the "lordes squier" provides yet another perspective on the narrative. Before the matter is finally closed, we also hear the opinions of "the lord, the lady, and ech man, save the frere" to what the squire "Jankyn spak, in this matere" (III [D] 2287–88).

In Chaucer's closure, in this extended process of response and comment, a private joke on the friar turns into a public one. Justice would seem to have come full circle with the gift of the fart and the friar's justifiable anger. In delightfully, and convincingly, extending the story beyond the private joke, Chaucer amplifies its satiric impact. The joke on the friar becomes progressively more social as each of his listeners hears and responds to the story of the "odious meschief" (III [D] 2190) perpetrated by "this false blasphemour" (III [D] 2213). Since the friar's typical earnings depend heavily on a discourse that is by definition not subjected to open commentary and cannot be verified—"glosynge" (III [D] 1790–93); "revelacioun" (III [D] 1854–68); "orisons" and the knowledge of "Cristes secree thynges" (III [D] 1870–71)—the publicity and commentary on Thomas's gift in the tale's closure seem particularly apt.

Closure, paradoxically, can also consist of comments that anticipate the literary construct they precede. Sometimes they provide at least one way of interpreting the discourse that follows. There are many instances of such anticipatory remarks in the *Canterbury Tales,* including those in prologues like the Reeve's, the Clerk's, and the Miller's, where the narrator's "And therfore, whoso list it nat yheere, / Turne over the leef and chese another tale" (I [A] 3176–77) surely signals a potential closure. The most piquant example, however, may well occur in the *Canon's Yeoman's Prologue,* where the Canon actually responds to the Yeoman's story before it is narrated. The Canon, who "drough hym neer and herde al thyng" (VIII [G] 685), is suspicious of the discourse, and indeed, of all discourse, or "mennes speche" (VIII [G] 687). Ordering the Yeoman to "spek no wordes mo" under pain of reprisal (VIII [G] 693), the Canon tells him, "Thou . . . discoverest that thou sholdest hyde" (VIII [G] 695–96). When the Canon sees that he cannot prevent the tale-telling, he flees "for verray sorwe and shame" (VIII [G] 702). His flight in itself establishes the subsequent disclosures as controversial and provides a significant comment on them.

In all these closures, Chaucer moves consistently—and sometimes abruptly—from speaker to listener, performer to audience. No performance in the *Canterbury* frame more fully illustrates this sense of discourse and its reception as a continuum than does the *Pardoner's Prologue and Tale*. Though its closure is roughly a variation on the type achieved through the narrator's comments on his or her own tale, it can also be described as both indefinite and compound. Here the engagement with an audience is virtually the Pardoner's theme, part of the literary structure of the prologue and tale, and thus from the first difficult to distinguish from that structure itself.

The ending of the tale (VI [C] 893ff.) is an astonishing series of forestalled closures. The Pardoner first indicates the close of his tale of the three rioters:

> Thus ended been thise homycides two,
> And eek the false empoysonere also. (VI [C] 893–94)

But Chaucer has already foreclosed the possibility of so simple and forthright an ending. The achieved telling of the tale is secondary to its instrumentality in moving the peasant audience. And so the Pardoner goes on with his emotional commentary, which begins

> O cursed synne of alle cursednesse!
> O traytours homycide, O wikkednesse!
> O glotonye, luxurie, and hasardrye! (VI [C] 895–87)—

and with his offering of pardon:

> Youre names I entre heer in my rolle anon;
> Into the blisse of hevene shul ye gon.
> I yow assoille, by myn heigh power,
> Yow that wol offre, as clene and eek as cleer
> As ye were born. (VI [C] 911–15)

This ending, however structurally licit, is compromised in turn because the Pardoner uses the revelation of his power over a peasant audience as a means of engaging the pilgrims as well. The next "ending" will thus add another social dimension to the tale's meaning, and also, quite unexpectedly and most movingly, another psychological dimension:

> . . . And lo, sires, thus I preche.
> And Jhesu Crist, that is oure soules leche,
> So graunte yow his pardoun to receyve,
> For that is best; I wol yow nat deceyve. (VI [C] 915–18)

The power and appeal of structural closure here would appear to be almost irresistible. The poem is already a masterpiece of characterization. But Chaucer is still not finished with it:

> But, sires, o word forgat I in my tale:
> I have relikes and pardoun in my male,
> As faire as any man in Engelond,
> Whiche were me yeven by the popes hond.
> If any of yow wole, of devocion,
> Offren and han myn absolucion,
> Com forth anon. . . . (VI [C] 919–25)

This ensuing denial of closure—adding either bottomless cynicism or misplaced humor to the Pardoner's portrait—deepens yet again the tale's psychological complexity, and opens the poem to further social commentary that the Pardoner can neither predict nor contain. For by inviting the Host and pilgrims to "offre," he has equated them with the peasants who have been the butt of his confession. In the backwash of the Host's devastating response (which is yet another possible closing), the Pardoner finally loses control of his discourse altogether: "So wroth he was, no word ne wolde he seye" (VI [C] 957). Our sense of an ending is satisfied at last by the Knight's peaceable reconciling of the two antagonists, and here we fully accept, with Chaucer, the essential importance of the listener's response in the makeup of human discourse.

This emphasis on response in the treatment of discourse is surely due in part to the period in which Chaucer wrote. His work is what Walter J. Ong describes as "early writing": "Generally speaking, literature becomes itself slowly, and the closer in time a literature is to an antecedent oral culture, the less literary or 'lettered' and the more oral-aural it will be."[24] The originality of narrative in an oral culture, in Ong's words, "lodges not in making up new stories but in managing a particular interaction with this audience at this time" and causing that audience to respond "vigorously."[25] While there is, of course, no question that Chaucer is writing a book—"Turne over the leef and chese another tale" (I [A] 3177)—his poetry has "residues" of an oral discourse: its amplifications, its occasional inconsistencies, its providing the reader, as Ong puts it, with "conspicuous helps for situating himself imaginatively." In both the *Decameron* and the *Canterbury Tales,* the frame story presents "fictional groups of men and women telling stories to one another . . . so that the reader can pretend to be one of the listening company."[26]

Nevertheless, the *Canterbury Tales* does not so much perpetuate an oral tradition as artfully imitate it. Indeed, the frame story intensifies the illusion of oral delivery, most powerfully by the interruption of narratives. Narrators also remark on their own rhetorical skills: the Squire draws attention to himself as speaker when he says, "It lyth nat in my tonge, n'yn my konnyng" (V [F] 35–42), as does the Franklin when he excuses himself for his "rude speche" (V [F] 718). In the *Clerk's,* the *Monk's,* and the *Nun's Priest's Tales,* among others, a present audience is also explicitly indicated when the narrators break in to address the listeners directly: "But o word, Lordynges, herkneth er I go" (IV [E] 1163); "Lordynges, ensample heerby may ye take" (VII 2239); and "Now goode men, I prey yow herkneth alle" (VII 3402). Sustained attention to the listener, as listener, is found as well in the events of the tales themselves. Notable examples are the court's responses to the strange knight in the *Squire's Tale* and the subjective miscommunication between Chaunticleer and Pertelote in the *Nun's Priest's Tale.*[27]

---

[24] Walter J. Ong, *Rhetoric, Romance, and Technology* (Cornell: Cornell UP, 1971) 25.

[25] Walter J. Ong, *Orality and Literacy: The Technologizing of the Word* (London: Methuen, 1982) 41–42.

[26] *Orality and Literacy* 103. The oral aspects of Chaucer's style have also been noted by Derek Brewer, who reminds us as well, however, that Chaucer "insists on the preservation of the detailed precision of his words and metrical forms in a way very unlike that of the truly oral poet"; see Brewer, *Chaucer: The Poet as Storyteller* (London: Macmillan, 1984) 79. See particularly *Troilus and Criseyde* 5.1793–99 and "Chaucers Wordes unto Adam, His Owne Scriveyn."

[27] The pervasive presence of audience in Chaucer's poetry is demonstrated in critical attempts to distinguish these "audiences" as fictional, implied, intended, and actual (see Paul Strohm, "Chaucer's Audience(s): Fictional, Implied, Intended, Actual," *Chaucer Review* 18 [1983]: 137–45), but there has as yet been no explanation for this "*presence of*

This consciously imitated oral quality shows Chaucer's pronounced interest in the social interactions of discourse. The *Canterbury Tales* does, as Ong says, provide fictive listeners with whom the reader can identify, but it goes beyond this. It also shows a consciousness of the psychology and the politics of their listening, of the processes that generate discourse or close it off. The Host, having suffered the "pitous tale" (VI [C] 302) of the Physician, calls for "triacle / Or elles a draughte of moyste and corny ale" (VI [C] 314–15) or "a myrie tale" (VI [C] 316), and the Knight, who interrupts the *Monk's Tale,* is unabashed in his dislike for narratives describing a "sodeyn fal" (VII 2773), asserting his preference for their opposite, for tales of folks who abide "in prosperitee" (VII 2777). The Friar and the Summoner's predictable rivalry, which surfaces in their squabble over the length of the Wife of Bath's "preambulacioun" (III [D] 837) in her prologue, constitutes only one of the many instances in which Chaucer finds misunderstanding as fascinating as understanding, if not more so. When the Wife of Bath closes her tale by returning to the issues of her prologue, she, like the narrator of the *Clerk's Tale,* points us to a discourse that revels in irresolution rather than resolution, in aperture rather than closure.

This view would seem to cast doubt on well-known recent readings that attempt to explain the *Tales* as a whole on the basis of one tale, or of the movement toward it. In these readings, as noted in Chapter 8, the

---

an audience as well as a poet" in Chaucer's work (Julian N. Wasserman and Robert J. Blanch, eds., *Chaucer in the Eighties* [Syracuse: Syracuse UP, 1986] xvi).

For general theoretical discussions on text and audience that bear on Chaucer, see Hans Georg Gadamer, *Truth and Method* (New York: Crossroads, 1985); Wolfgang Iser, *The Act of Reading: A Theory of Aesthetic Response* (Baltimore: Johns Hopkins UP, 1978); and Hans Robert Jauss, *Aesthetic Experience and Literary Hermeneutics,* trans. Michael Shaw (Minneapolis: U of Minnesota P, 1982). On the whole subject, see Bertrand Bronson, "Chaucer's Art in Relation to His Audience," in *Five Studies in Literature* (Berkeley: U of California P, 1940); Ruth Crosby, "Chaucer and the Custom of Oral Delivery," *Speculum* 13 (1938): 413–38; Dieter Mehl, "The Audience of Chaucer's Troilus and Criseyde," in *Chaucer and Middle English Studies in Honor of Rossell Hope Robbins,* ed. B. Rowland (London: Allen and Unwin, 1974) 173–89; Anne Middleton, "The Idea of Public Poetry in the Reign of Richard II," *Speculum* 53 (1978): 94–114; Walter J. Ong, "The Writer's Audience Is Always a Fiction," *PMLA* 90 (1975): 9–21; Derek A. Pearsall, "The Troilus Frontispiece and Chaucer's Audience," *Yearbook of English Studies* 7 (1977): 68–74; Pearsall, *The Canterbury Tales* (London: Allen and Unwin, 1985); Edmund Reiss, "Chaucer and His Audience," *Chaucer Review* 14 (1980): 390–402; Paul Strohm, "Chaucer's Audience," *Literature and History* 5 (1977): 26–41; Strohm, "Chaucer's Audience(s): Fictional, Implied, Intended, Actual," *Chaucer Review* 18 (1983) 137–45; Strohm, *Social Chaucer* (Cambridge: Harvard UP, 1989) 47–83; and W. Daniel Wilson, "Readers in Texts," *PMLA* 96 (1981): 848–63.

Canon's Yeoman's, the *Second Nun's,* and the *Manciple's Tales* are regarded as preparing for the *Parson's Tale* and having "the effect of an ironical *De contemptu mundi*—they let us see the vanity of earthly pursuits, the mutability of human deeds, the disappointing uselessness of human striving, the corruptness of human nature."[28] The *Manciple's Tale* is seen as preparing us "for the Parson not just by rehearsing one of the fables the Parson is going to reject but by casting doubt upon the whole poetic enterprise"; the Parson's "sacramental language of penance" acts finally to define and unify everything that has gone before.[29]

By asserting this hierarchy and resolution, and claiming that "all the individual Canterbury tales must be seen in the context of the last, the *Parson's Tale,*"[30] such readings are of course consistent with Smith's description of structural closure. But Chaucer's more innovative, if not radical, treatment of closure throughout the *Canterbury Tales* would seem to counsel against these interpretations. They may reflect not so much Chaucer's intention as the readers' assumption that "finality," "completion," and "composure" must inhere in the very structure of poetry.[31]

If the Retraction belongs where we find it, the *Parson's Tale* emphatically does not "knytte up al this feeste and make an ende" (X [I] 47).[32]

---

[28] Donald Howard, *The Idea of the Canterbury Tales* (Berkeley: U of California P, 1976) 304. See my discussion of this view in relation to the *Manciple's Tale,* in chapter 8 above.

[29] Lee Patterson, "The *Parson's Tale* and the Quitting of the *Canterbury Tales,*" *Traditio* 34 (1978): 377–79. The earliest instance of this trend in Chaucer criticism to assert the structural closure of the *Canterbury Tales*—along with thematic unity—is Ralph Baldwin's *The Unity of "The Canterbury Tales"* (Anglistica, vol. 5 Copenhagen: Rosenkilde and Bagger, 1955): "For though the *Canterbury Tales* is incomplete, it cannot be properly called unfinished. The ending is as neatly calculated as the beginning. Even the conventional opening metaphor, the springtime, has fostered one conspicuous, symbolic tree, the tree of Penitence, whose roots thrust through and whose branches overspread the world of the Canterbury pilgrims" (110). See also Howard, *The Idea of the Canterbury Tales* 304, 385–87; and V. A. Kolve, *Chaucer and the Imagery of Narrative: The First Five Canterbury Tales* (Stanford: Stanford UP, 1984) 369–71.

[30] Florence Ridley, "The State of Chaucer Studies: A Brief Survey," *Studies in the Age of Chaucer* 1 (1979): 14.

[31] We recall Carolyn Dinshaw's observation that reading *Troilus and Criseyde* "like a man" imposes a structure that is not necessarily Chaucer's (*Chaucer's Sexual Poetics* 51).

[32] Peter W. Travis considers Chaucer's use of language in the Retraction as "substantially different than that which deconstructionists are wont to employ and attack" and refers to the Retraction as "an illustration of the 'pragmatics' of language, demonstrating how the meaning of every utterance is actively constructed in a complex exchange that adheres to rules both conventional and 'free,' between speaker and listener, author and reader." See Travis, "Deconstructing Chaucer's Retraction," *Exemplaria* 3.1 (Spring 1991): 150.

Moving out from the built-in, fictional audience of the Canterbury pilgrimage, Chaucer addresses yet another audience, listeners or readers. Even here, where one might most ardently look for conventional closure or summation, the discourse is reciprocal:

> Now preye I to hem alle that herkne this litel tretys or rede, that if ther be any thyng in it that liketh hem, that therof they thanken our Lord Jhesu Crist. . . . And if ther be any thyng that displese hem, I preye hem also that they arrette it to the defaute of myn unkonnynge and nat to my wyl. . . . Wherfore I biseke yow mekely. . . .

The passage is at once a bow to conventional expectation and an escape from it. In thus asking the audience to complete the text, Chaucer again evades structural closure in favor of a continuing process that involves listener as well as speaker, reader as well as writer. In this light, it also seems highly doubtful that Chaucer, had he ever "completed" the tales and brought his pilgrims back to the Tabard, could have prevented a discussion (if not a brawl) revolving around Harry Bailly's decision on the best performance. Launched with a plan for closure, with the Host to judge "which of yow that bereth hym *best of alle*" (I [A] 796; italics mine), the tales expose us, rather, to the manifold forces—delightful, troublesome, and inevitable—that make such closure all but impossible.

Chaucer's sense both of the reciprocity of discourse and of the relation of discourse to closure is by no means evident only in the *Canterbury Tales* or in the works that are nominally "unfinished." It seems, rather, to be a deep-seated instinct or conviction that is present in the whole Chaucer corpus. Apparent in his treatment of the *Book of the Duchess* and in his dream visions generally, it takes various forms throughout his career, surfacing most notably in *Troilus and Criseyde,* where the narrator is both speaker and listener, at once the source of the narrative and part of the audience for the story he tells. It is an instinct, finally, to which we might attribute Chaucer's most characteristic narrative convention, the frame narration that finds extensive and successful expression in the *Canterbury Tales.*

Looking back at Chaucer's early frame narratives from the perspective of the *Canterbury Tales,* one finds in each of them an emphasis on communication and response that could, in itself, account for their typical disinclination to closure. The *Book of the Duchess* is only the first of many poems in which Chaucer's interest in the communicative interplay (here between the frame's dreamer-narrator and the Black Knight in the dream) counsels against closure. These tendencies are present as well in the *Parliament of Fowls,* in which choices and decisions are repeatedly deferred and the main issue, the formel eagle's selection of a mate, is never resolved. Both highly dialogic, especially in their framing, the *House of Fame* and the *Legend of Good Women* are simply unfinished, whether intentionally or not.

Always a means of concentrating on discourse as a generative transaction between speaker and listener, the frame narrative is most fully realized in the *Canterbury Tales.* Here, in a context that seeks to approximate living speech, the frame amply accommodates Chaucer's sense of discourse as a reciprocal process that evolves rather than one that reaches a conclusion. The fictive frame provides Chaucer with a whole gamut of narrative voices and audience responses and with the psychological and social mechanisms that bring those responses into play. His pilgrims supply the interruptions and competitions, the exposures and self-exposures, the sympathies and enmities that underlie communication and miscommunication. In short, they everywhere exemplify the social dynamics that militate against simple resolution. As treated in the *Canterbury Tales,* discourse *requires* a listener as well as a speaker. It cannot be closed without that listener's active participation. The degree to which Chaucer varies the sense of closure, and thus the manner and placement of audience reception, may contribute to masking a theme of substantial importance. Indeed, on the evidence of a text variously and persuasively attentive to the engagement between speaker and audience, the *Canterbury Tales* seems not so much a drama, or a "drama of style,"[33] as a drama of the reception of discourse.

Chaucer shares with the humanists the idea of speech as a map of human character and a way of reading society. He presents in the *Canterbury Tales* a copia of the human motives—social, psychological, and political—that generate alternately communication and misunderstanding. What is his alone, however, is the inference that the connection between speech and human nature makes closure, be it fictive or theoretical, all but impossible; and his treatment of closure, in turn, is only one feature of a whole poetic that is at bottom dialogic and social. The denial of

---

[33] C. David Benson, *Chaucer's Drama of Style: Poetic Variety and Contrast in the Canterbury Tales* (Chapel Hill: U of North Carolina P, 1986).

structural closure in the *Canterbury Tales* is characteristic of Chaucer's attitude toward inquiry and knowledge generally. In his epistemology, nothing is ever complete. This view is suggested not so much by direct statement as by the geography of his discourse; it is a world characterized by interaction, dialectical relations, and open process. This is the deepest implication of the early humanists' theory of discourse, and Chaucer is the only one to have realized it fully.

BIBLIOGRAPHY

Abelard, Peter. *Letters of Direction*. In *The Letters of Abelard and Heloise,* trans. Betty Rad-
ice. New York: Penguin, 1974.
Amodio, Mark C. "Oral Poetics in Post-Conquest England." In *Oral Poetics in Middle
English Poetry,* ed. Mark C. Amodio, 1–28. New York: Garland, 1994.
Aquinas, St. Thomas. *Truth.* vol. 1. Trans. Robert W. Mulligan, S. J. Chicago: Regnery,
1952.
Ashley, Kathleen M. "Renaming the Sins: A Homiletic Topos of Linguistic Instability
in the *Canterbury Tales.*" In *Sign, Sentence, Discourse: Language in Medieval Thought and
Literature,* ed. Julian N. Wasserman and Lois Roney, 272–89. Syracuse: Syracuse UP,
1989.
Augustine, Saint. *The Confessions of St. Augustine.* Trans. Rex Warner. New York: New
American Library, 1963.
Baker, Donald C., ed. *The Manciple's Tale.* In *A Variorum Edition of the Works of Geoffrey
Chaucer.* Vol. 2, pt. 10. Norman: U of Oklahoma P, 1984.
Bakhtin, M. M. "Discourse in The Novel." In *The Dialogic Imagination: Four Essays,* ed.
Michael Holquist. Trans. Caryl Emerson and Michael Holquist, 259–422. Austin: U
of Texas P, 1981.
Baldwin, Ralph. *The Unity of "The Canterbury Tales."* Anglistica, vol. 5 Copenhagen:
Rosenkilde and Bagger, 1955.
Baron, Hans. *In Search of Florentine Civic Humanism: Essays on the Transition from Medieval
to Modern Thought.* 2 vols. Princeton: Princeton UP, 1988.
———. *The Crisis of the Early Renaissance.* Princeton: Princeton UP, 1955.
Bellamy, J. G. *The Law of Treason in England in the Later Middle Ages.* Cambridge Studies
in English Legal History. Cambridge: Cambridge UP, 1970.
Bennett, J. A. W. *"The Parlement of Foules": An Interpretation.* Oxford: Clarendon, 1957.
Benson, C. David. *Chaucer's Drama of Style: Poetric Variety and Contrast in "The Canter-
bury Tales."* Chapel Hill: U of North Carolina P, 1986.
———. *Chaucer's Troilus and Criseyde.* London: Unwin Hyman, 1990.
Berger, Harry, Jr. "The F Fragment of *The Canterbury Tales:* Part I." *Chaucer Review* 1
(1966–67): 88–102.
Besserman, Lawrence. " 'Glossynge Is a Glorious Thyng': Chaucer's Biblical Exegesis."
In *Chaucer and Scriptural Tradition,* ed. David Lyle Jeffrey, 65–73. Ottawa: U of Ot-
tawa P, 1984.

Bird, Ruth. *The Turbulent London of Richard II*. London: Longmans, 1949.

Bloomfield, Morton. *The Seven Deadly Sins: An Introduction to the History of a Religious Concept*. East Lansing: U of Michigan P, 1952.

Boccaccio, Giovanni. *Decameron, Filocolo*. Vol. 4 of *Tutte le Opere di Giovanni Boccaccio*. Milano: Arnoldo Mondadori, 1983.

————. *The Decameron*. Trans. Mark Musa and Peter Bondanella. New York: Norton, 1982.

————. *De casibus virorum illustrium*. Vol. 9 of *Tutte Le Opere di Giovanni Boccaccio*. Milano: Arnoldo Mondadori, 1983.

————. *The Fates of Illustrious Men*. Trans. Louis Brewer Hall. New York: Ungar, 1965.

Boethius. *The Consolation of Philosophy (Boece)*. Trans. Geoffrey Chaucer. In *The Riverside Chaucer*, ed. Larry D. Benson, et al. 3rd ed. Boston: Houghton, 1987.

Boitani, Piero. *Chaucer and the Imaginary World of Fame*. Cambridge: Cambridge UP, 1984.

————. "The *Monk's Tale*: Dante and Boccaccio." *Medium Aevum* 45 (1976): 50–69.

Braeger, Peter C. "The Portrayal of Fortune in the Tales of the Monk's Tale." In *Rebels and Rivals: The Contestive Spirit in "The Canterbury Tales."* Ed. Susanna Greer Fein, David Raybin, and Peter C. Braeger. SMC XXIX, Medieval Institute Publications (Kalamazoo, Mi: Western Michigan U., 1991). 223–26.

Brewer, Derek. *Chaucer: The Poet as Storyteller*. London: Macmillan, 1984.

————. "Some Metonymic Relationships in Chaucer's Poetry." *Poetica* 1 (1974): 1–20.

Bronson, Bertrand. "Chaucer's Art in Relation to His Audience." In *Five Studies in Literature*, 1–53. University of California Publications in English 8, no. 1. Berkeley: U of California P, 1940.

Brushfield, T. N. *Obsolete Punishments, II: The Cucking Stool. Journal of Architecture, Archaeology, and History*. Society of Chester, VI. (1857–59).

Burlin, Robert B. *Chaucerian Fiction*. Princeton: Princeton UP, 1977.

Burnley, J. D. *Chaucer's Language and the Philosophers' Tradition*. Cambridge, Eng.: Brewer, 1979.

Burrow, John. "Poems without Endings." *Studies in the Age of Chaucer* 13 (1991): 17–37.

Caie, Graham D. "The Significance of Marginal Glosses in the Earliest Manuscripts of *The Canterbury Tales*." In *Chaucer and Scriptural Tradition*, ed. David Lyle Jeffrey, 75–88. Ottawa: U of Ottawa P (1984).

Chapman, C. O. "Chaucer and the Gawain-Poet: A Conjecture." *Modern Language Notes* 68 (1953): 521–24.

Chaucer, Geoffrey. *The Complete Poetry and Prose of Geoffrey Chaucer*. Ed. John Fisher. New York: Holt, 1977.

————. *The Complete Works of Geoffrey Chaucer*. Ed. Walter W. Skeat. Vol. 7: *Chaucerian and Other Pieces*. Oxford: Clarendon P, 1897.

————. *The Miller's Tale*. Ed. Constance B. Hieatt. New York: U of Western Ontario P, 1970.

————. *The Parlement of Foulys*. Ed. Derek Brewer. Manchester: Manchester UP, 1960.

————. *The Riverside Chaucer*. Ed. Larry D. Benson, et al. 3rd ed. Boston: Houghton, 1987.

————. *Troilus and Criseyde: A New Edition of "The Book of Troilus."* Ed. Barry A. Windeatt. New York: Longman, 1984.

Childs, Wendy. "Anglo-Italian Contacts in the Fourteenth Century." In *Chaucer and the Italian Trecento,* ed. Piero Boitani, 65–87. Cambridge: Cambridge UP, 1983.

Cicero, Marcus Tullius. *De inventione, De optimo genere, Oratorum topica.* Trans. H. M. Hubbell. Loeb Classical Library. Cambridge: Harvard UP, 1949.

———. *De oratore.* Trans. E. W. Sutton and H. Rackham. Loeb Classical Library. Cambridge: Harvard UP, 1942.

Clemen, Wolfgang. *Chaucer's Early Poetry.* Trans. G. A. M. Sym. New York: Barnes, 1964.

The Cloud of Unknowing and Other Works. Ed. and Trans. Clifton Wolters. New York: Penguin Books, 1961.

Clouston, W. A. "On the Magical Elements in Chaucer's 'Squire's Tale,' with Analogues." *Chaucer's Squire's Tale.* 263–471. London: Chaucer Society, 2nd ser. 23, 26 (1987–89).

Coghill, Nevill. "Chaucer's Narrative Art in *The Canterbury Tales*." In *Chaucer and Chaucerians: Critical Studies in Middle English Literature,* ed. Derek Brewer, 114–39. University: U of Alabama P, 1966.

———. *The Poet Chaucer.* London: Oxford UP, 1949.

Colie, Rosalie. *Paradoxia Epidemica: The Renaissance Tradition of Paradox.* Princeton: Princeton UP, 1966.

Cooper, Helen. *The Structure of the Canterbury Tales.* Athens: U of Georgia P, 1984.

Coulton, G. G. *Medieval Panorama: The English Scene from Conquest to Reformation.* New York: Meridian, 1955.

Crosby, Ruth. "Chaucer and the Custom of Oral Delivery." *Speculum* 13 (1938): 413–38.

Curtis, Ernst Robert. "Mittelalter-Studien. XVIII." *Zeitschrift für romanische Philologie* 63 (1943): 225–74.

Dante Alighieri. *Inferno.* Trans. Charles S. Singleton. Vol. 2 of *The Divine Comedy.* Bollingen Series 80. Princeton: Princeton UP, 1970.

———. *Il convivio* 2. Trans. Philip H. Wicksteed. London: Dent, 1931.

———. *De vulgari eloquentia. Literature in the Vernacular.* Trans. Sally Purcell. Manchester, Eng.: Carcanet New Press, 1981.

Davenport, W. A. "Patterns in Middle English Dialogues." In *Medieval English Studies Presented to George Kane,* ed. Edward Donald Kennedy, Ronald Waldron, and Joseph S. Wittig, 127–45. Wolfeboro, NH: Boydell and Brewer, 1988.

David, Alfred. *The Strumpet Muse.* Bloomington: Indiana UP, 1976.

Dean, James. "Chaucer's *Book of the Duchess:* A Non-Boethian Interpretation," *Modern Language Quarterly* 46 (1985): 235–49.

———. "The Ending of the *Canterbury Tales.*" *Texas Studies in Literature and Language* 21 (1979): 17–33.

d'Entrèves, A. P. *Dante as Political Thinker.* Oxford: Clarendon, 1952.

Diekstra, F. N. M. "Chaucer's Digressive Mode and the Moral of the Manciple's Tale." *Neophilologus* 67 (1983): 131–48.

DiMarco, Vincent D. "A Note on Canace's Magic Ring." *Anglia* 99 (1981): 399–405.

Dinshaw, Carolyn. *Chaucer's Sexual Poetics.* Madison: U of Wisconsin P, 1989.

Ebin, Lois. "Lydgate's Views on Poetry." *Annuale Mediaevale* 18 (1977): 76–106.

Erasmus, Desiderius. "The Tongue/Lingua." In *Collected Works of Erasmus*. Vol. 29. *Literary and Educational Writings,* ed. and trans. Elaine Fantham and Erika Rummel, 249–412. Toronto: U of Toronto P, 1989.

Faral, Edmond. *Les Arts poétiques du XIIe et du XIIIe siècle.* Paris: E. Champion, 1924.

Farmer, Sharon. "Persuasive Voices: Clerical Images of Medieval Wives," *Speculum* 61 (1986): 517–43.

Finlayson, John. "The *Roman de la Rose* and Chaucer's Narrators." *Chaucer Review* 24 (1990): 187–210.

Fleming, John V. "Jean de Meun and the Ancient Poets." In *Rethinking "The Romance of the Rose": Text, Image, Reception,* ed. Kevin Brownlee and Sylvia Huot, 81–100. Philadelphia: U of Pennsylvania P, 1992.

Fradenburg, Louise. "The Manciple's Servant's Tongue: Politics and Poetry in the *Canterbury Tales.*" *English Literary History* 52 (1985): 85–118.

Frakes, Jerold C. " 'Ther nis na moore to seye': Closure in the *Knight's Tale.*" *Chaucer Review* 22 (1987): 1–7.

Froissart, Jean. *Le Paradys d'Amour.* Ed. Peter F. Dembowski. Geneva: Librairie Droz S.A., 1986.

Fromm, Erich. *Man for Himself.* New York: Rinehart, 1947.

Fulk, R. D. "Reinterpreting the *Manciple's Tale.*" *Journal of English and Germanic Philology* 78 (1979): 485–93.

Fyler, John. *Chaucer and Ovid.* New Haven: Yale UP, 1979.

Gadamer, Hans Georg. *Truth and Method.* New York: Crossroads, 1985.

Ganim, John. "Chaucer and the Noise of the People." *Exemplaria: A Journal of Theory in Medieval and Renaissance Studies* 2 (1990): 71–88.

———. *Chaucerian Theatricality.* Princeton: Princeton UP, 1990.

Gardner, John. *The Life and Times of Chaucer.* New York: Knopf, 1977.

Garin, Eugenio. *L'umanesimo italiano: filosofia e vita civile nel Rinascimento.* Bari: Laterza, 1952.

———. *Italian Humanism: Philosophy and Civic Life in the Renaissance.* Trans. Peter Munz. Oxford: Blackwell, 1965.

Godman, Peter. "Chaucer and Boccaccio's Latin Works." In *Chaucer and the Italian Trecento,* ed. Piero Boitani, 269–95. Cambridge: Cambridge UP, 1983.

Göller, Karl Heinz. "Chaucer's *Squire's Tale:* 'The knotte of the tale.' " In *Chaucer und Seine Zeit: Symposium für Walter F. Schirmer.* Buchreihe der Anglia: Zeitschrift für Englische Philologie 14, ed. Arno Esch, 163–88. Tübingen: Max Niemeyer, 1968.

Green, Richard Firth. *Poets and Princepleasers: Literature and the English Court in the Late Middle Ages.* Toronto: U of Toronto P, 1980.

Grudin, Michaela Paasche. "Chaucer's *Clerk's Tale* as Political Paradox." *Studies in the Age of Chaucer* 11 (1989): 63–92.

Guillaume de Lorris, and Jean de Meung. *Le Roman de la Rose.* Ed. Felix Lecoy, 3 vols. Paris: H. Champion, 1965–70.

Gunn, M. F. *The Mirror of Love: A Reinterpretation of "The Romance of the Rose."* Lubbock: Texas Tech, 1952.

Haas, Renate. "Chaucer's *Monk's Tale:* An Ingenious Criticism of Early Humanist Conceptions of Tragedy." *Humanistica Lovaniensia* 36 (1987): 44–70.

Hahn, Thomas. "Teaching the Resistant Woman: The Wife of Bath and the Academy." *Exemplaria: A Journal of Theory in Medieval and Renaissance Studies* 4 (Fall 1992): 431–40.

Haller, Robert S. "Chaucer's *Squire's Tale* and the Uses of Rhetoric." *Modern Philology* 62 (1965): 285–95.

Hanning, Robert W. "I Shal Finde It in a Maner Glose: Versions of Textual Harrassment in Medieval Literature." In *Medieval Texts and Contemporary Readers,* ed. Laurie A. Finke and Martin B. Shichtman, 27–50. Ithaca: Cornell UP, 1987.

Harding, Alan. "The Revolt Against the Justices." In *The English Rising of 1381,* ed. R. H. Hilton and T. H. Aston, 165–93. New York: Cambridge UP, 1984.

Hardman, Phillipa. "Chaucer's Tyrants of Lombardy." *The Review of English Studies,* n.s., 31 (1980): 172–78.

Harwood, Britton J. "Language and the Real: Chaucer's Manciple." *Chaucer Review* 6 (1972): 268–79.

Hazelton, Richard. "The *Manciple's Tale:* Parody and Critique." *Journal of English and Germanic Philology* 62 (1963): 1–31.

Hector, L. C. and Barbara F. Harvey. *The Westminster Chronicle.* Oxford: Clarendon, 1982.

Homer, *The Odyssey.* Vol. 1. Loeb Classical Library. (1960).

———. *The Odyssey.* Trans. Robert Fitzgerald. New York: Doubleday, 1963.

Howard, Donald R. *Chaucer: His Life, His Works, His World.* New York: E. P. Dutton, 1987.

———. *The Idea of "The Canterbury Tales."* Berkeley: U of California P, 1976.

Hult, David F. "Language and Dismemberment: Abelard, Origen, and the *Romance of the Rose.*" In *Rethinking "The Romance of the Rose": Text, Image, Reception,* ed. Kevin Brownlee and Sylvia Huot, 101–30. Philadelphia: U of Pennsylvania P, 1992.

———. Preface: "Concepts of Closure." *Yale French Studies* 67 (1984): iii–vi.

Hussey, S. S. *Chaucer: An Introduction.* London: Methuen, 1971.

Hutchison, Harold F. *The Hollow Crown: A Life of Richard II.* New York: John Day, 1961.

Huizinga, Johan. *Homo Ludens: A Study of the Play Element in Culture.* Boston: Beacon, 1950.

Iser, Wolfgang. *The Act of Reading: A Theory of Aesthetic Response.* Baltimore: Johns Hopkins UP, 1978.

Jauss, Hans Robert. *Aesthetic Experience and Literary Hermeneutics.* Trans. Michael Shaw. Minneapolis: U of Minnesota P, 1982.

Jensen, Emily. "Male Competition as a Unifying Motif in Fragment A of the *Canterbury Tales.*" *Chaucer Review* 24 (1990): 320–28.

Jones, H. S. V. "The Squire's Tale." In *Sources and Analogues of Chaucer's Canterbury Tales,* ed. W. F. Bryan and Germaine Dempster, 357–76. Chicago: U of Chicago P, 1941.

Jordan, Robert M. *Chaucer's Poetics and the Modern Reader.* Berkeley: U of California P, 1987.

———. "The Question of Genre: Five Chaucerian Romances." In *Chaucer at Albany,* ed. Rossell Hope Robbins, 77–103. New York: Burt Franklin, 1975.

Kahrl, Stanley J. "Chaucer's *Squire's Tale* and the Decline of Chivalry." *Chaucer Review* 7 (1973): 194–209.

Kaske, R. E. "The Knight's Interruption of *The Monk's Tale*." *English Literary History*, 24 (1957): 249–68.

Kellogg, Alfred L. "The Evolutions of *The Clerk's Tale*: A Study in Connotation." In *Chaucer, Langland, Arthur: Essays in Middle English Literature,* ed. Alfred L. Kellogg, 276–329. New Brunswick: Rutgers UP, 1972.

Kermode, Frank. *The Sense of an Ending: Studies in the Theory of Fiction.* New York: Oxford UP, 1967.

Kittredge, George Lyman. *Chaucer and His Poetry.* Cambridge: Harvard UP, 1915.

———. "Chaucer's Discussion of Marriage." *Modern Philology* 9 (1912): 435–67.

Knapp, Peggy Ann. *Chaucer and the Social Contest.* New York: Routledge, 1990.

———. "Robyn the Miller's Thrifty Work." In *Sign, Sentence, Discourse: Language in Medieval Thought and Literature,* ed. Julian N. Wasserman and Lois Roney, 294–308. Syracuse: Syracuse UP, 1989.

Knight, Stephen. "Chaucer and the Sociology of Literature." *Studies in the Age of Chaucer* 2 (1980): 15–51.

———. *Ryming Craftily: Meaning in Chaucer's Poetry.* London: Angus and Robertson, 1973.

Kolve, V. A. *Chaucer and the Imagery of Narrative: The First Five Canterbury Tales.* Stanford: Stanford UP, 1984.

Lawlor, John. "The Pattern of Consolation in the *Book of the Duchess*." *Speculum* 31 (1956): 640–48.

Lawton, David. *Chaucer's Narrators.* Vol. 13 of *Chaucer Studies.* Cambridge, Eng.: Brewer, 1985.

Lewis, C. S. *The Allegory of Love: A Study in Medieval Tradition.* New York: Oxford UP, 1936.

Liber Albus: The White Book of the City of London. Ed. and trans. Henry Thomas Riley. London: Richard Griffin, 1861.

Lille, Alain de. *The Complaint of Nature.* Trans. Douglas M. Moffat. Yale Studies in English 36. Ed. Albert S. Cook. New York: Holt, 1908.

Lindahl, Carl. *Earnest Games: Folkloric Patterns in the "Canterbury Tales."* Bloomington: Indiana UP, 1987.

Lydgate, John. *Lydgate's Fall of Princes, Part III.* Ed. Henry Bergen. Early English Text Society E. S. London: Oxford UP, 1924; reprint. 1942.

Machaut, Guillaume de. *Le Jugement du Roy de Behaigne* and *Remede de Fortune.* Ed. James I. Wimsatt and William W. Kibler. Athens and London: U of Georgia P, 1988.

Manly, John M. "Chaucer and the Rhetoricians." *Proceedings of the British Academy* 12 (1926): 95–133.

Mann, Jill. "Chaucer and the Medieval Latin Poets: The Satiric Tradition." In *Geoffrey Chaucer: Writers and Their Background,* 172–83. London: Bell, 1974; Ohio UP, 1975.

———. "Satisfaction and Payment in Middle English Literature." *Studies in the Age of Chaucer* 5 (1983): 17–48.

———. "The Authority of the Audience in Chaucer." In *Poetics: Theory and Practice in Medieval English Literature,* ed. Piero Boitani and Anna Torti, 1–12. Woodbridge: Brewer, 1991.

———. "Chaucer and Atheism." Presidential Address. *Studies in the Age of Chaucer* 17 (1995): 5–19.

Mannyng, Robert. *Handlyng Synne.* Ed. Frederick J. Furnivall. Early English Text Society, o.s., 119, 123. London, 1901.

Martin, Wallace. *Recent Theories of Narrative.* Ithaca: Cornell UP, 1986.

McCall, John P. "The Squire in Wonderland." *Chaucer Review* 1 (1966): 103–09.

McGerr, Rosemarie P. "Meaning and Ending in a 'Paynted Proces': Resistance to Closure in *Troilus and Criseyde.*" In *Chaucer's "Troilus and Criseyde": "Subgit to Alle Poesye": Essays in Criticism,* ed. R. A. Shoaf, 179–98. Binghamton, NY: Medieval and Renaissance Texts and Studies, 1992.

McKeon, Richard. "Rhetoric in the Middle Ages." *Speculum* 17 (1942): 1–32.

Mehl, Dieter. "The Audience of Chaucer's Troilus and Criseyde." In *Chaucer and Middle English Studies in Honor of Rossell Hope Robbins,* ed. B. Rowland, 173–89. London: Allen and Unwin, 1974.

Memorials of London and London Life in the XIIIth, XIVth, and XVth Centuries: A.D. 1276–1419. Ed. and trans. Henry Thomas Riley. London: Longmans, Green, and Co. 1868.

Middle English Dictionary. Ed. Hans Kurath and Sherman M. Kuhn. Ann Arbor: U of Michigan P, 1954.

Middleton, Anne. "The Idea of Public Poetry in the Reign of Richard II." *Speculum* 53 (1978): 94–114.

Miller, D. A. *Narrative and Its Discontents: Problems of Closure in the Traditional Novel.* Princeton: Princeton UP, 1981.

Miller, J. Hillis. "Narrative and History." *English Literary History* 41 (1974): 455–73.

Minnis, A. J. *Chaucer and Pagan Antiquity.* Cambridge, Eng.: Brewer, 1982.

Mooney, Michael. *Vico in the Tradition of Rhetoric.* Princeton: Princeton UP, 1985.

Moore, R. I. *The Formation of a Persecuting Society: Power and Deviance in Western Europe, 950–1250.* Oxford: Blackwell, 1987.

Murphy, James J., ed. *Medieval Eloquence: Studies in the Theory and Practice of Medieval Rhetoric.* Berkeley: U of California P, 1978.

———. *Rhetoric in the Middle Ages: A History of Rhetorical Theory from Saint Augustine to the Renaissance.* Berkeley: U of California P, 1974.

Muscatine, Charles. *Chaucer and the French Tradition.* Berkeley: U of California P, 1957.

———. *The Old French Fabliaux.* New Haven: Yale UP, 1986.

Myers, A. R., ed. *Historia Anglicana.* In *English Historical Documents IV: 1327–1485.* New York: Oxford UP, 1969.

Neville, Marie. "The Function of the *Squire's Tale* in the Canterbury Scheme." *Journal of English and Germanic Philology* 50 (1951): 167–79.

Nykrog, Per. *L'Amour et la Rose: Le Grand Dessein de Jean de Meun.* Harvard Studies in Romance Languages 41. Lexington, Kentucky: French Forum Publishers, 1986.

Olson, Paul A. *The "Canterbury Tales" and the Good Society.* Princeton: Princeton UP, 1986.

———. "*The Parlement of Foules:* Aristotle's *Politics* and the Foundations of Human Society," *Studies in the Age of Chaucer* 2 (1980): 53–69.

Ong, Walter J. *Orality and Literacy: The Technologizing of the Word.* New York: Methuen, 1982.

————. *Rhetoric, Romance, and Technology.* Cornell: Cornell UP, 1971.

————. "The Writer's Audience Is Always a Fiction." *Publications of the Modern Language Association* 90 (1975): 9–21.

Osberg, Richard H. "Between the Motion and the Act: Intentions and Ends in Chaucer's *Troilus.*" *English Literary History* 48 (1981): 257–70.

Paré, Gerard Marie. *Le Roman de la Rose et la Scolastique Courtoise.* Paris: J. Vrin, 1941.

————. *Les Idées et les lettres au XIIIe siècle: le Roman de la Rose.* Montreal: Centre de psychologie et de philosophie, 1947.

Parks, Ward. "Oral Tradition and the *Canterbury Tales.*" In *Oral Poetics in Middle English Poetry,* ed. Mark C. Amodio, 149–79. New York: Garland, 1994.

Patterson, Lee W. " 'No Man His Reson Herde': Peasant Consciousness, Chaucer's Miller and the Structure of *The Canterbury Tales.*" *South Atlantic Quarterly* 86 (1987): 457–95.

————. "The 'Parson's Tale' and the Quitting of the *Canterbury Tales.*" *Traditio* 34 (1978): 331–80.

Payne, Robert O. *Chaucer and the Key of Remembrance: A Study of Chaucer's Poetics.* New Haven: Yale UP, 1963.

Pearsall, Derek A. *The Canterbury Tales.* Boston: Allen and Unwin, 1985.

————. *The Life of Geoffrey Chaucer: A Critical Biography.* Cambridge, MA: Blackwell, 1992.

————. "The Squire as Story-Teller." *University of Toronto Quarterly* 34 (1964): 82–92.

————. "The Troilus Frontispiece and Chaucer's Audience." *Yearbook of English Studies* 7 (1977): 68–74.

Petrarca, Francesco. *De sui ipsius et multorum ignorantia, Opera omnia.* 3 vols. Ridgewood, NJ: Gregg Press, 1965.

————. *Epistolae rerum senilium.* In *Chaucer: Sources and Backgrounds,* ed. Robert P. Miller, 137–40. New York: Oxford UP, 1977.

Petrarch's Remedies for Fortune Fair and Foul: Book I: Remedies for Prosperity. Ed. and trans. Conrad H. Rawski. Bloomington: Indiana UP, 1991.

Petty, George R., Jr. "Power, Deceit, and Misinterpretation: Uncooperative Speech in the *Canterbury Tales. Chaucer Review* 27 (1993): 413–23.

Phillips, Helen. "Structure and Consolation in the *Book of the Duchess.*" *Chaucer Review* 16 (1981): 107–118.

Plato. *The Collected Dialogues of Plato.* Ed. Edith Hamilton and Huntington Cairns. Bollingen Series 71. Princeton: Princeton UP, 1961.

Pulsiano, Phillip. "Redeemed Language and the Ending of *Troilus and Criseyde.*" In *Sign, Sentence, Discourse: Language in Medieval Thought and Literature,* ed. Julian N. Wasserman and Lois Roney, 153–74. Syracuse: Syracuse UP, 1989.

Rambuss, Richard. " 'Process of tyme': History, Consolation, and Apocalypse in the *Book of the Duchess.*" *Exemplaria* 2 (1990): 549–83.

Reed, Thomas L., Jr. *Middle English Debate Poetry and the Aesthetics of Irresolution.* Columbia: U of Missouri P, 1990.

Regalado, Nancy. " 'Des contraires choses': la fonction poétique de la citation et des exampla dans le 'Roman de la Rose' de Jean de Meun." *Litterature* 41 (Feb. 1981): 62–81.

Reiss, Edmund. "Biblical Parody: Chaucer's 'Distortions' of Scripture." In *Chaucer and Scriptural Tradition,* ed. David Lyle Jeffrey, 47–61. Ottawa: U of Ottawa P, 1984.

———. "Chaucer and His Audience." *Chaucer Review* 14 (1980): 390–402.

Rich, Adrienne. "Teaching Language in Open Admissions." In *On Lies, Secrets, and Silence: Selected Prose 1966–1978,* 51–68. New York: Norton, 1979.

Ridley, Florence. "The State of Chaucer Studies: A Brief Survey." *Studies in the Age of Chaucer* 1 (1979): 3–16.

Robertson, D. W. *A Preface to Chaucer.* Princeton: Princeton UP, 1962.

Root, R. K. *The Poetry of Chaucer.* 2nd ed. Boston: Houghton, 1906.

Rosenberg, Bruce A. "The Contrary Tales of the Second Nun and the Canon's Yeoman." *Chaucer Review* 2 (1968): 278–91.

Rowe, Donald. *Through Nature to Eternity: Chaucer's "Legend of Good Women."* Lincoln: U of Nebraska P, 1988.

Ruggiers, Paul G. *The Art of The Canterbury Tales.* Madison: U of Wisconsin P, 1965.

Salter, Elizabeth. *Fourteenth-Century English Poetry: Contexts and Readings.* Oxford: Oxford UP, 1983.

Sarraute, Natalie. *L'Ère du Soupçon: Essais sur le Roman.* Paris: Gallimard-Idees, 1956.

Scattergood, V. J. "The Manciple's Manner of Speaking." *Essays in Criticism* 24 (1974): 124–46.

Schildgen, Brenda Deen. "Jerome's *Prefatory Epistles* to the Bible and the *Canterbury Tales.*" *Studies in the Age of Chaucer* 15 (1993): 111–130.

Schultz, James A. "Classical Rhetoric, Medieval Poetics, and the Medieval Vernacular Prologue," *Speculum* 59 (1984): 1–15.

Severs, Burke. "Is the *Manciple's Tale* a Success?" *Journal of English and Germanic Philology* 51 (1952): 1–16.

Shumaker, Wayne. "Chaucer's *Manciple's Tale* as Part of a Canterbury Group." *University of Toronto Quarterly* 22 (1953): 147–56.

Sklute, Larry. *The Virtue of Necessity: Inconclusiveness and Narrative Form in Chaucer's Poetry.* Columbus: Ohio State UP, 1984.

Smith, Barbara Herrnstein. *Poetic Closure: A Study of How Poems End.* Chicago: U of Chicago P, 1968.

Spearing, A. C. *Medieval Dream-Poetry.* Cambridge: Cambridge UP, 1976.

Speirs, John. *Chaucer the Maker.* London: Faber and Faber, 1964.

Stillinger, Thomas C. *The Song of Troilus: Lyric Authority in the Medieval Book.* Philadelphia: U of Pennsylvania P, 1992.

Stillwell, Gardiner. "Chaucer in Tartary." *Review of English Studies* 24 (1948): 177–88.

Stock, Brian. *The Implications of Literacy: Written Language and Models of Interpretation in the Eleventh and Twelfth Centuries.* Princeton: Princeton UP, 1983.

Storm, Melvin. "The Tercelet as Tiger: Bestiary Hypocrisy in the Squire's Tale." *English Language Notes* 14 (1977): 172–74.

Strohm, Paul. "Chaucer's Audience(s): Fictional, Implied, Intended, Actual." *Chaucer Review* 18 (1983): 137–45.

———. "Chaucer's Audience." *Literature and History* 5 (1977): 26–44.

———. "Form and Social Statement in *Confessio Amantis* and *The Canterbury Tales.*" *Studies in the Age of Chaucer* 1 (1979): 17–40.

———. *Social Chaucer.* Cambridge: Harvard UP, 1989.

Tatlock, John S. P. and Arthur G. Kennedy. *A Concordance to the Complete Works of Geoffrey Chaucer and to "The Romaunt of the Rose."* Washington, DC: Carnegie Institution, 1927.

Trask, Richard M. "The Manciple's Problem." *Studies in Short Fiction* 14 (1977): 109–16.

Travis, Peter W. "Deconstructing Chaucer's Retraction." *Exemplaria* 3 (1991): 135–58.

Trinkaus, Charles. *The Scope of Renaissance Humanism.* Ann Arbor: U of Michigan, 1983.

Usk, Thomas. "*The Testament of Love* by Thomas Usk: A New Edition." Ed. Virginia Bording Jellech. Diss. Washington University, 1970.

Vance, Eugene. "Marvelous Signals: Poetics, Sign Theory, and Politics in Chaucer's *Troilus.*" *New Literary History* 10 (1979): 293–337.

Vinsauf, Geoffrey of. *The New Poetics.* Trans. Jane Baltzell Kopp. In *Three Medieval Rhetorical Arts.* Ed. James J. Murphy. Berkeley: U of California, 1971.

Wallace, David. "Chaucer and Boccaccio's Early Writings." In *Chaucer and the Italian Trecento,* ed. Piero Boitani, 141–67. Cambridge, Eng.: Cambridge UP, 1983.

———. "*Troilus* and the *Filostrato*: Chaucer as Translator of Boccaccio." In *Chaucer's "Troilus and Criseyde": "Subgit to Alle Poesye": Essays in Criticism,* ed. R. A. Shoaf, 257–67. Binghamton, NY: Medieval and Renaissance Texts and Studies, 1992.

Walsingham. *Historia Anglicana. English Historical Documents IV: 1327–1485.* Ed. A. R. Myers. New York: Oxford UP, 1969.

The Westminster Chronicle. Ed. L. C. Hector and Barbara F. Harvey. Oxford: Clarendon, 1982.

Wasserman, Julian N., and Robert J. Blanch, eds. *Chaucer in the Eighties.* Syracuse: Syracuse UP, 1986.

Wenzel, Siegfried. "Chaucer and the Language of Contemporary Preaching." *Studies in Philology* 73 (1976): 138–61.

Whiting, B. J. "Gawain: His Reputation, His Courtesy and His Appearance in Chaucer's *Squire's Tale.*" *Mediaeval Studies* 9 (1947): 189–234.

Whittock, Trevor. *A Reading of the Canterbury Tales.* Cambridge: Cambridge UP, 1968.

Wilson, W. Daniel. "Readers in Texts." *Publications of the Modern Language Association* 96 (1981): 848–63.

Wimsatt, James I. *Chaucer and His French Contemporaries: Natural Music in the Fourteenth Century.* Toronto: U of Toronto P, 1991.

Windeatt, Barry A. "Chaucer and the *Filostrato.*" In *Chaucer and the Italian Trecento,* ed. Piero Boitani, 163–83. Cambridge: Cambridge UP, 1983.

———. *Chaucer's Dream Poetry: Sources and Analogues.* Totowa, NJ: Rowman and Littlefield, 1982.

———. "Literary Structures in Chaucer." In *The Cambridge Chaucer Companion,* ed. Piero Boitani and Jill Mann, 195–212. Cambridge: Cambridge UP, 1986.

Winnett, Susan. "Coming Unstrung: Women, Men, Narrative, and Principles of Pleasure." *Publications of the Modern Language Association* 105 (1990): 505–18.

INDEX

Abelard, Peter
  and Christian view of speech, 3–4, 4n9
  definition of spoken sentence, 39,
    39n21
Aers, David, 57n5
Alexander, Archbishop of York, 23n48
Amodio, Mark C., 2n2
amplificatio, 118n9, 156n18
  and society of the poet, 156–59
Aquinas, Thomas, 4, 4n11
Aristotle, 8n23
Ashley, Kathleen M., 19–20n38
Aston, T. H., 42n25
audience, 19–20, 25, 31–32, 83, 176–78,
  177–78n27. *See also* discourse: the
  listener
Augustine, St., 3–4, 5n13, 82n39

Bacon, Roger, 122–23n15
Baker, Donald C., 149–50n1, 158n21
Bakhtin, M. M., 19n37, 19–20n38,
  63n16, 88n8, 104–5n16
Baldwin, Ralph, 179n29
Baron, Hans, 2n4, 6n19, 48n37
Barthes, Roland, 166n7
Basevorn, Robert of, 74n30
Bellamy, J. G., 21n42
Bennett, J. A. W., 47, 47n33, 52n41
Benson, C. David, 56n2, 57n5, 58n6,
  115–16n4, 181n33
Benson, Larry D., 1n1, 34n8, 144n13

Beowulf
  digressions, 118n9
  and speech, 3
Bergen, Henry, 96n19
Berger, Harry Jr., 115n3
Besserman, Lawrence, 104n15, 105n17
Bible: Chaucer's use of, 103–6, 103n14,
  104nn15 and 16, 105n17
Bird, Ruth, 21n43
Bishop, Ian, 57n5
Blake, John, 23n48
Blanch, Robert J., 177–78n27
Bloomfield, Morton, 4n11
Boccaccio, Giovanni, 2, 6n18
  closure, 168
  Corbaccio, 37
  credulousness, 159, 159n25
  Decameron, 105–6, 105n18, 112,
    127n23, 168, 170, 170–71n18, 177
  De casibus, 5–7, 6n17, 9–12, 10nn27
    and 28, 11nn29 and 30, 41n23, 83,
    95–96, 96n18, 159, 159n25
  Filostrato, 56, 56n2, 57, 57nn3 and 4,
    58n6, 72n26, 73n28, 76n32, 77n34
  Giotto, 127n23
  and Jean de Meun, 63n14, 142n10
  relationship between poetry and
    knowledge, 140–42, 145
Boethius, 40, 48–49n38, 87
Boitani, Piero, 12–13n33, 19n37, 35,
  35n10, 58n6, 165, 165nn2 and 4
Bondanella, Peter, 127–28n23

193